Sasaki and Miyano

CONTENTS

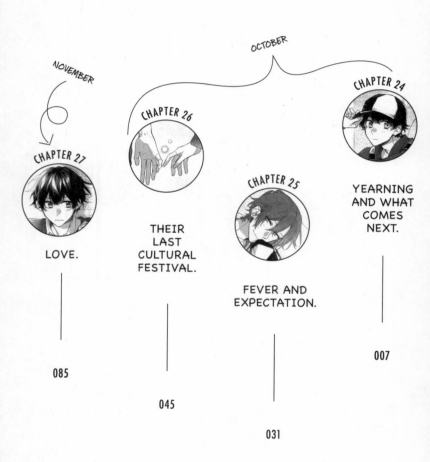

IF YOU'RE
TIRED.

111

THE GUY
I LIKE IS
POPULAR,
AND IT
BOTHERS
ME.

Sasaki and Miyano

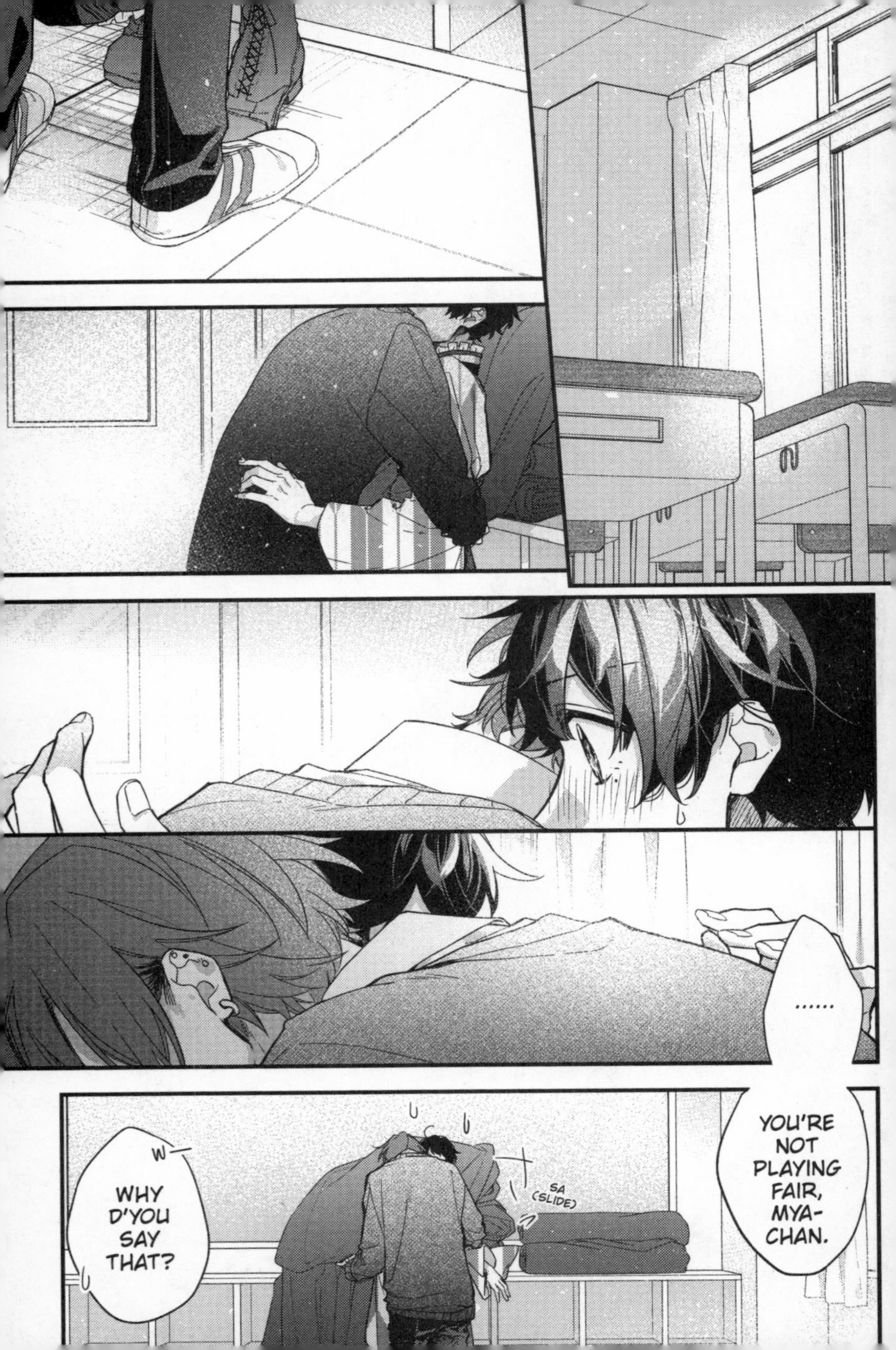
......
YOU'RE NOT PLAYING FAIR, MYA-CHAN.
SA (SLIDE)
W—
WHY D'YOU SAY THAT?

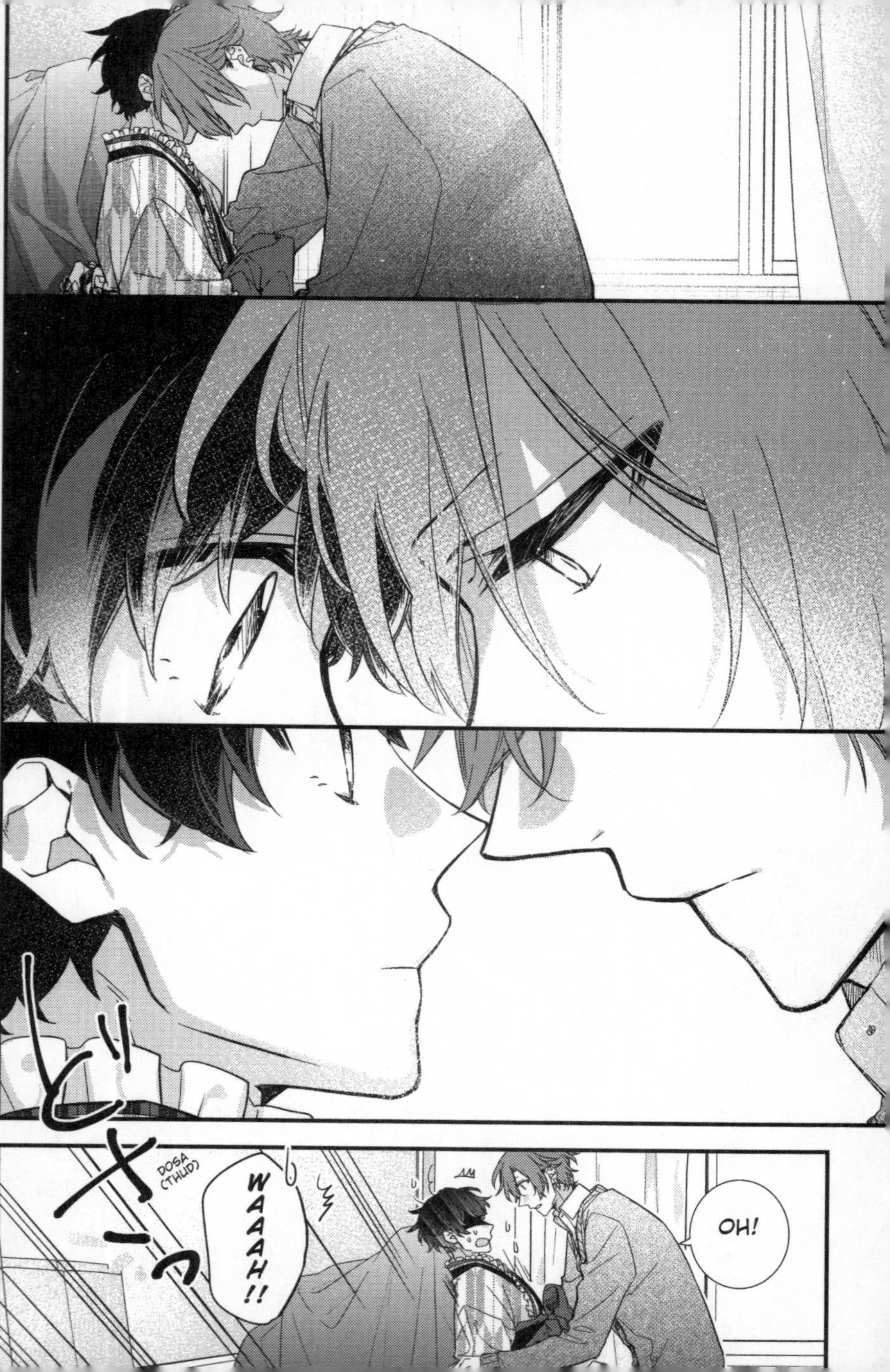

OH!
WAAAH!!
DOSA (THUD)
どさーっ

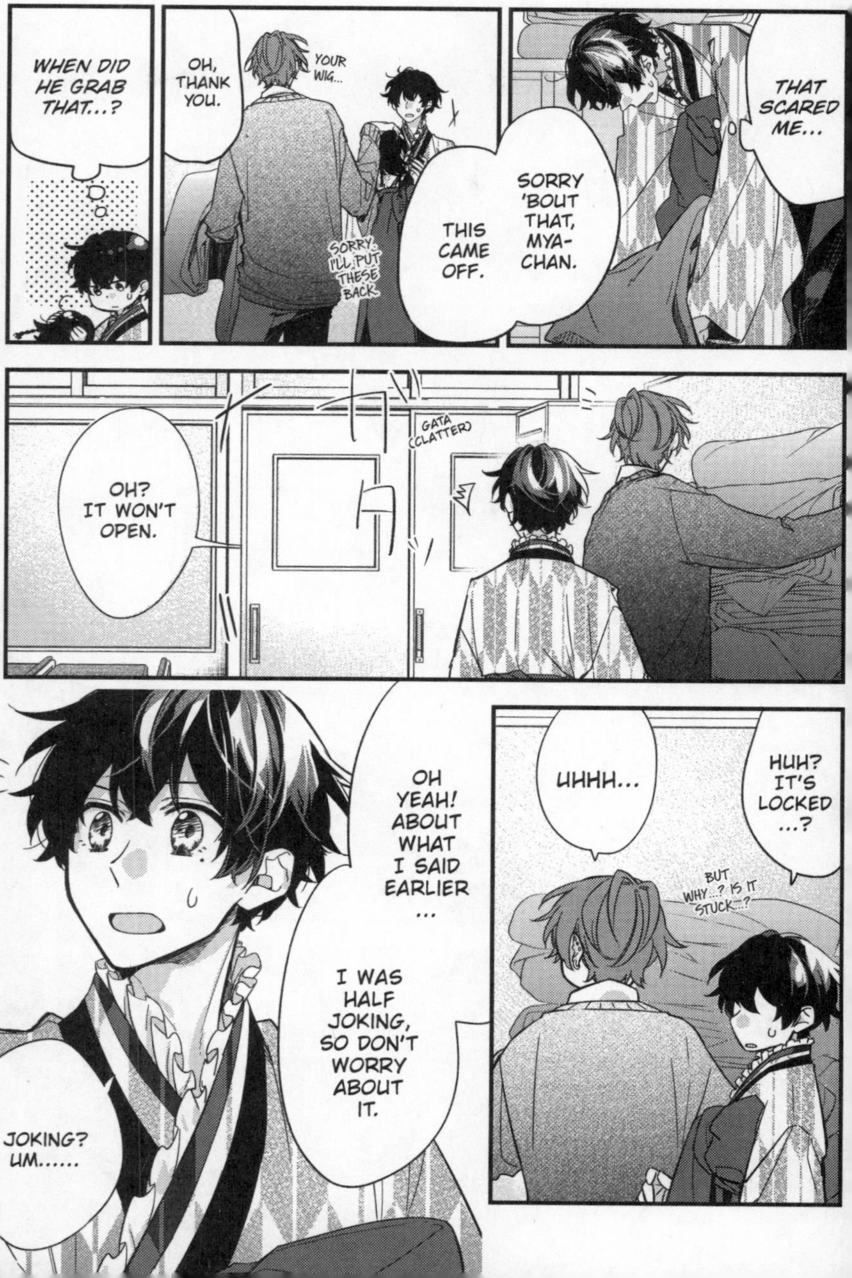
THAT SCARED ME...
SORRY 'BOUT THAT, MYA-CHAN.
THIS CAME OFF.
YOUR WIG...
OH, THANK YOU.
SORRY. I'LL PUT THESE BACK
WHEN DID HE GRAB THAT...?
GATA (CLATTER)
OH? IT WON'T OPEN.
HUH? IT'S LOCKED ...?
BUT WHY...? IS IT STUCK...?
UHHH...
OH YEAH! ABOUT WHAT I SAID EARLIER ...
I WAS HALF JOKING, SO DON'T WORRY ABOUT IT.
JOKING? UM......

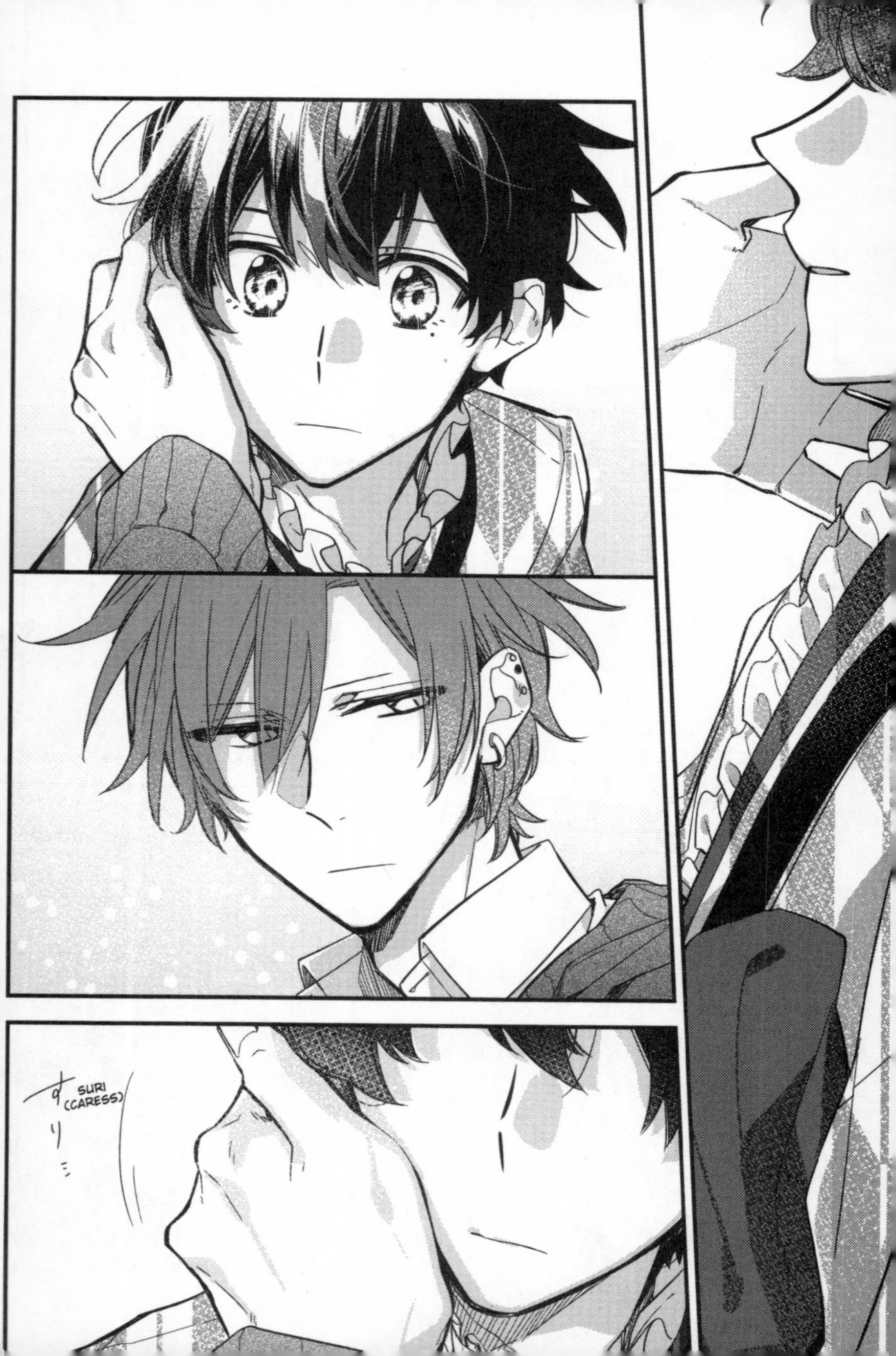
すりッ
SURI (CARESS)

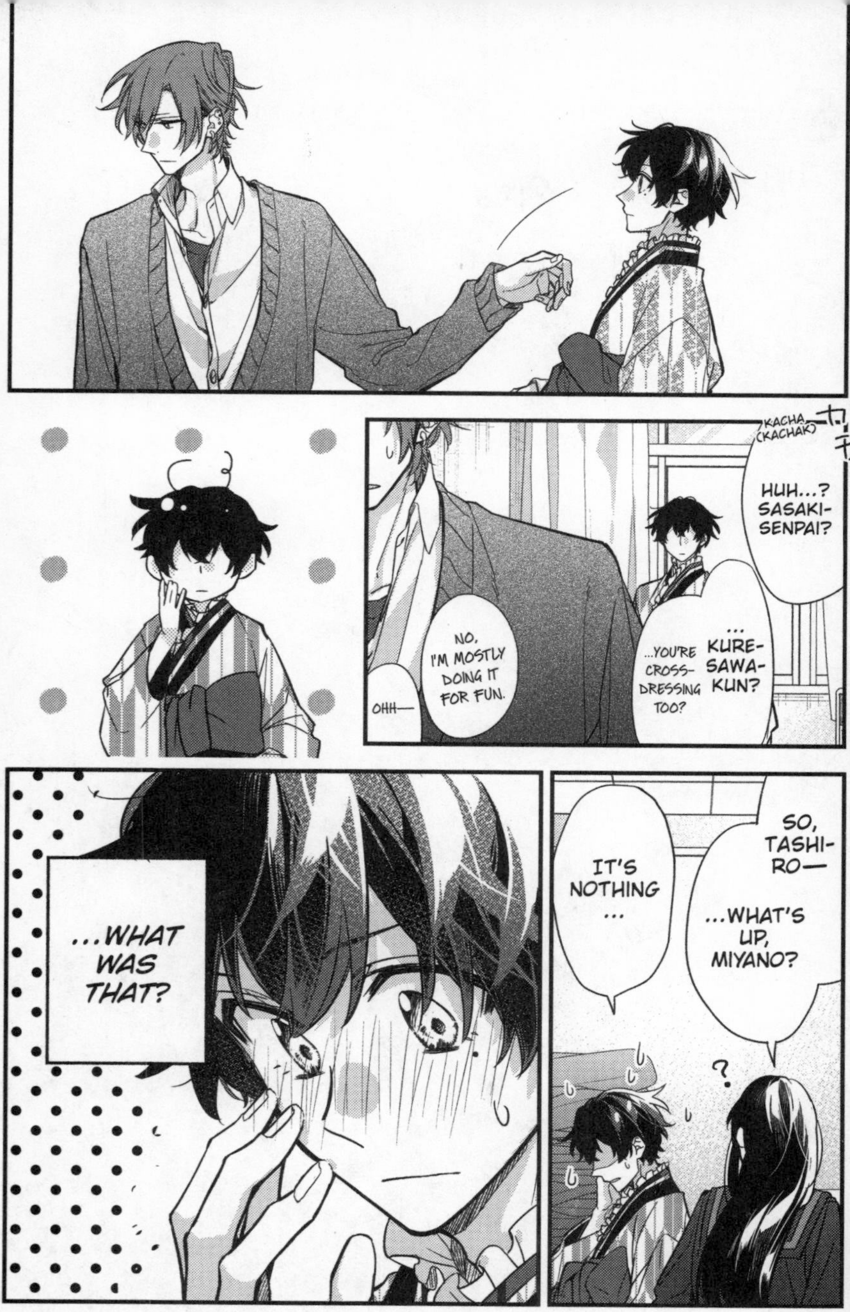
KACHA (KACHAK)
HUH...? SASAKI-SENPAI?
...KURE-SAWA-KUN?
...YOU'RE CROSS-DRESSING TOO?
NO, I'M MOSTLY DOING IT FOR FUN.
OHH—
SO, TASHIRO—
...WHAT'S UP, MIYANO?
IT'S NOTHING...
...WHAT WAS THAT?

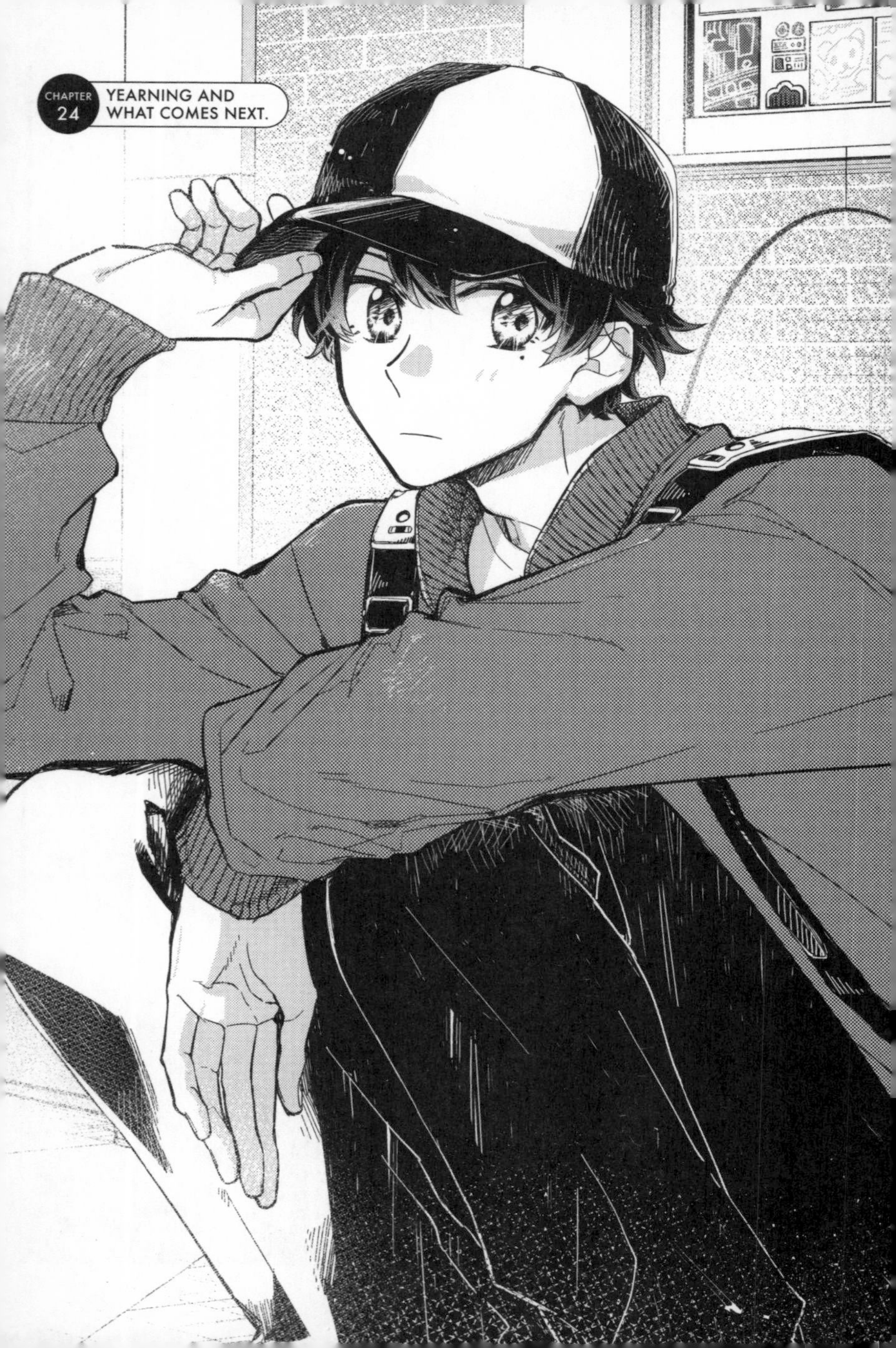
CHAPTER 24
YEARNING AND WHAT COMES NEXT.

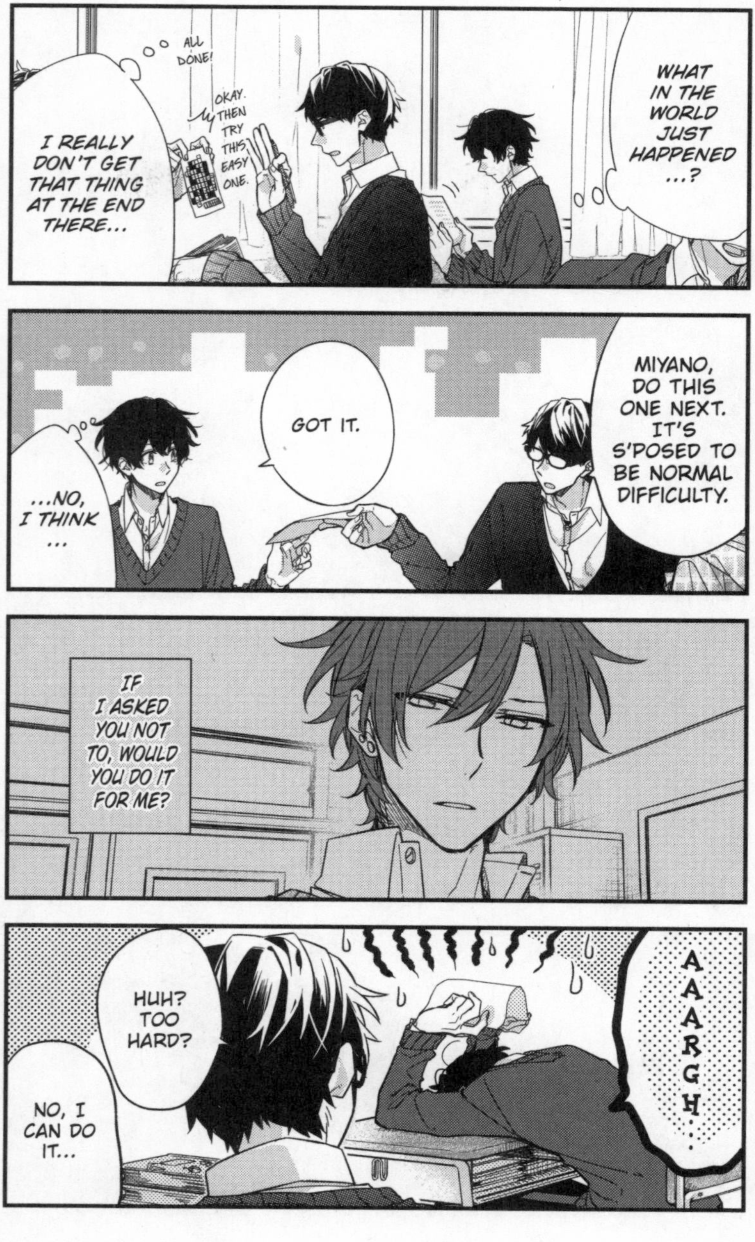
WHAT IN THE WORLD JUST HAPPENED ...?
ALL DONE!
OKAY. THEN TRY THIS EASY ONE.
I REALLY DON'T GET THAT THING AT THE END THERE...
MIYANO, DO THIS ONE NEXT. IT'S S'POSED TO BE NORMAL DIFFICULTY.
GOT IT.
...NO, I THINK ...
IF I ASKED YOU NOT TO, WOULD YOU DO IT FOR ME?
AAARGH...
HUH? TOO HARD?
NO, I CAN DO IT...

THAT WAS PROBABLY POSSESSIVENESS.

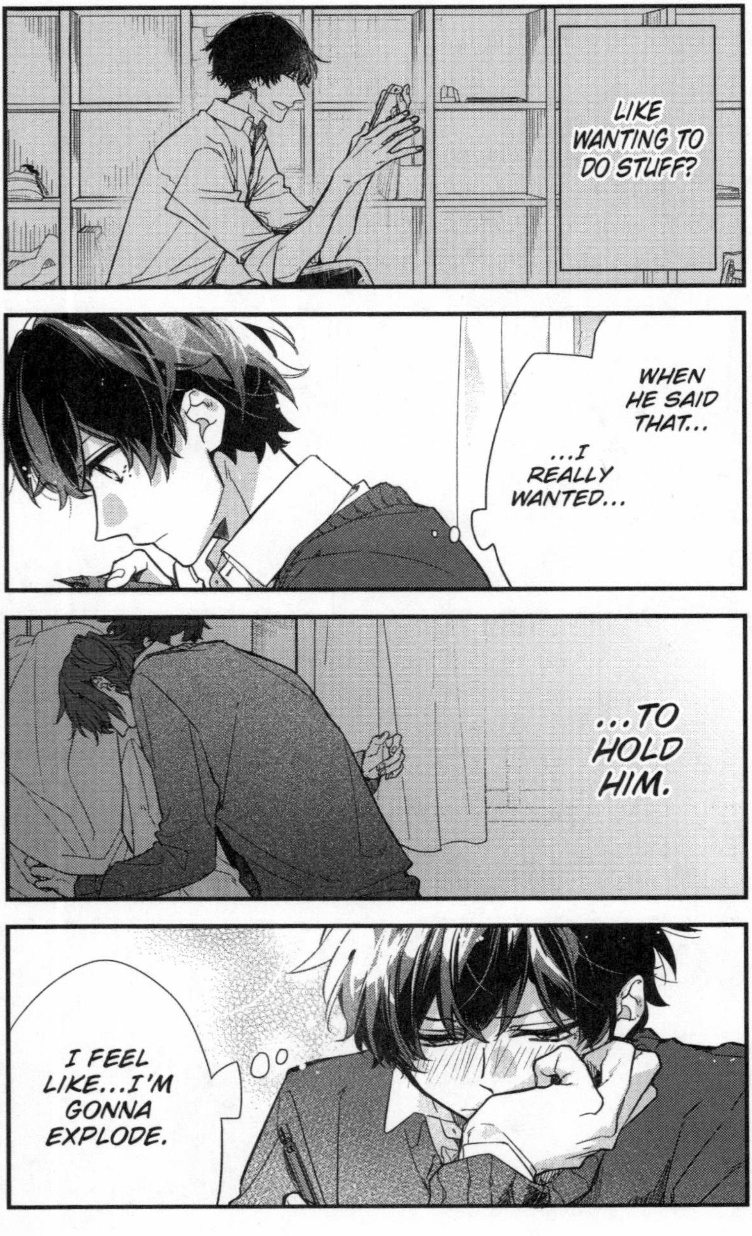
LIKE WANTING TO DO STUFF?
WHEN HE SAID THAT...
...I REALLY WANTED...
...TO HOLD HIM.
I FEEL LIKE...I'M GONNA EXPLODE.

OVERFLOWING EMOTIONS.

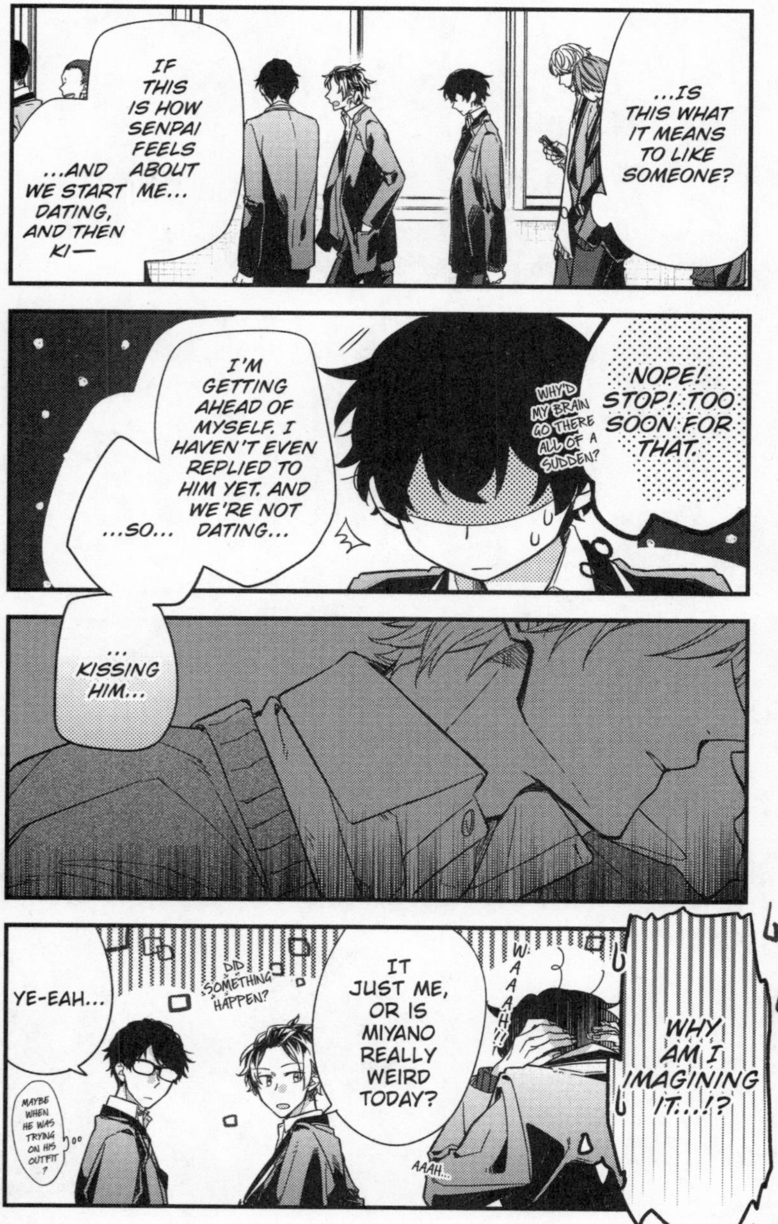
...IS THIS WHAT IT MEANS TO LIKE SOMEONE?
IF THIS IS HOW SENPAI FEELS ABOUT ME...
...AND WE START DATING, AND THEN KI—
NOPE! STOP! TOO SOON FOR THAT.
WHY'D MY BRAIN GO THERE ALL OF A SUDDEN?
I'M GETTING AHEAD OF MYSELF. I HAVEN'T EVEN REPLIED TO HIM YET. AND WE'RE NOT DATING...
...SO...
...KISSING HIM...
WHY AM I IMAGINING IT...!?
WAAAAH!!
AAAH...
IT JUST ME, OR IS MIYANO REALLY WEIRD TODAY?
DID SOMETHING HAPPEN?
YE-EAH...
MAYBE WHEN HE WAS TRYING ON HIS OUTFIT?

RESTLESS EMOTIONS.

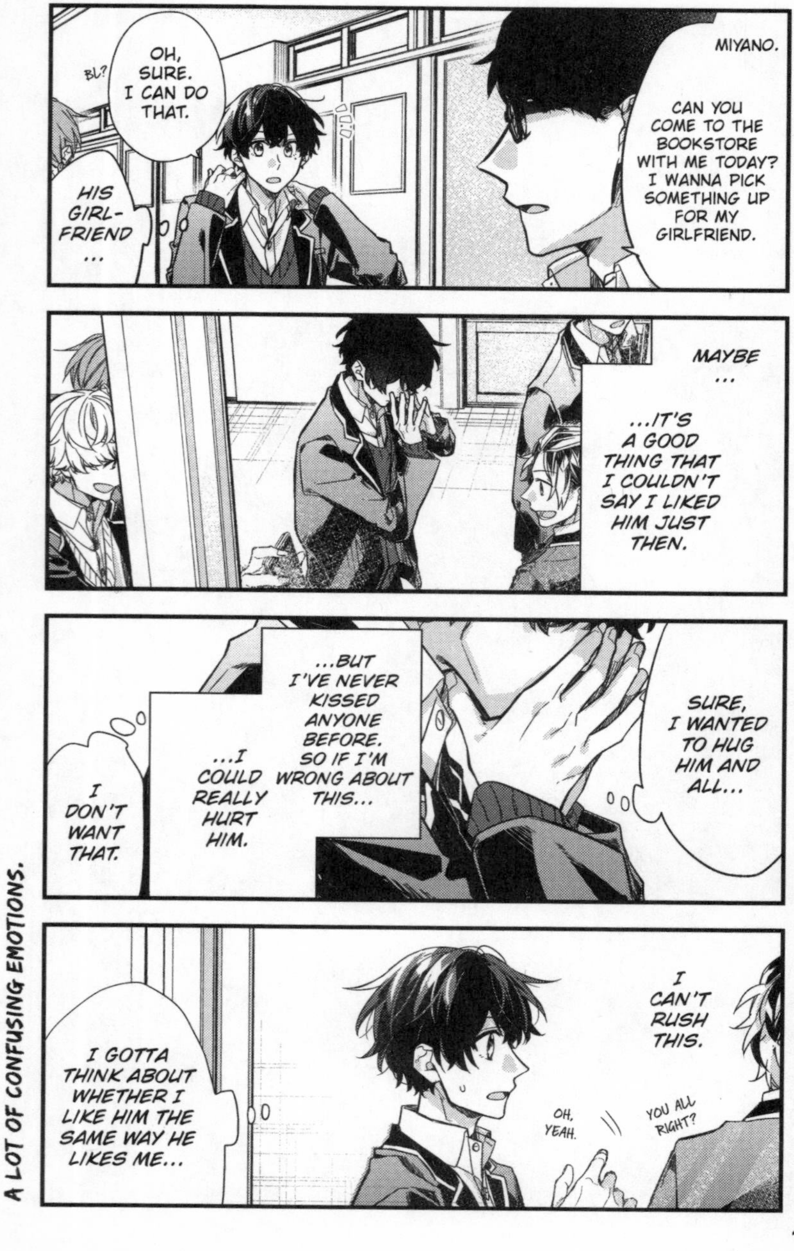
MIYANO.
CAN YOU COME TO THE BOOKSTORE WITH ME TODAY? I WANNA PICK SOMETHING UP FOR MY GIRLFRIEND.
OH, SURE. I CAN DO THAT.
BL?
HIS GIRL-FRIEND...
MAYBE...
...IT'S A GOOD THING THAT I COULDN'T SAY I LIKED HIM JUST THEN.
SURE, I WANTED TO HUG HIM AND ALL...
...BUT I'VE NEVER KISSED ANYONE BEFORE. SO IF I'M WRONG ABOUT THIS...
...I COULD REALLY HURT HIM.
I DON'T WANT THAT.
I CAN'T RUSH THIS.
YOU ALL RIGHT?
OH, YEAH.
I GOTTA THINK ABOUT WHETHER I LIKE HIM THE SAME WAY HE LIKES ME...

A LOT OF CONFUSING EMOTIONS.

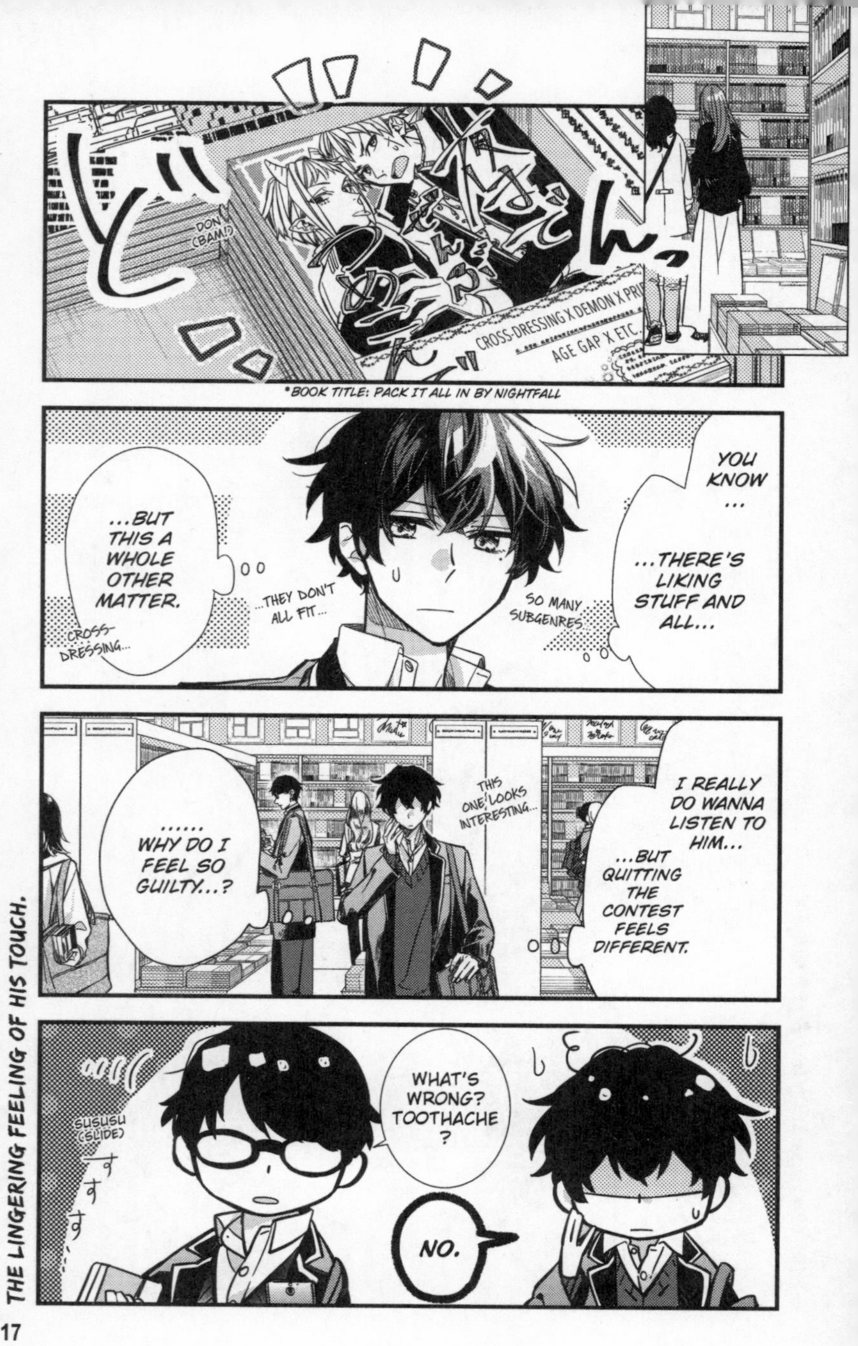
DON (BAM!)
CROSS-DRESSING X DEMON X PRI
AGE GAP X ETC.
*BOOK TITLE: PACK IT ALL IN BY NIGHTFALL
YOU KNOW ...
...THERE'S LIKING STUFF AND ALL...
SO MANY SUBGENRES...
...THEY DON'T ALL FIT...
...BUT THIS A WHOLE OTHER MATTER.
CROSS-DRESSING...
I REALLY DO WANNA LISTEN TO HIM...
...BUT QUITTING THE CONTEST FEELS DIFFERENT.
THIS ONE LOOKS INTERESTING...
...... WHY DO I FEEL SO GUILTY...?
WHAT'S WRONG? TOOTHACHE?
NO.
SUSUSU (SLIDE)
すすす

THE LINGERING FEELING OF HIS TOUCH.

CONDITIONED RESPONSE OF THE GIRLFRIEND-OBSESSED.

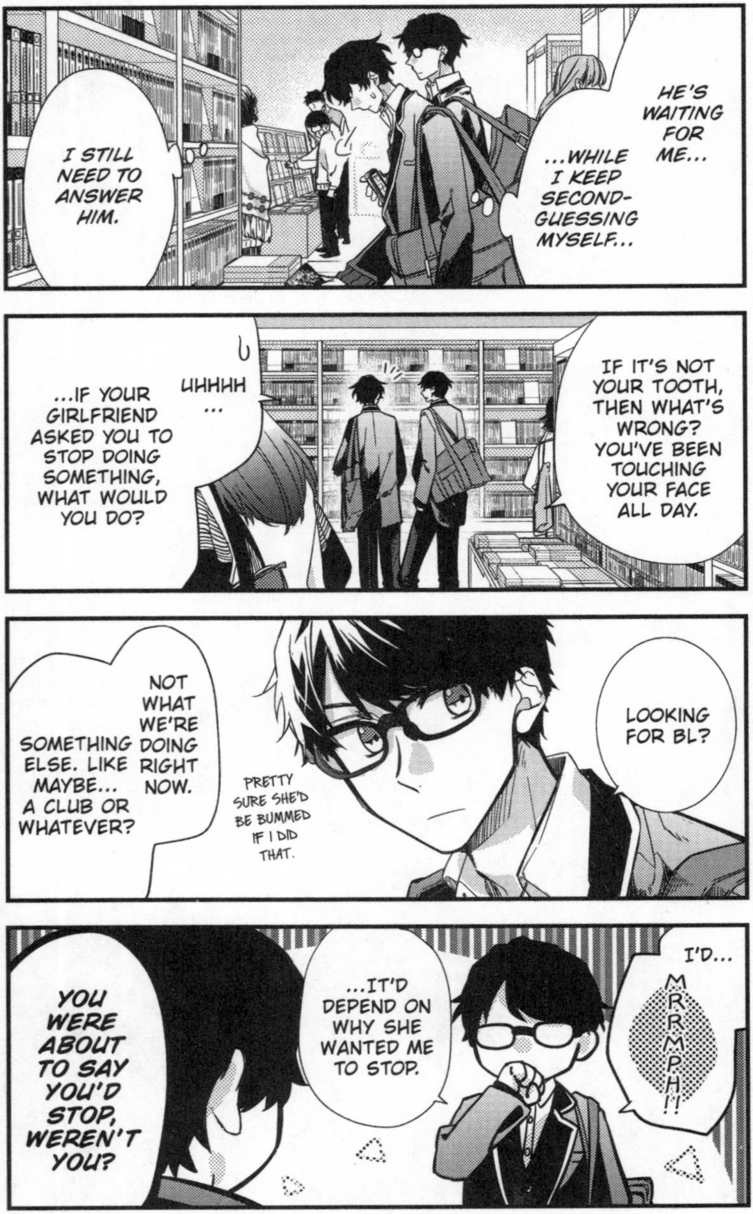
HE'S WAITING FOR ME...
...WHILE I KEEP SECOND-GUESSING MYSELF...
I STILL NEED TO ANSWER HIM.
IF IT'S NOT YOUR TOOTH, THEN WHAT'S WRONG? YOU'VE BEEN TOUCHING YOUR FACE ALL DAY.
UHHHH ...
...IF YOUR GIRLFRIEND ASKED YOU TO STOP DOING SOMETHING, WHAT WOULD YOU DO?
LOOKING FOR BL?
PRETTY SURE SHE'D BE BUMMED IF I DID THAT.
NOT WHAT WE'RE DOING RIGHT NOW.
SOMETHING ELSE. LIKE MAYBE... A CLUB OR WHATEVER?
I'D...
MRRMPH!!
...IT'D DEPEND ON WHY SHE WANTED ME TO STOP.
YOU WERE ABOUT TO SAY YOU'D STOP, WEREN'T YOU?

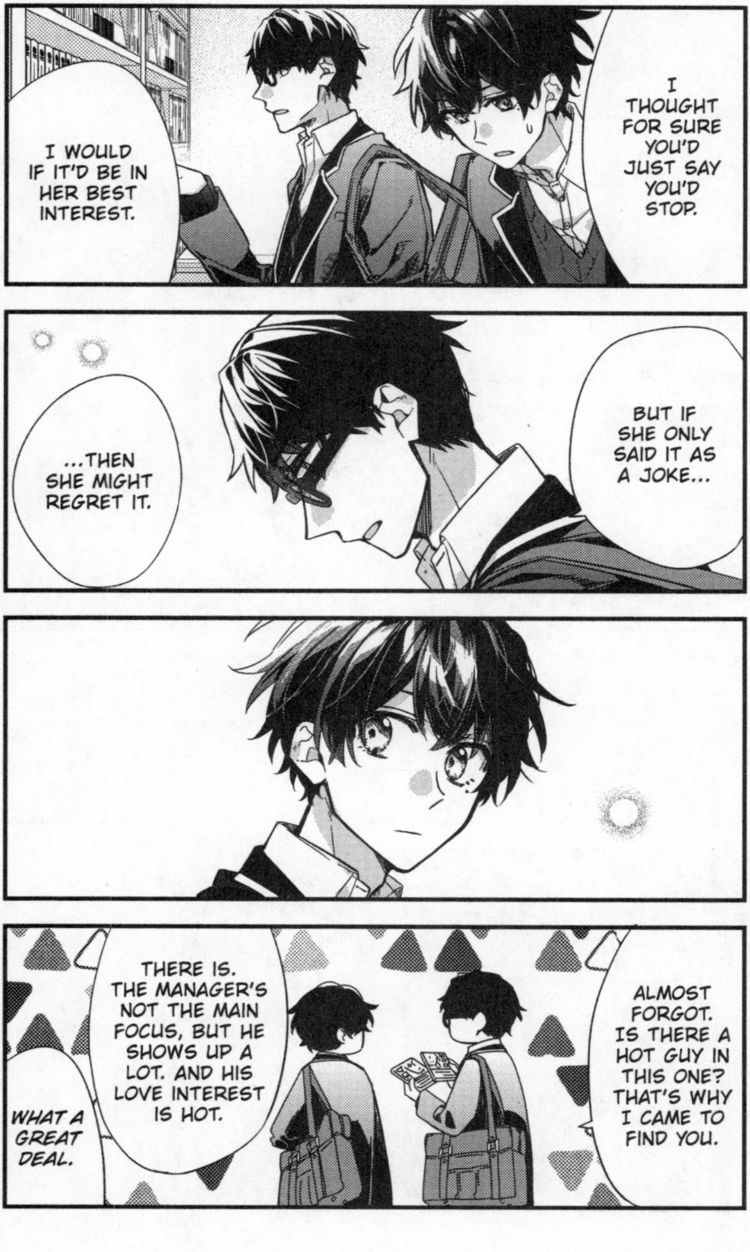
I THOUGHT FOR SURE YOU'D JUST SAY YOU'D STOP.
I WOULD IF IT'D BE IN HER BEST INTEREST.
BUT IF SHE ONLY SAID IT AS A JOKE...
...THEN SHE MIGHT REGRET IT.
ALMOST FORGOT. IS THERE A HOT GUY IN THIS ONE? THAT'S WHY I CAME TO FIND YOU.
THERE IS. THE MANAGER'S NOT THE MAIN FOCUS, BUT HE SHOWS UP A LOT. AND HIS LOVE INTEREST IS HOT.
WHAT A GREAT DEAL.

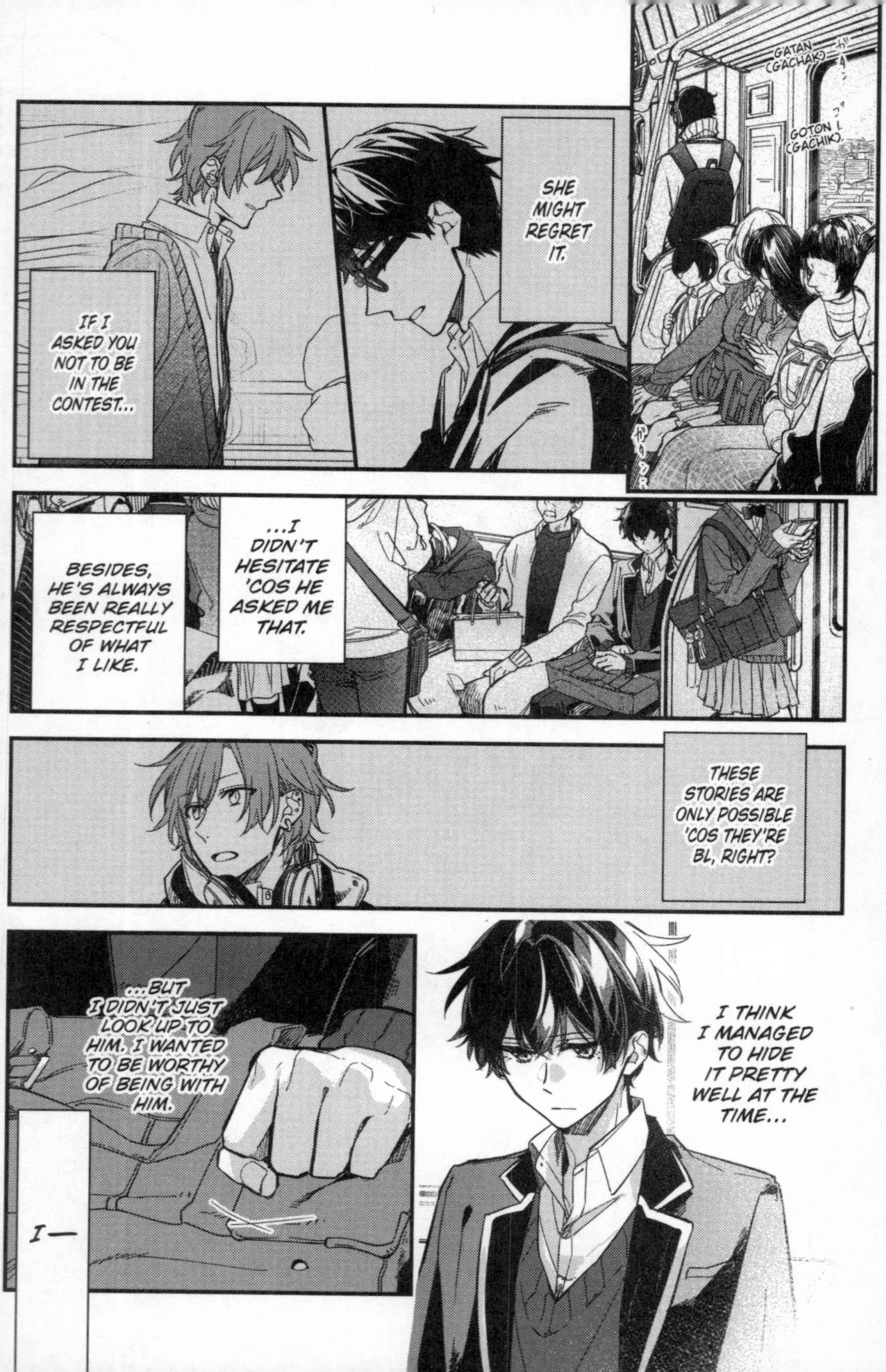
GATAN (GACHAK)
GOTON (GACHIK)
SHE MIGHT REGRET IT.
IF I ASKED YOU NOT TO BE IN THE CONTEST...
...I DIDN'T HESITATE 'COS HE ASKED ME THAT.
BESIDES, HE'S ALWAYS BEEN REALLY RESPECTFUL OF WHAT I LIKE.
THESE STORIES ARE ONLY POSSIBLE 'COS THEY'RE BL, RIGHT?
I THINK I MANAGED TO HIDE IT PRETTY WELL AT THE TIME...
...BUT I DIDN'T JUST LOOK UP TO HIM. I WANTED TO BE WORTHY OF BEING WITH HIM.
I—

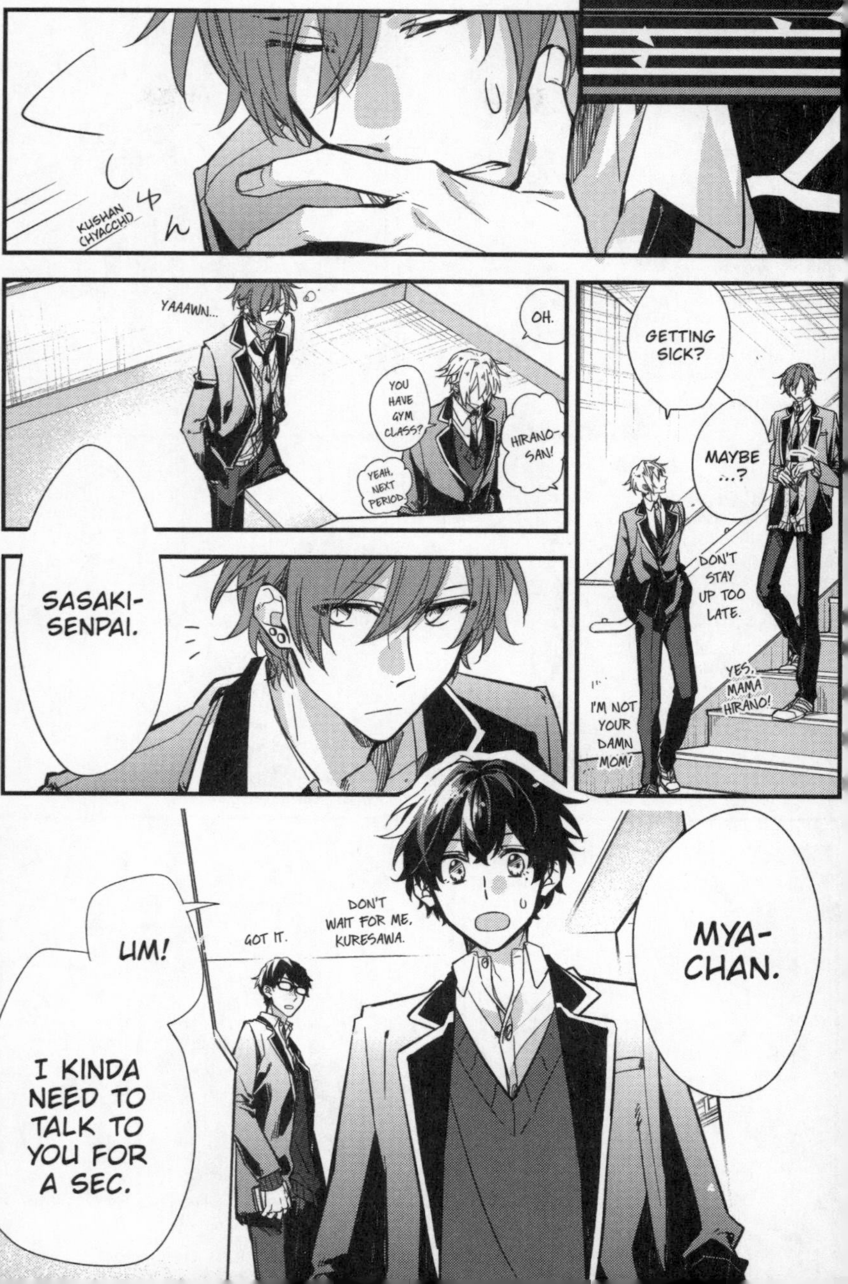
しゅん
KUSHAN CHYACCHD
GETTING SICK?
MAYBE ...?
DON'T STAY UP TOO LATE.
YES, MAMA HIRANO!
I'M NOT YOUR DAMN MOM!
OH.
HIRANO-SAN!
YOU HAVE GYM CLASS?
YEAH, NEXT PERIOD.
YAAAWN...
SASAKI-SENPAI.
MYA-CHAN.
DON'T WAIT FOR ME, KURESAWA.
GOT IT.
UM!
I KINDA NEED TO TALK TO YOU FOR A SEC.

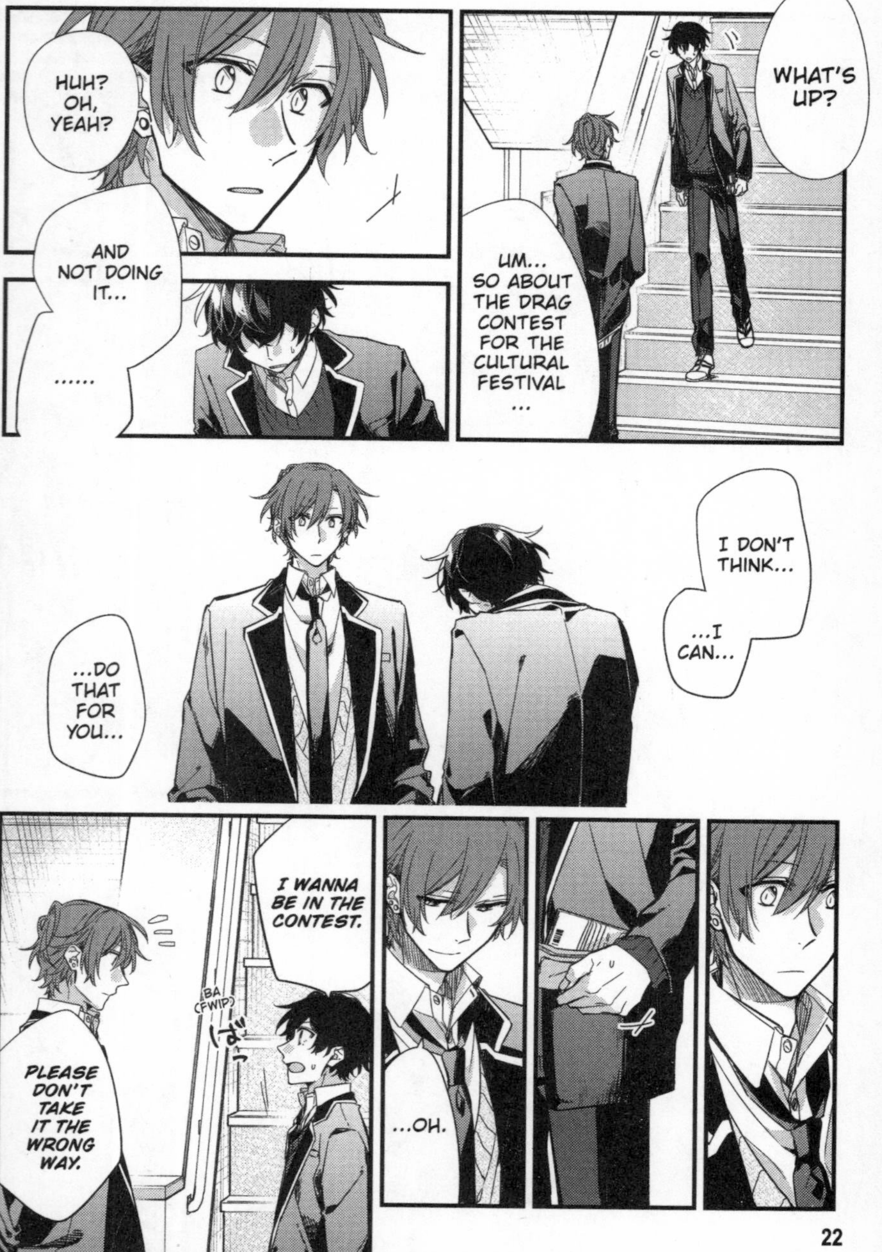
WHAT'S UP?
UM... SO ABOUT THE DRAG CONTEST FOR THE CULTURAL FESTIVAL ...
HUH? OH, YEAH?
AND NOT DOING IT...
......
I DON'T THINK...
...I CAN...
...DO THAT FOR YOU...
...OH.
I WANNA BE IN THE CONTEST.
BA (FWIP)
PLEASE DON'T TAKE IT THE WRONG WAY.

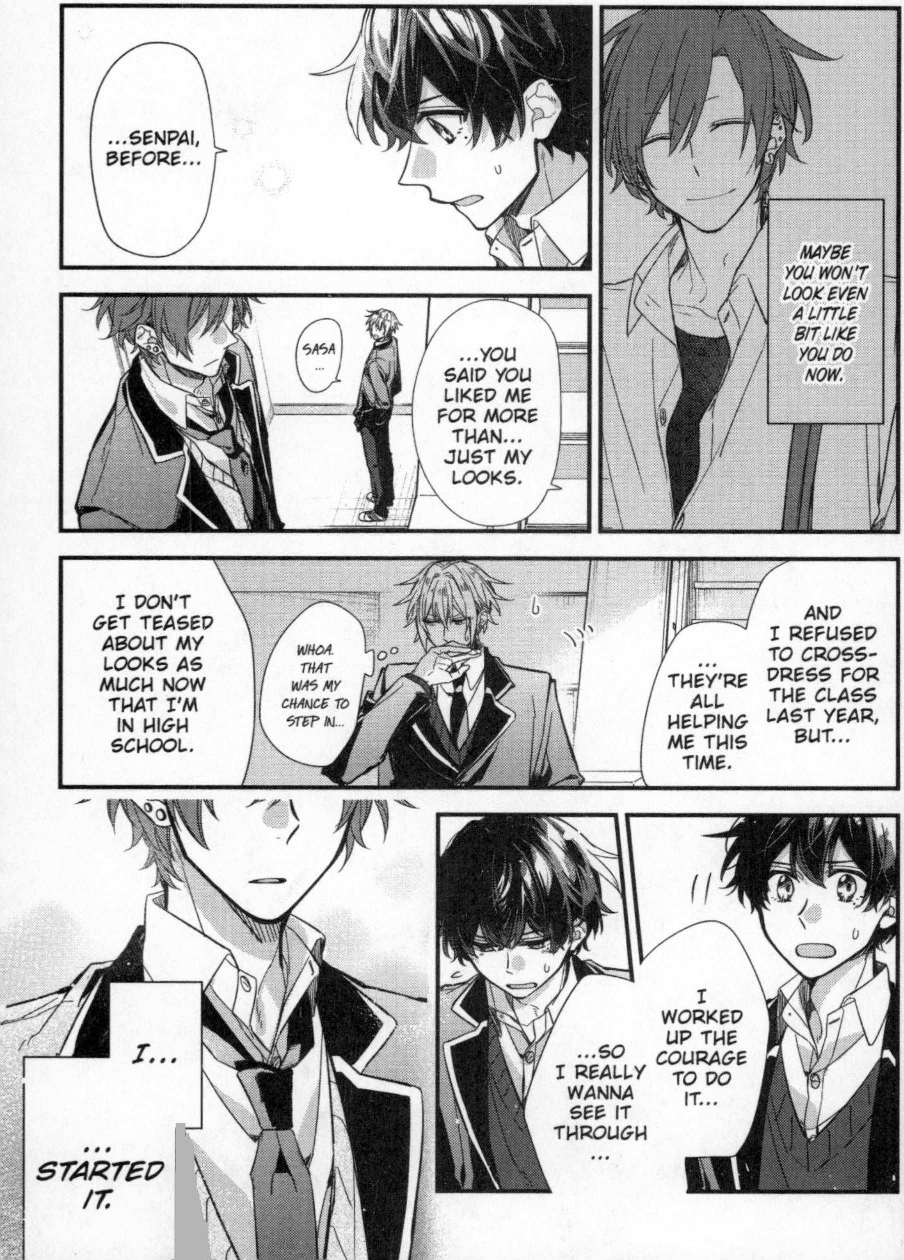
MAYBE YOU WON'T LOOK EVEN A LITTLE BIT LIKE YOU DO NOW.
...SENPAI, BEFORE...
...YOU SAID YOU LIKED ME FOR MORE THAN... JUST MY LOOKS.
SASA ...
AND I REFUSED TO CROSS-DRESS FOR THE CLASS LAST YEAR, BUT...
... THEY'RE ALL HELPING ME THIS TIME.
WHOA. THAT WAS MY CHANCE TO STEP IN...
I DON'T GET TEASED ABOUT MY LOOKS AS MUCH NOW THAT I'M IN HIGH SCHOOL.
I WORKED UP THE COURAGE TO DO IT...
...SO I REALLY WANNA SEE IT THROUGH ...
I...
... STARTED IT.

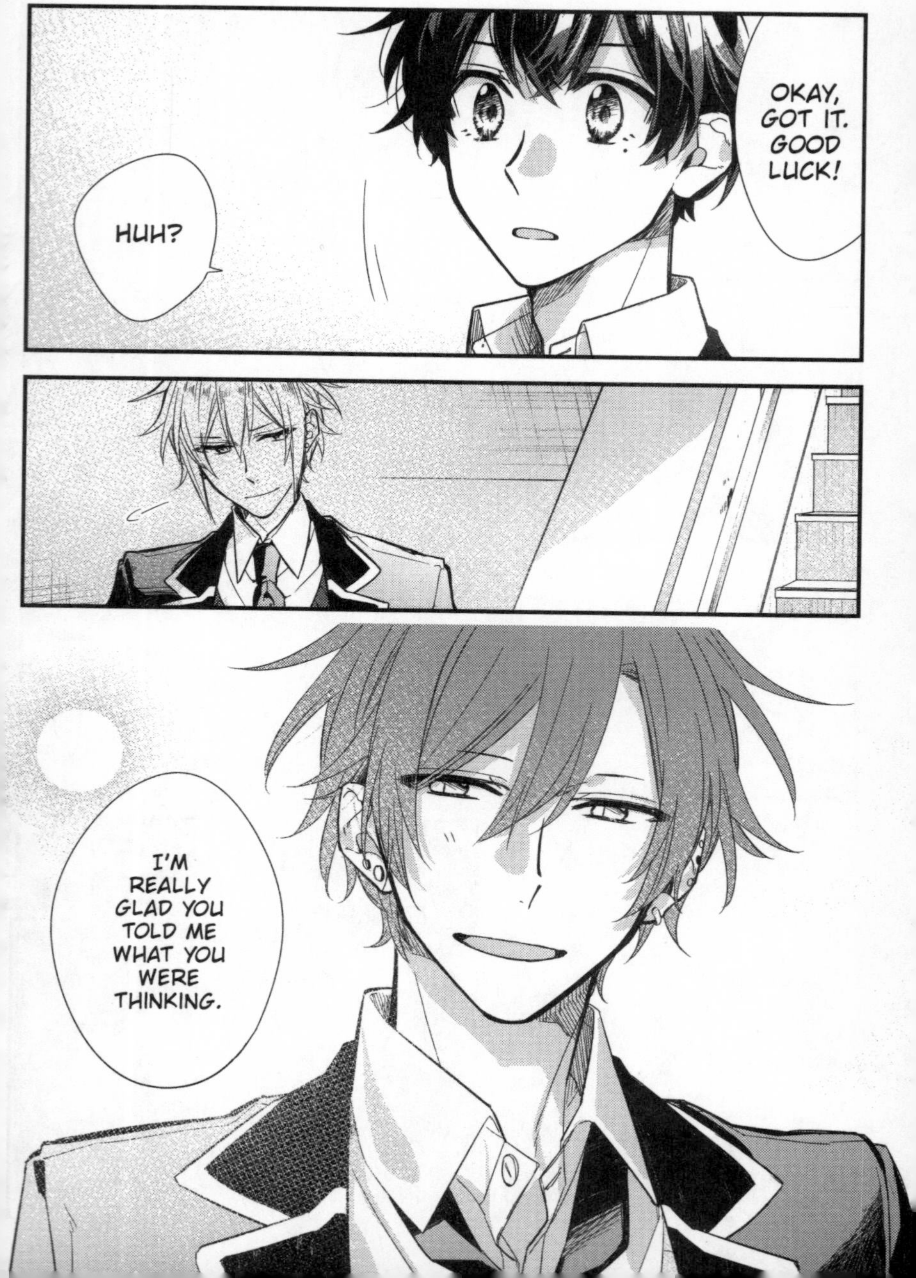
OKAY, GOT IT. GOOD LUCK!
HUH?
I'M REALLY GLAD YOU TOLD ME WHAT YOU WERE THINKING.

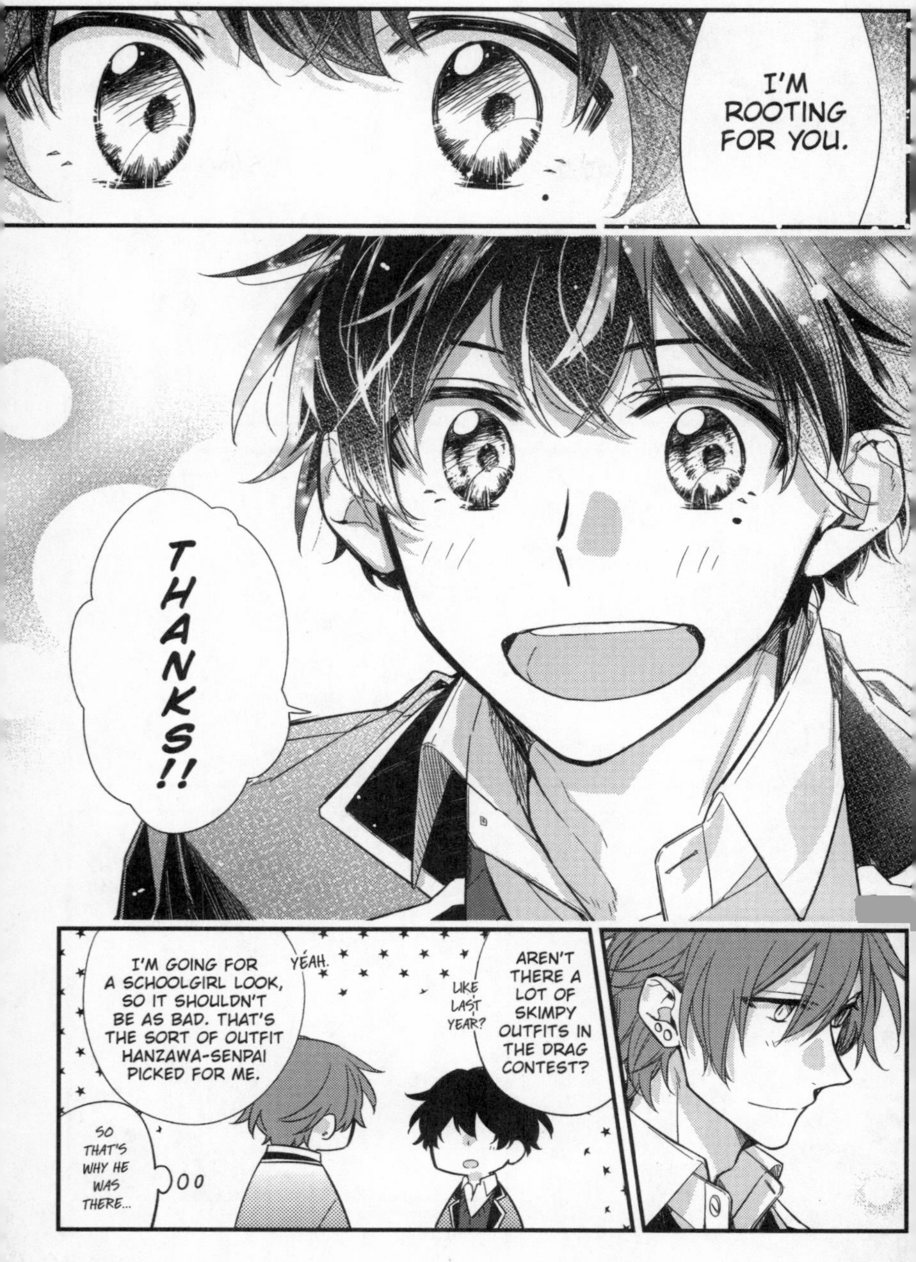
I'M ROOTING FOR YOU.
THANKS!!
AREN'T THERE A LOT OF SKIMPY OUTFITS IN THE DRAG CONTEST?
LIKE LAST YEAR?
YEAH.
I'M GOING FOR A SCHOOLGIRL LOOK, SO IT SHOULDN'T BE AS BAD. THAT'S THE SORT OF OUTFIT HANZAWA-SENPAI PICKED FOR ME.
SO THAT'S WHY HE WAS THERE...

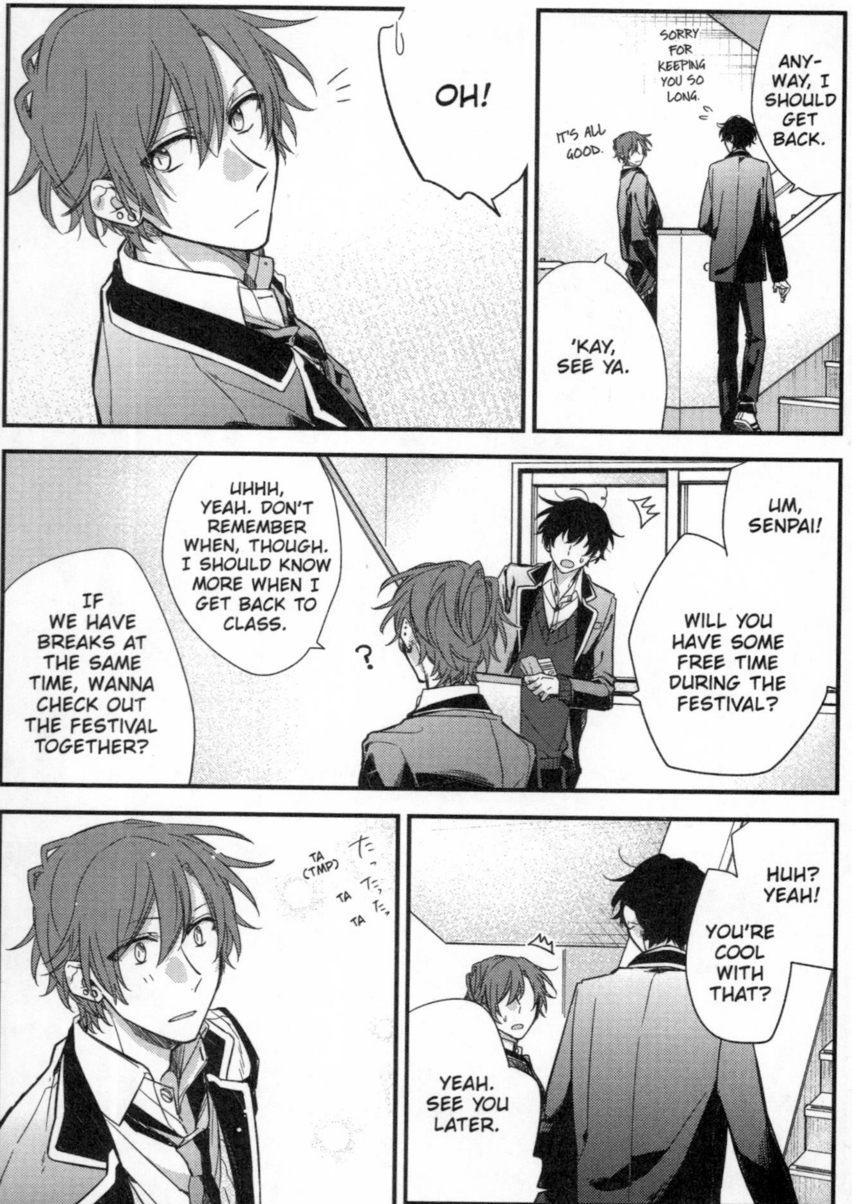
ANY-WAY, I SHOULD GET BACK.
SORRY FOR KEEPING YOU SO LONG.
IT'S ALL GOOD.
'KAY, SEE YA.
OH!
UM, SENPAI!
WILL YOU HAVE SOME FREE TIME DURING THE FESTIVAL?
UHHH, YEAH. DON'T REMEMBER WHEN, THOUGH. I SHOULD KNOW MORE WHEN I GET BACK TO CLASS.
?
IF WE HAVE BREAKS AT THE SAME TIME, WANNA CHECK OUT THE FESTIVAL TOGETHER?
HUH? YEAH!
YOU'RE COOL WITH THAT?
YEAH. SEE YOU LATER.
TA (TMP)
TA
TA

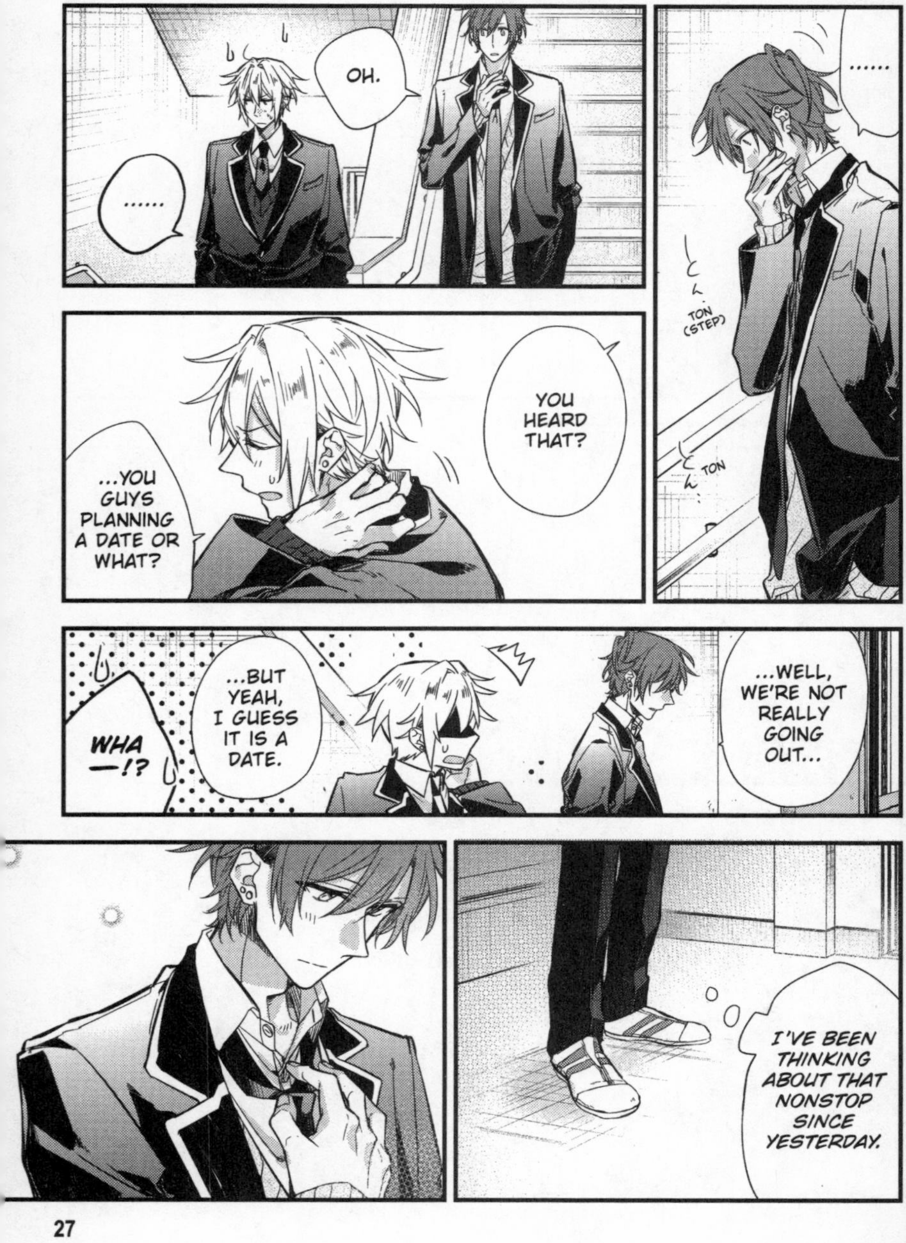
......
とん
TON (STEP)
とん
TON
OH.
......
YOU HEARD THAT?
...YOU GUYS PLANNING A DATE OR WHAT?
...WELL, WE'RE NOT REALLY GOING OUT...
...BUT YEAH, I GUESS IT IS A DATE.
WHA—!?
I'VE BEEN THINKING ABOUT THAT NONSTOP SINCE YESTERDAY.

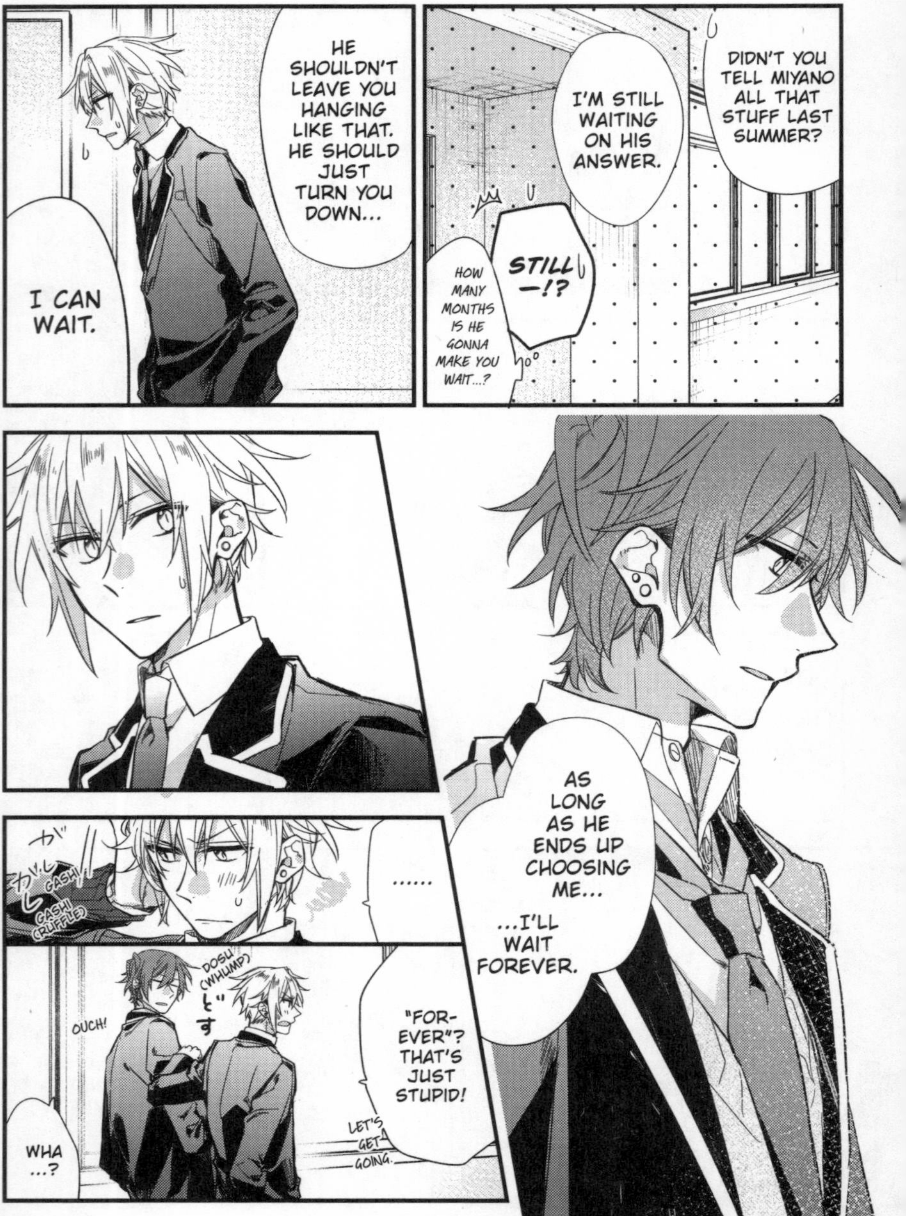
DIDN'T YOU TELL MIYANO ALL THAT STUFF LAST SUMMER?
I'M STILL WAITING ON HIS ANSWER.
STILL—!?
HOW MANY MONTHS IS HE GONNA MAKE YOU WAIT...?
HE SHOULDN'T LEAVE YOU HANGING LIKE THAT. HE SHOULD JUST TURN YOU DOWN...
I CAN WAIT.
AS LONG AS HE ENDS UP CHOOSING ME...
...I'LL WAIT FOREVER.
......
GASHI GASHI (RUFFLE)
"FOR-EVER"? THAT'S JUST STUPID!
DOSU (WHUMP)
OUCH!
LET'S GET GOING.
WHA...?

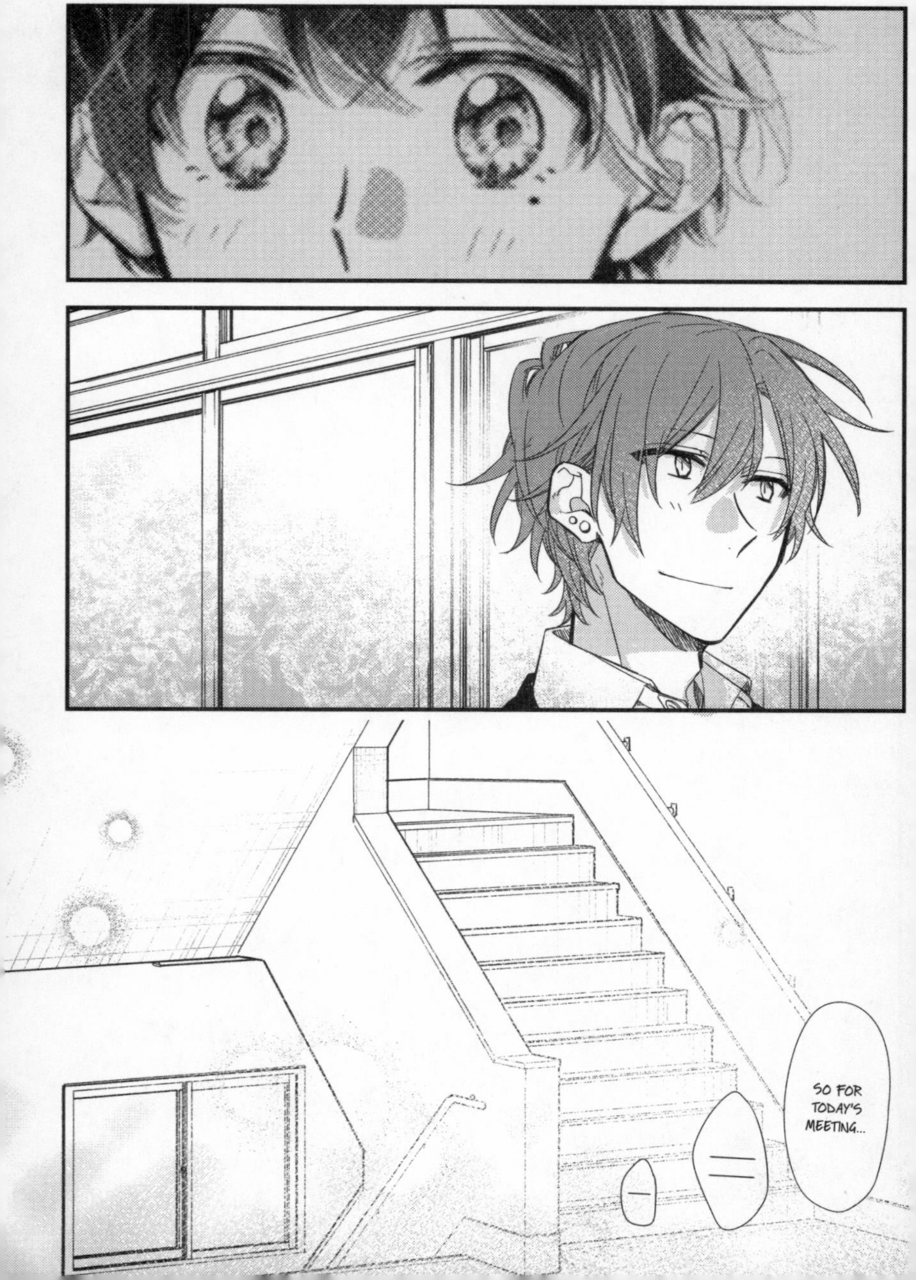
SO FOR TODAY'S MEETING...

Sasaki and Miyano

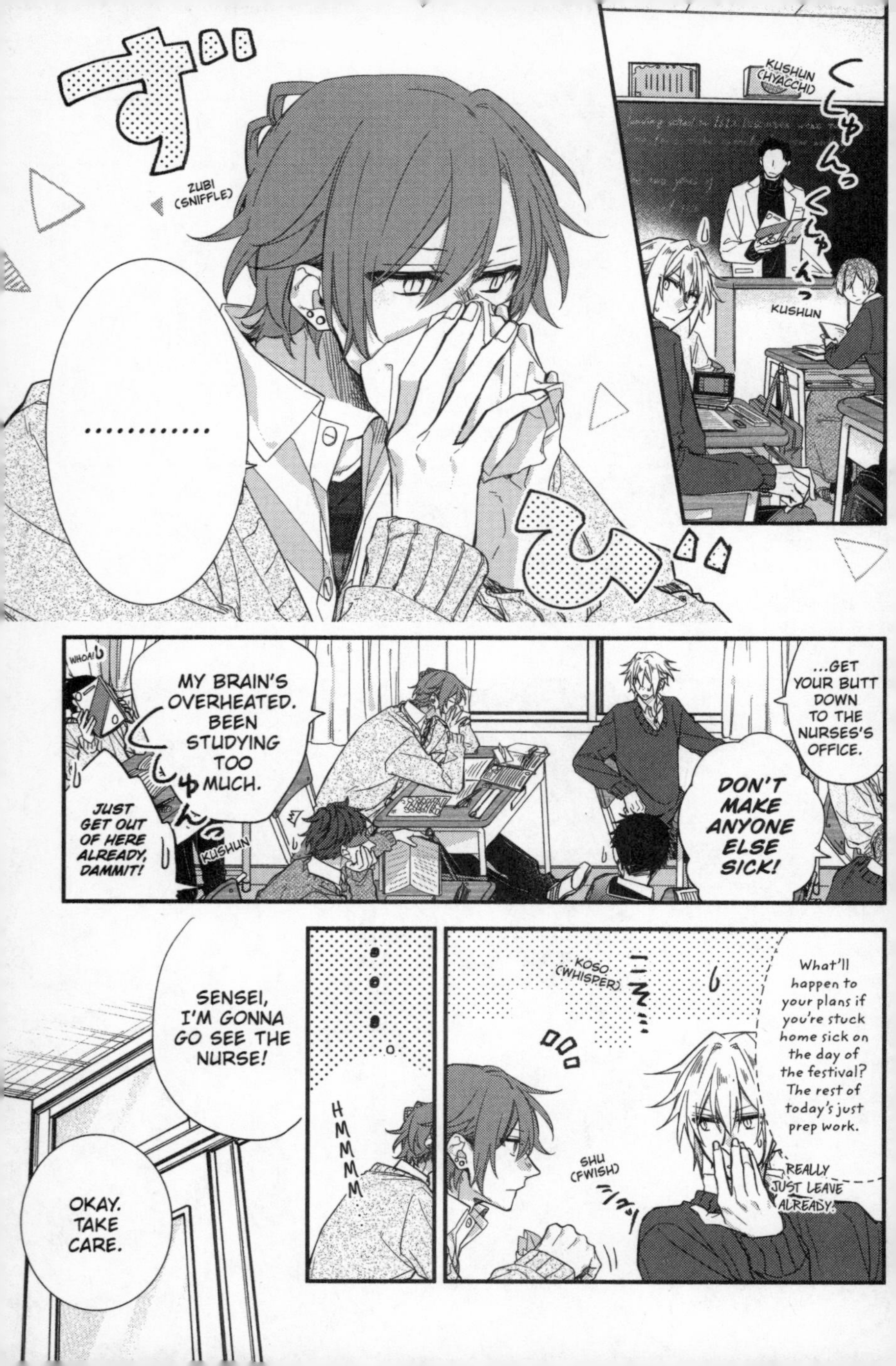
KUSHUN (HYACCHI)
くしゅんっ くしゅんっ
KUSHUN
ZUBI (SNIFFLE)
ずびっ
....
...GET YOUR BUTT DOWN TO THE NURSES'S OFFICE.
DON'T MAKE ANYONE ELSE SICK!
MY BRAIN'S OVERHEATED. BEEN STUDYING TOO MUCH.
KUSHUN
JUST GET OUT OF HERE ALREADY, DAMMIT!
WHOA!
What'll happen to your plans if you're stuck home sick on the day of the festival? The rest of today's just prep work.
KOSO (WHISPER)
REALLY JUST LEAVE ALREADY!
SHU (FWISH)
HMMMM
SENSEI, I'M GONNA GO SEE THE NURSE!
OKAY. TAKE CARE.

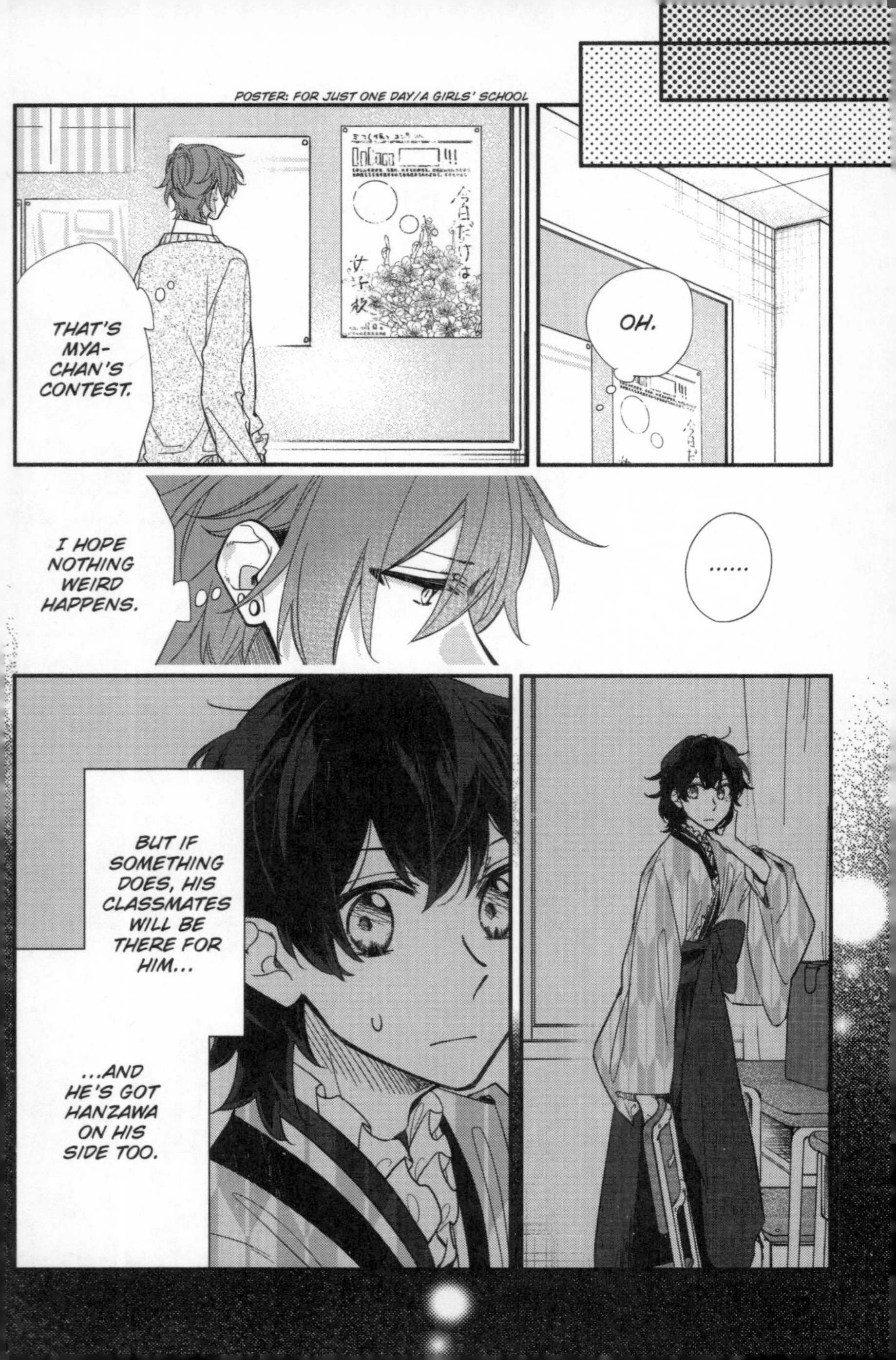
OH.
POSTER: FOR JUST ONE DAY/A GIRLS' SCHOOL
THAT'S MYA-CHAN'S CONTEST.
......
I HOPE NOTHING WEIRD HAPPENS.
BUT IF SOMETHING DOES, HIS CLASSMATES WILL BE THERE FOR HIM...
...AND HE'S GOT HANZAWA ON HIS SIDE TOO.

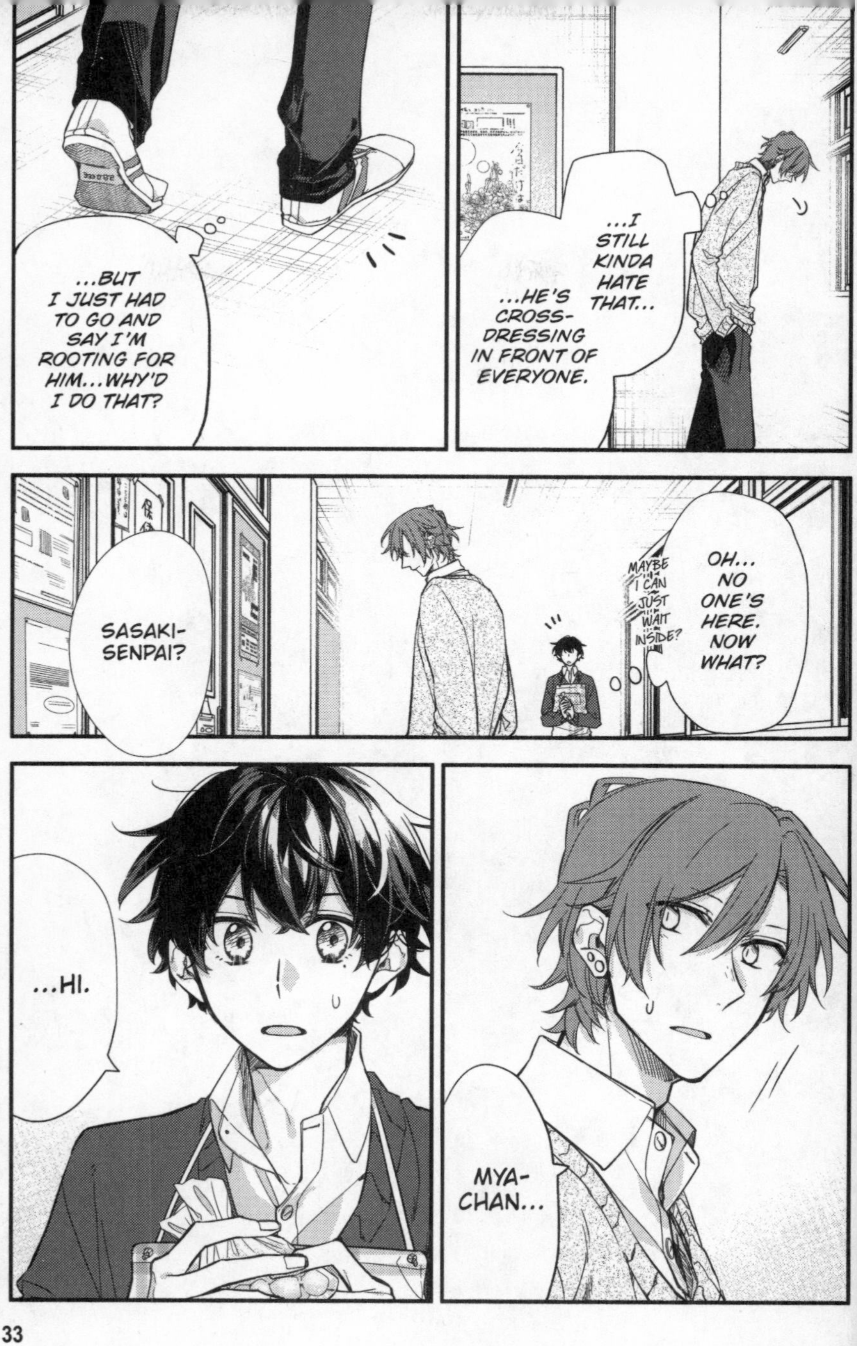
...I STILL KINDA HATE THAT...
...HE'S CROSS-DRESSING IN FRONT OF EVERYONE.
...BUT I JUST HAD TO GO AND SAY I'M ROOTING FOR HIM...WHY'D I DO THAT?
OH... NO ONE'S HERE. NOW WHAT?
MAYBE I CAN JUST WAIT INSIDE?
SASAKI-SENPAI?
MYA-CHAN...
...HI.

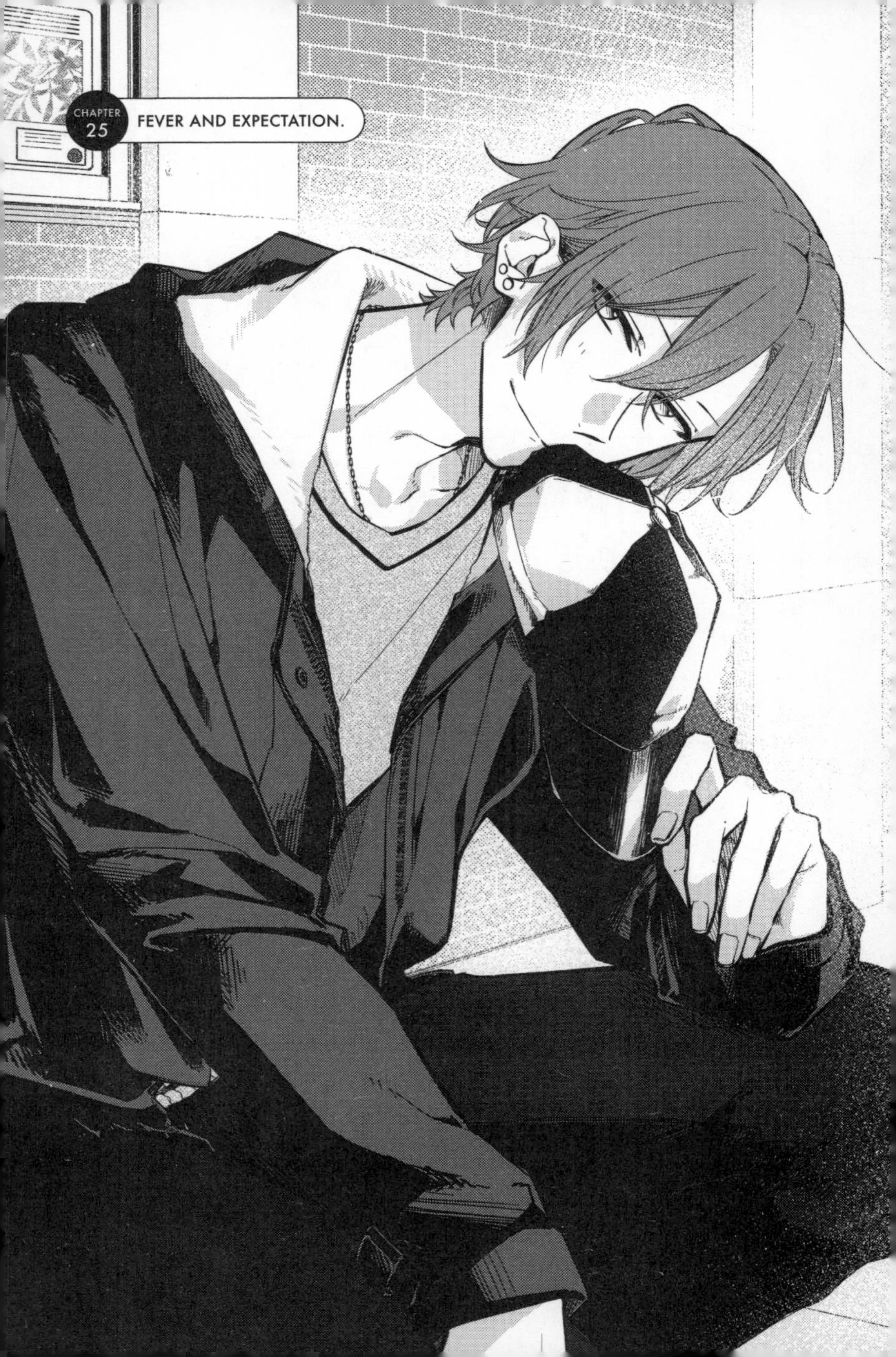
CHAPTER 25
FEVER AND EXPECTATION.

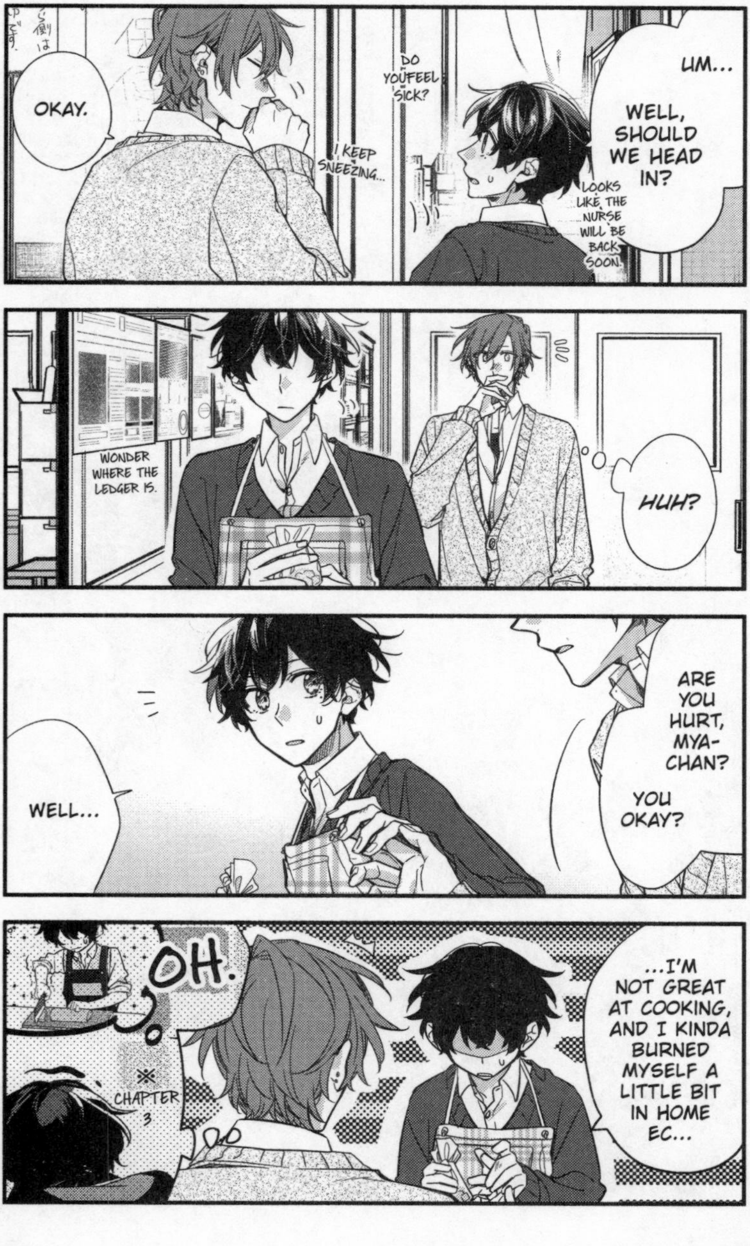
UM...
WELL, SHOULD WE HEAD IN?
LOOKS LIKE THE NURSE WILL BE BACK SOON.
DO YOU FEEL SICK?
I KEEP SNEEZING...
OKAY.
HUH?
WONDER WHERE THE LEDGER IS.
ARE YOU HURT, MYA-CHAN?
YOU OKAY?
WELL...
...I'M NOT GREAT AT COOKING, AND I KINDA BURNED MYSELF A LITTLE BIT IN HOME EC...
OH.
※ CHAPTER 3

HE'S CLUMSY.

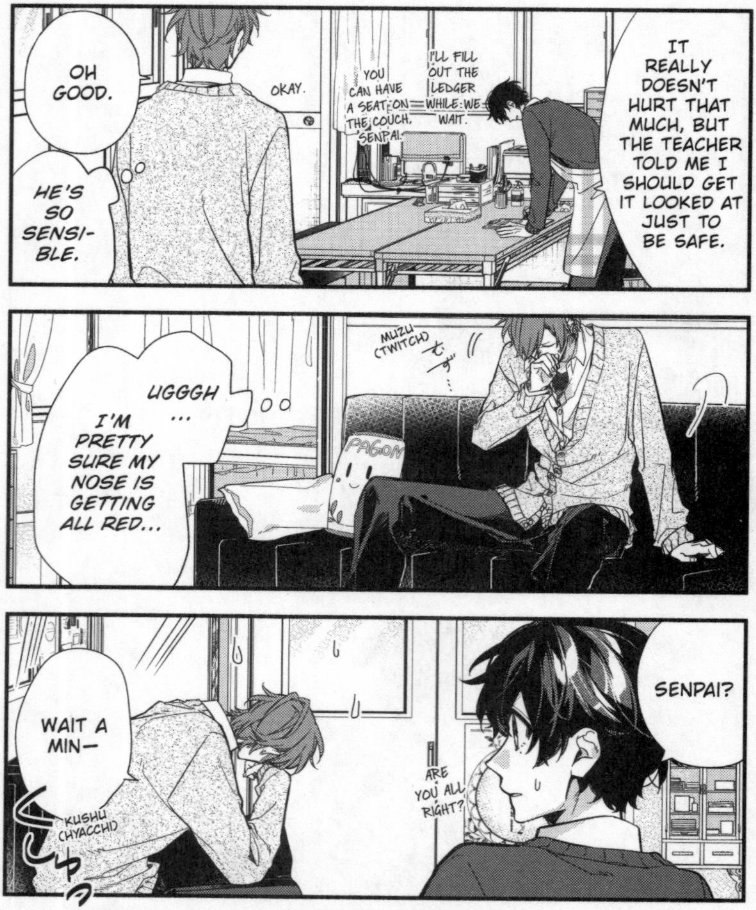
IT REALLY DOESN'T HURT THAT MUCH, BUT THE TEACHER TOLD ME I SHOULD GET IT LOOKED AT JUST TO BE SAFE.
I'LL FILL OUT THE LEDGER WHILE WE WAIT.
YOU CAN HAVE A SEAT ON THE COUCH, SENPAI.
OKAY.
OH GOOD.
HE'S SO SENSIBLE.
MUZU (TWITCH)
PAGON
UGGGH...
I'M PRETTY SURE MY NOSE IS GETTING ALL RED...
SENPAI?
ARE YOU ALL RIGHT?
WAIT A MIN—
KUSHU (CHYACCHI)
...NEED A TISSUE?
HIS SNEEZES ARE PRETTY CUTE...
...THANKS.
CAN'T HIDE THE SNEEZES.

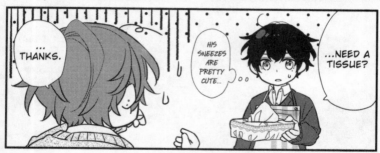

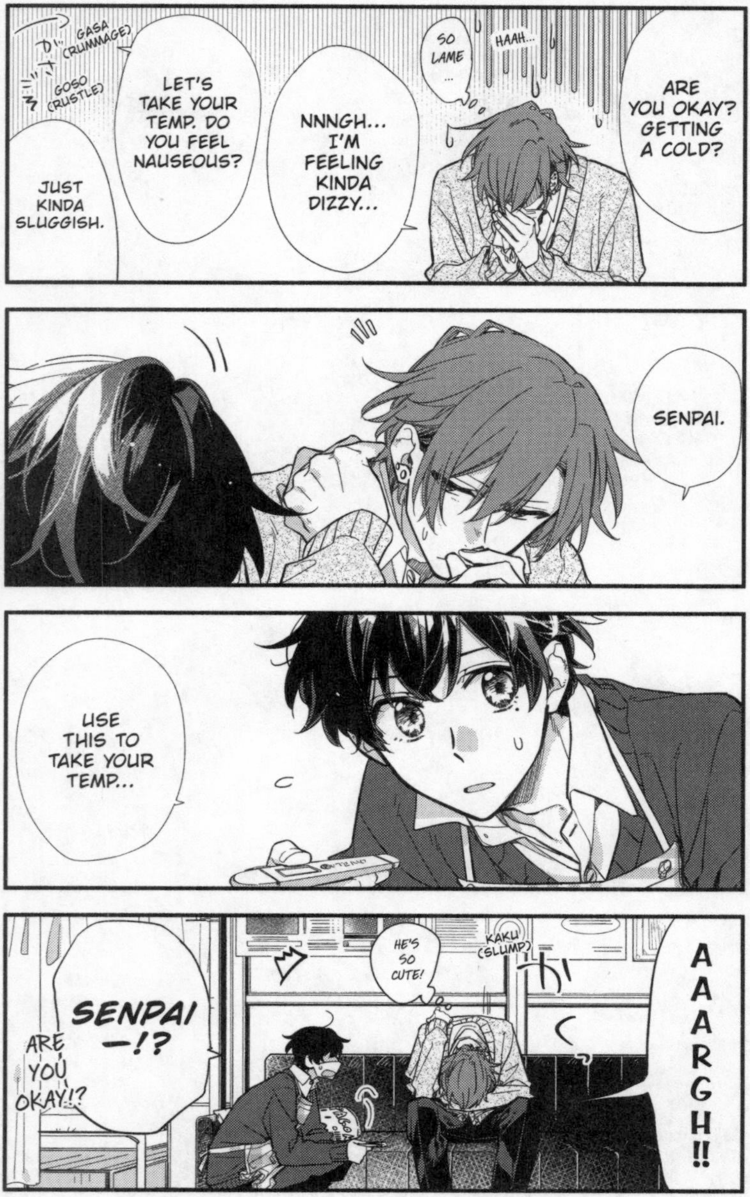
ARE YOU OKAY? GETTING A COLD?
HAAH...
SO LAME ...
NNNGH... I'M FEELING KINDA DIZZY...
LET'S TAKE YOUR TEMP. DO YOU FEEL NAUSEOUS?
GASA (RUMMAGE)
GOSO (RUSTLE)
JUST KINDA SLUGGISH.
SENPAI.
USE THIS TO TAKE YOUR TEMP...
AAAARGH!!
KAKU (SLUMP)
HE'S SO CUTE!
SENPAI—!?
ARE YOU OKAY!?

FEVER RISING.

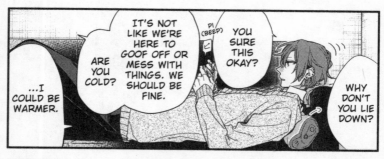

WHY DON'T YOU LIE DOWN?
YOU SURE THIS OKAY?
PI (BEEP)
IT'S NOT LIKE WE'RE HERE TO GOOF OFF OR MESS WITH THINGS. WE SHOULD BE FINE.
ARE YOU COLD?
...I COULD BE WARMER.
......
HE'S LOOKING ALL OVER.
GASA (RUMMAGE)
BLANKET, BLANKET... NOT HERE ...
GASA
IT'S NOT LIKE MYA-CHAN HELPS OUT HERE OR ANYTHING. HE'S ON THE DISCIPLINARY COMMITTEE...
...AND I'M THE OLDER ONE OF US TOO.
SENPAI.
A BOLD UNDERCLASSMAN.
I COULDN'T FIND A BLANKET. ARE YOU OKAY WITH A DUVET INSTEAD?
I GRABBED IT OFF ONE OF THE BEDS.
BASA (FLUMP)
SURE, THANKS.
KOFF!
URGH!
KOFF!
YOU ALL RIGHT?
YEAH...

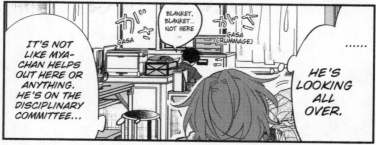

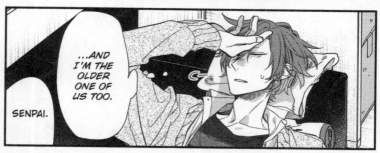

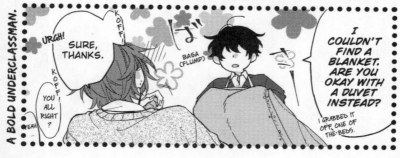

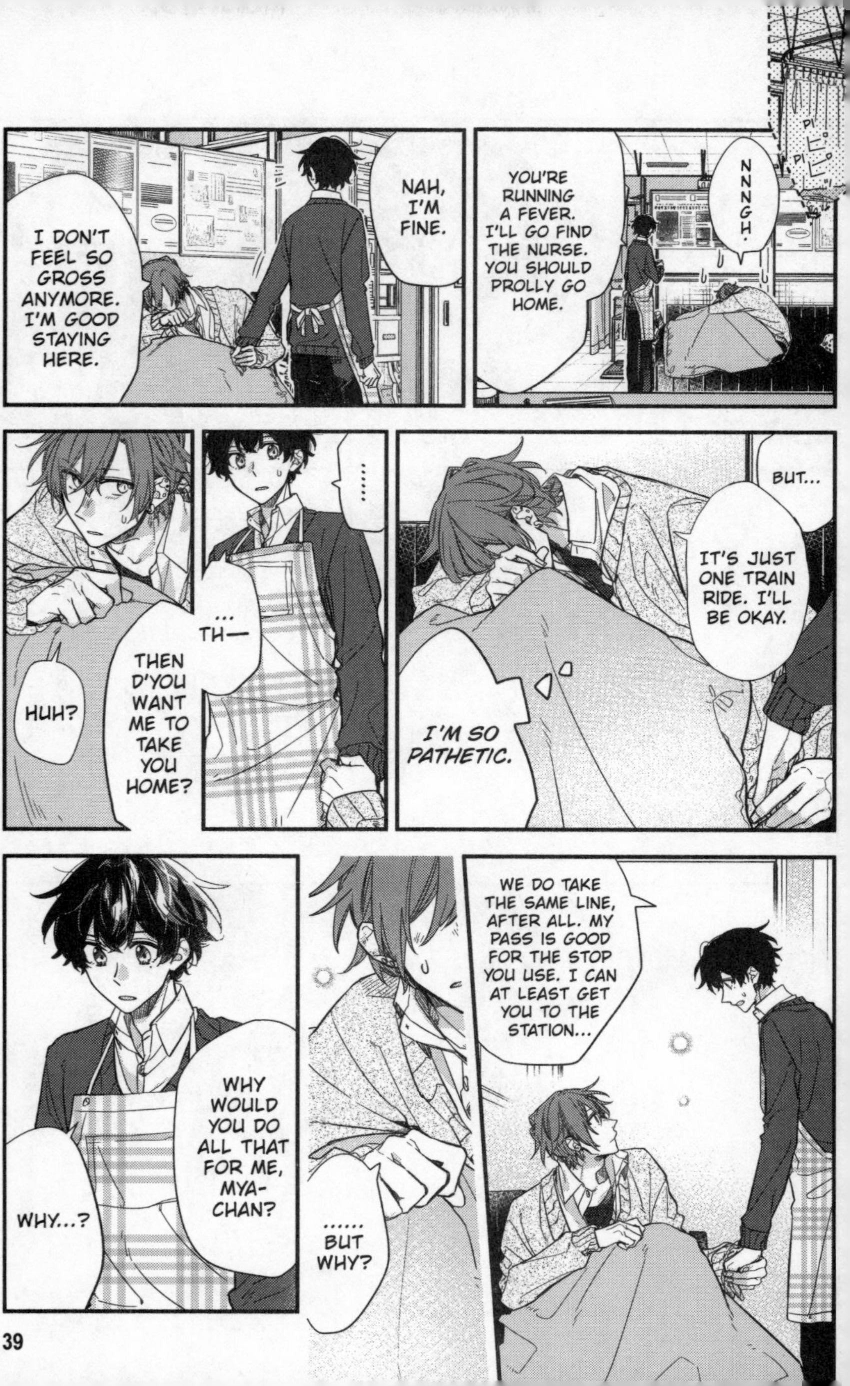
PI
PI
NNNGH.
YOU'RE RUNNING A FEVER. I'LL GO FIND THE NURSE. YOU SHOULD PROLLY GO HOME.
NAH, I'M FINE.
I DON'T FEEL SO GROSS ANYMORE. I'M GOOD STAYING HERE.
BUT...
IT'S JUST ONE TRAIN RIDE. I'LL BE OKAY.
I'M SO PATHETIC.
......
... TH—
THEN D'YOU WANT ME TO TAKE YOU HOME?
HUH?
WE DO TAKE THE SAME LINE, AFTER ALL. MY PASS IS GOOD FOR THE STOP YOU USE. I CAN AT LEAST GET YOU TO THE STATION...
...... BUT WHY?
WHY WOULD YOU DO ALL THAT FOR ME, MYA-CHAN?
WHY...?

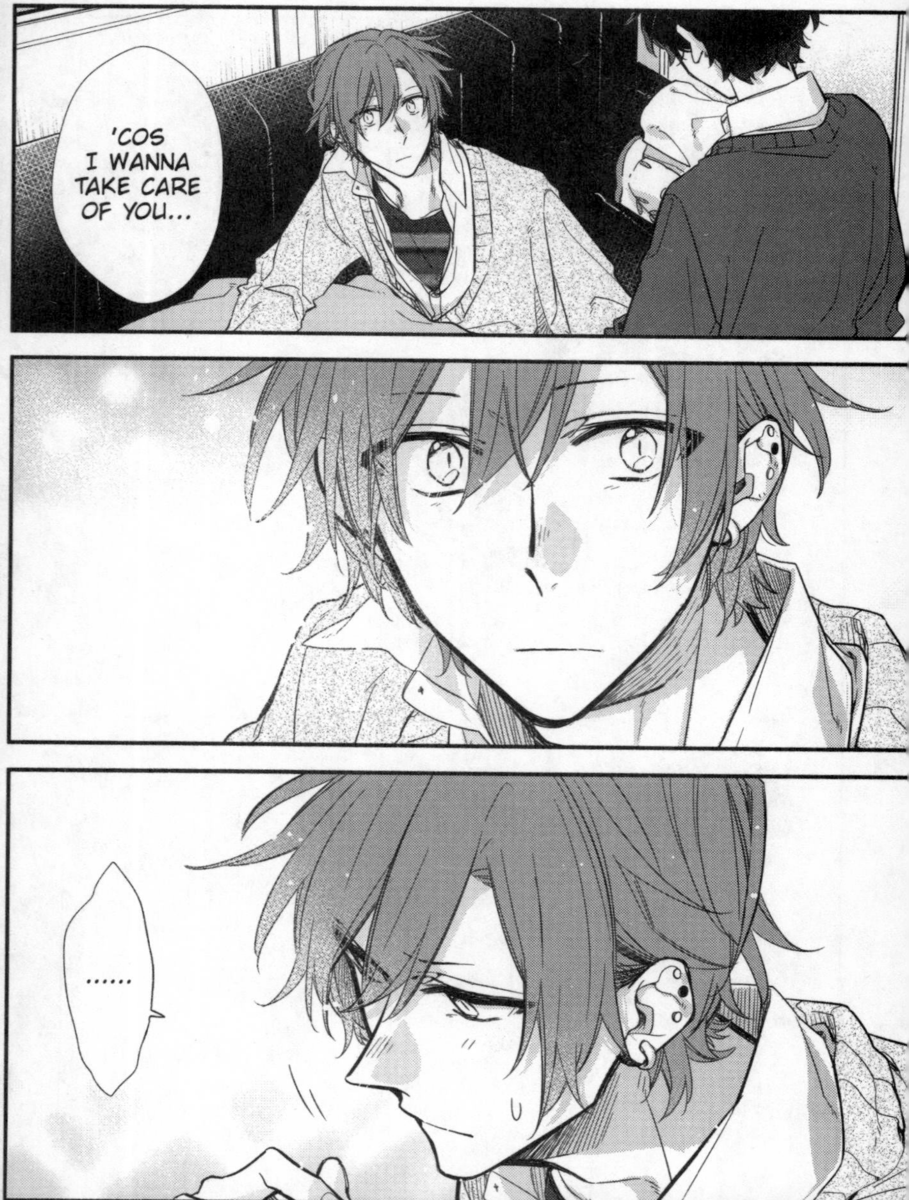
'COS I WANNA TAKE CARE OF YOU...
......

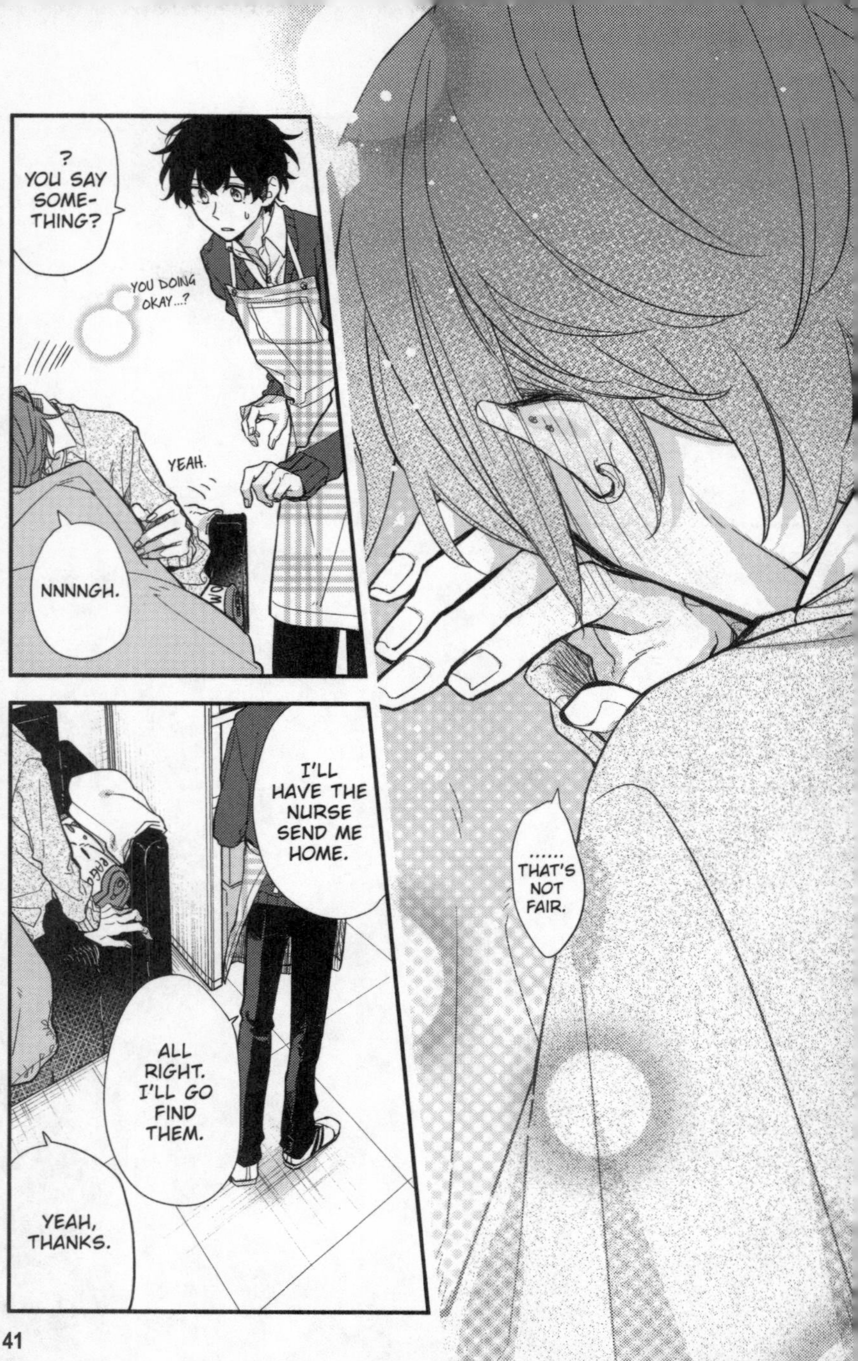

......THAT'S NOT FAIR.
? YOU SAY SOME-THING?
YOU DOING OKAY...?
YEAH.
NNNNGH.
I'LL HAVE THE NURSE SEND ME HOME.
ALL RIGHT. I'LL GO FIND THEM.
YEAH, THANKS.

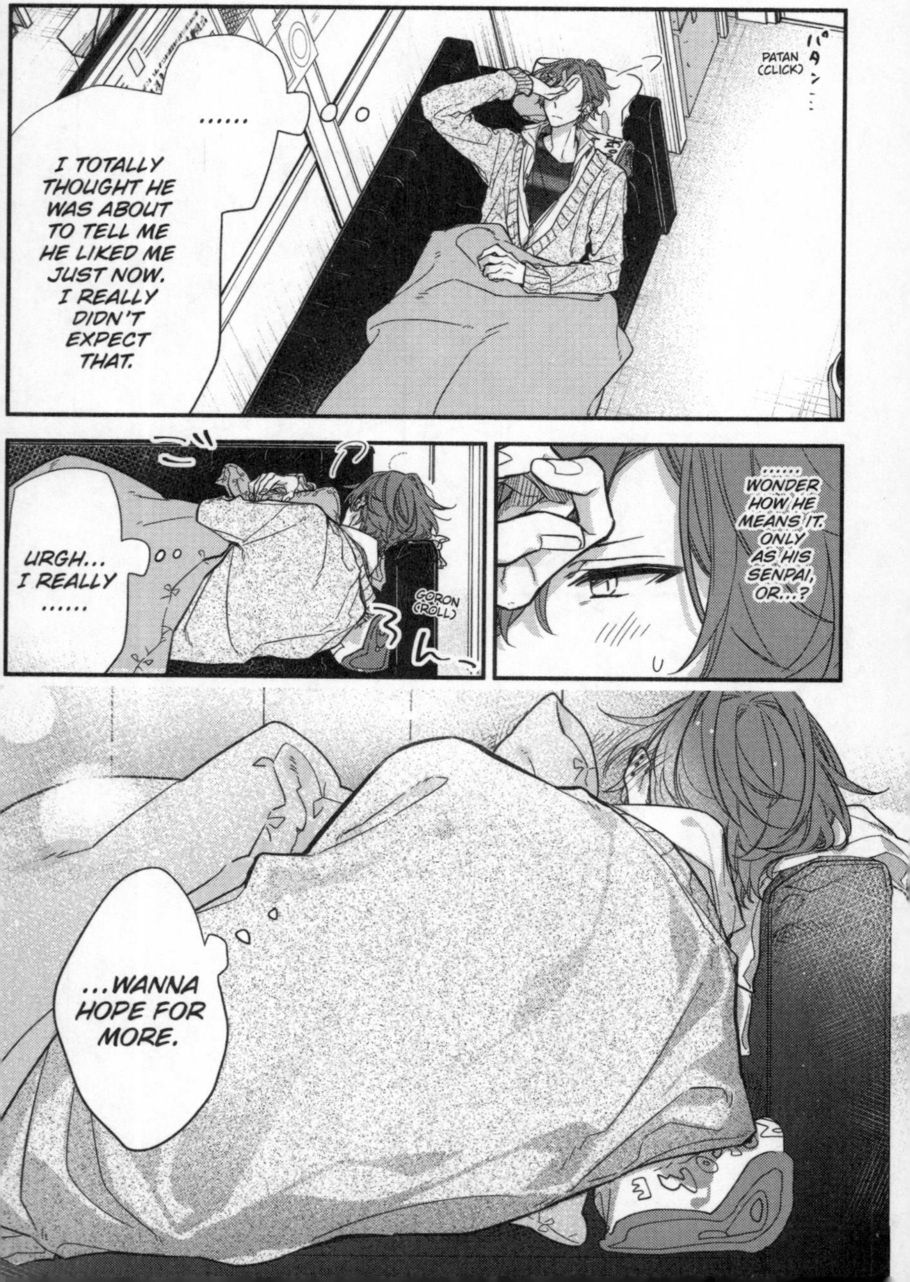
PATAN (CLICK)
......
I TOTALLY THOUGHT HE WAS ABOUT TO TELL ME HE LIKED ME JUST NOW. I REALLY DIDN'T EXPECT THAT.
......WONDER HOW HE MEANS IT. ONLY AS HIS SENPAI, OR...?
GORON (ROLL)
URGH... I REALLY ......
...WANNA HOPE FOR MORE.

Sasaki and Miyano

Sasaki and Miyano

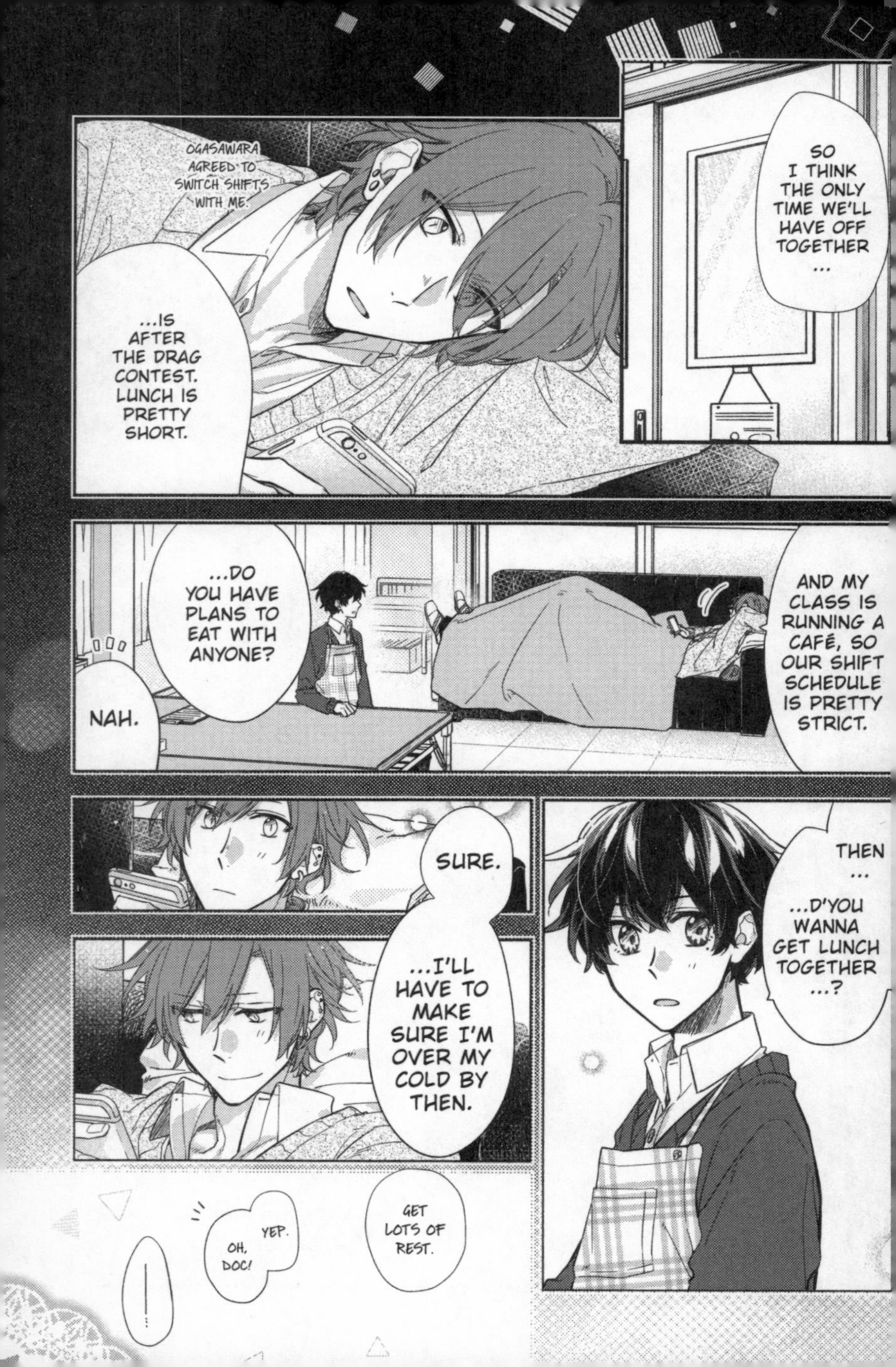
SO I THINK THE ONLY TIME WE'LL HAVE OFF TOGETHER ...
OGASAWARA AGREED TO SWITCH SHIFTS WITH ME.
...IS AFTER THE DRAG CONTEST. LUNCH IS PRETTY SHORT.
AND MY CLASS IS RUNNING A CAFÉ, SO OUR SHIFT SCHEDULE IS PRETTY STRICT.
...DO YOU HAVE PLANS TO EAT WITH ANYONE?
NAH.
THEN ... ...D'YOU WANNA GET LUNCH TOGETHER ...?
SURE.
...I'LL HAVE TO MAKE SURE I'M OVER MY COLD BY THEN.
GET LOTS OF REST.
YEP.
OH, DOC!

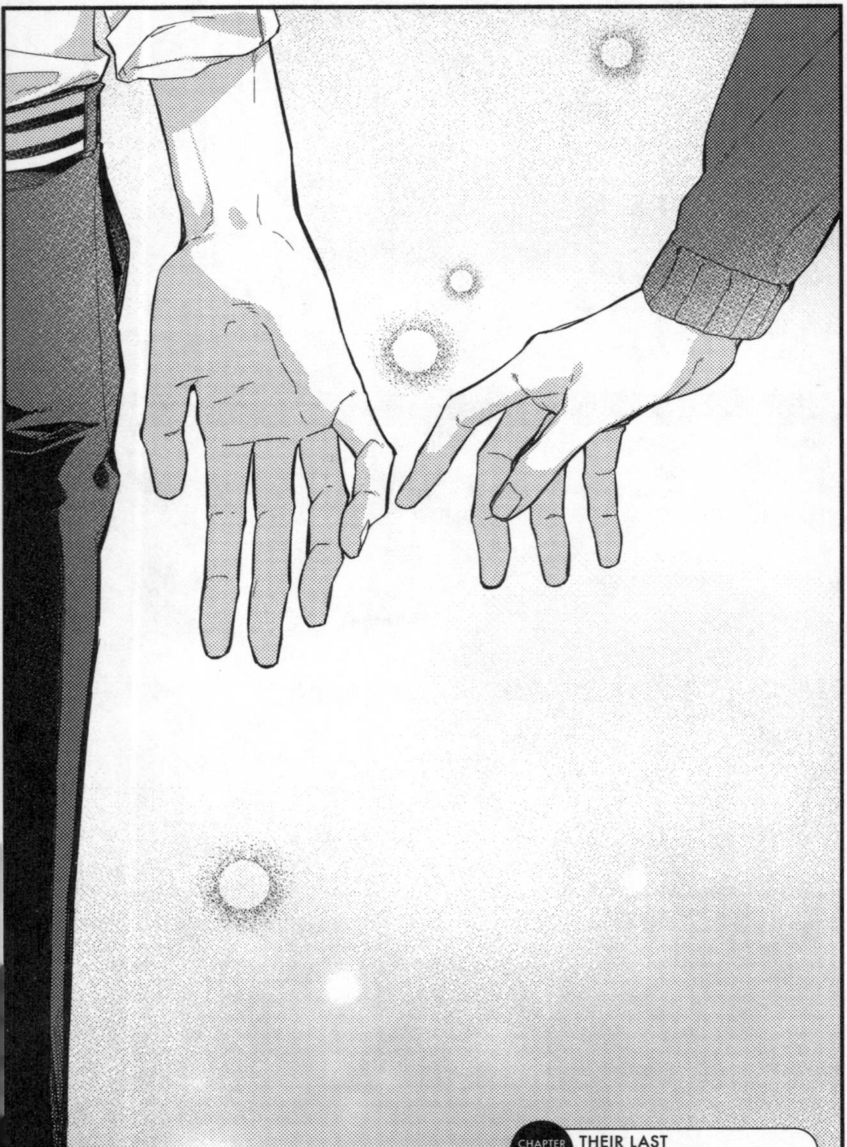
CHAPTER 26
THEIR LAST CULTURAL FESTIVAL.

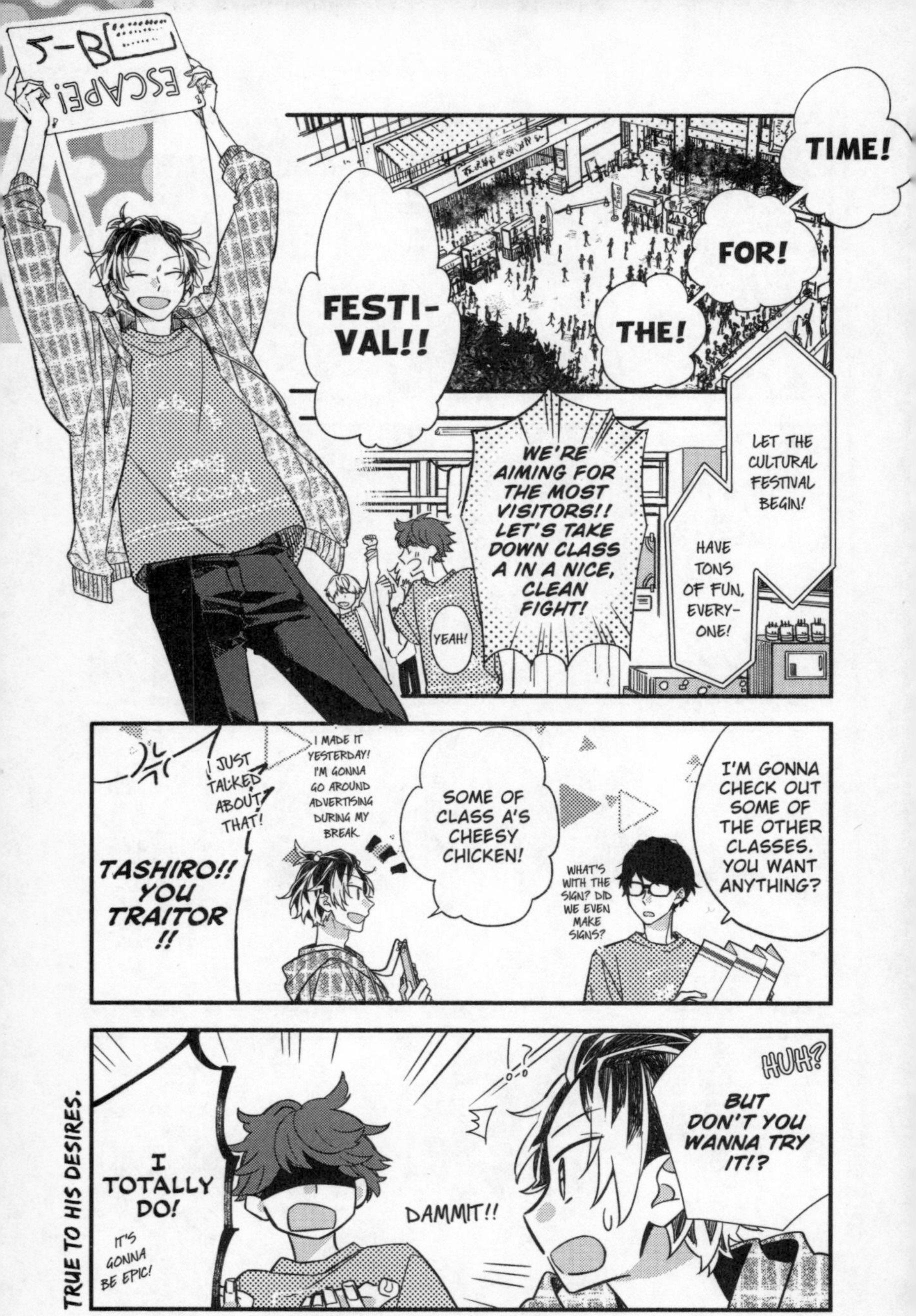
TIME!
FOR!
THE!
FESTI-VAL!!
ESCAPE!
LET THE CULTURAL FESTIVAL BEGIN!
HAVE TONS OF FUN, EVERY-ONE!
WE'RE AIMING FOR THE MOST VISITORS!! LET'S TAKE DOWN CLASS A IN A NICE, CLEAN FIGHT!
YEAH!
I'M GONNA CHECK OUT SOME OF THE OTHER CLASSES. YOU WANT ANYTHING?
WHAT'S WITH THE SIGN? DID WE EVEN MAKE SIGNS?
SOME OF CLASS A'S CHEESY CHICKEN!
I MADE IT YESTERDAY! I'M GONNA GO AROUND ADVERTISING DURING MY BREAK.
I JUST TALKED ABOUT THAT!
TASHIRO!! YOU TRAITOR!!
HUH?
BUT DON'T YOU WANNA TRY IT!?
DAMMIT!!
I TOTALLY DO!
IT'S GONNA BE EPIC!
TRUE TO HIS DESIRES.

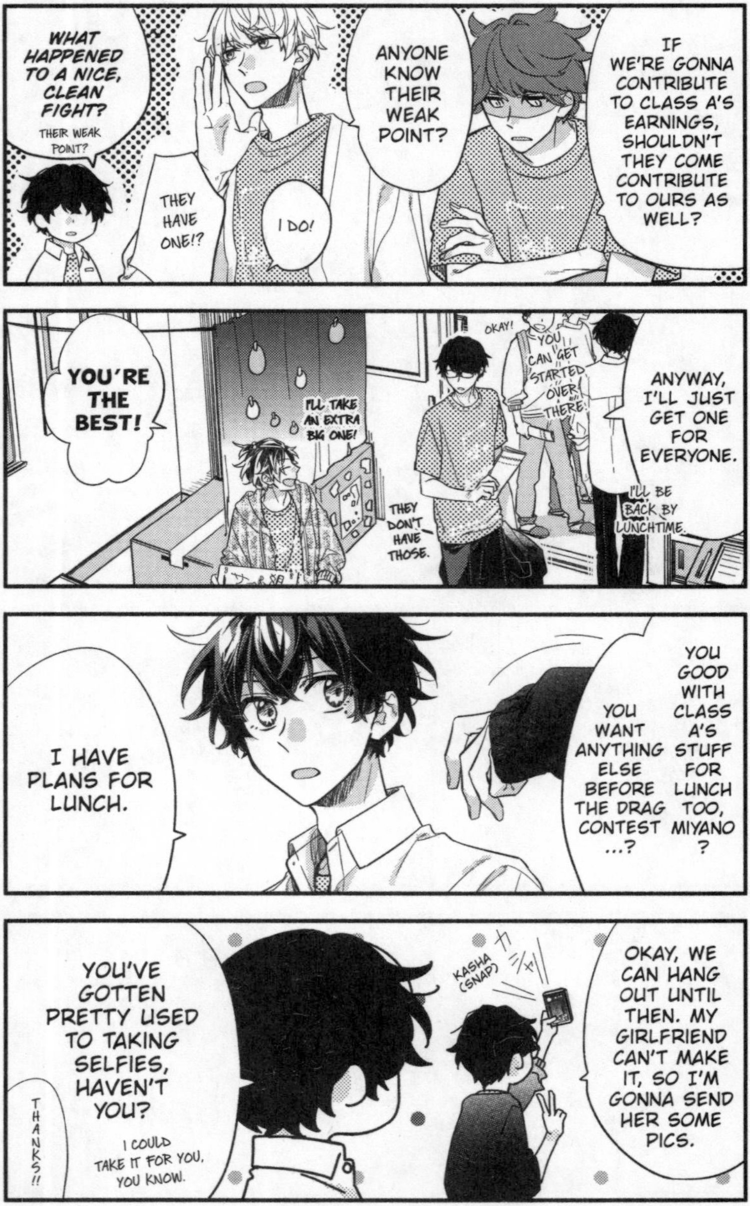
IF WE'RE GONNA CONTRIBUTE TO CLASS A'S EARNINGS, SHOULDN'T THEY COME CONTRIBUTE TO OURS AS WELL?
ANYONE KNOW THEIR WEAK POINT?
I DO!
THEY HAVE ONE!?
WHAT HAPPENED TO A NICE, CLEAN FIGHT?
THEIR WEAK POINT?
ANYWAY, I'LL JUST GET ONE FOR EVERYONE.
I'LL BE BACK BY LUNCHTIME.
YOU CAN GET STARTED OVER THERE.
OKAY!
THEY DON'T HAVE THOSE.
I'LL TAKE AN EXTRA BIG ONE!
YOU'RE THE BEST!
YOU GOOD WITH CLASS A'S STUFF FOR LUNCH TOO, MIYANO?
YOU WANT ANYTHING ELSE BEFORE THE DRAG CONTEST...?
I HAVE PLANS FOR LUNCH.
OKAY, WE CAN HANG OUT UNTIL THEN. MY GIRLFRIEND CAN'T MAKE IT, SO I'M GONNA SEND HER SOME PICS.
KASHA (SNAP)
YOU'VE GOTTEN PRETTY USED TO TAKING SELFIES, HAVEN'T YOU?
I COULD TAKE IT FOR YOU, YOU KNOW.
THANKS!!

MUCH EXCITEMENT.

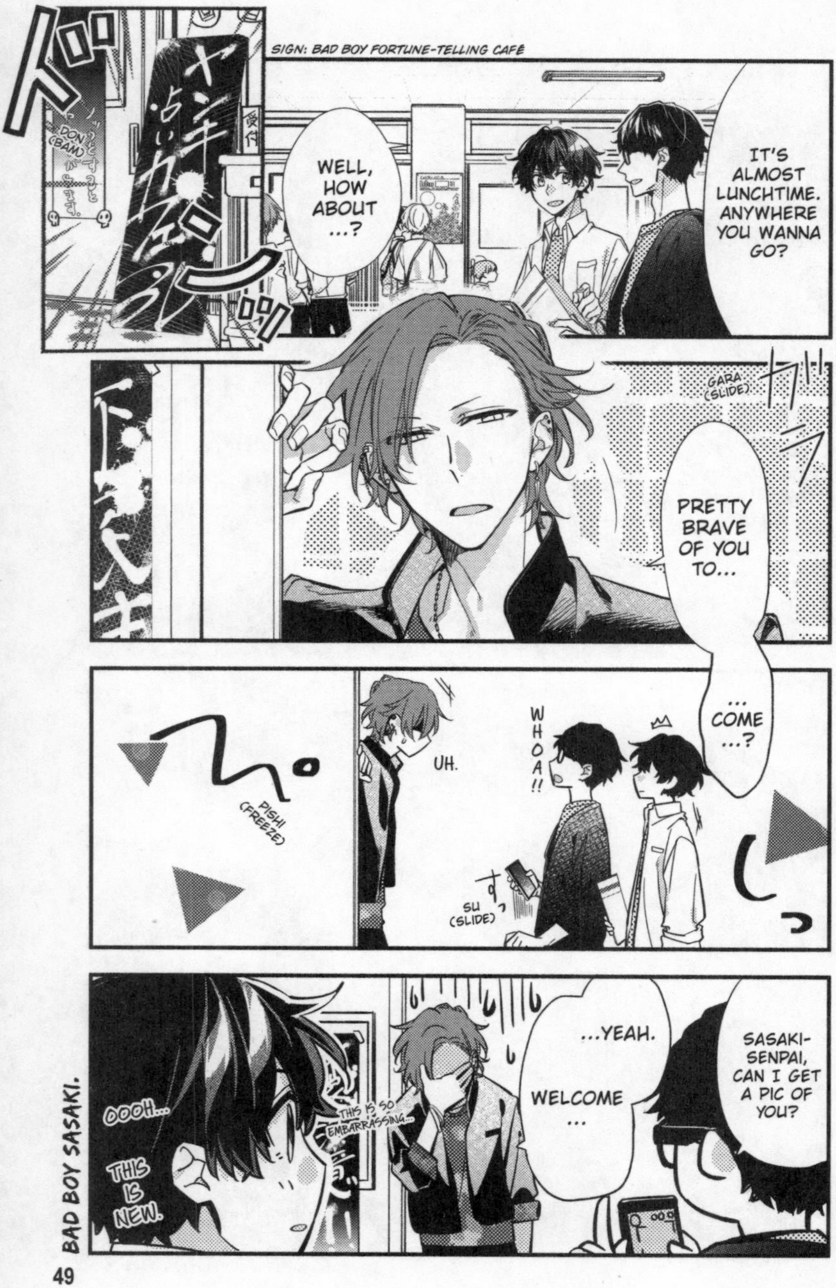
SIGN: BAD BOY FORTUNE-TELLING CAFÉ
IT'S ALMOST LUNCHTIME. ANYWHERE YOU WANNA GO?
WELL, HOW ABOUT ...?
DON (BAM)
GARA (SLIDE)
PRETTY BRAVE OF YOU TO...
... COME ...?
WHOA!!
UH.
SU (SLIDE)
PISHI (FREEZE)
SASAKI-SENPAI, CAN I GET A PIC OF YOU?
...YEAH.
WELCOME ...
THIS IS SO EMBARRASSING...
OOOH...
THIS IS NEW.
BAD BOY SASAKI.

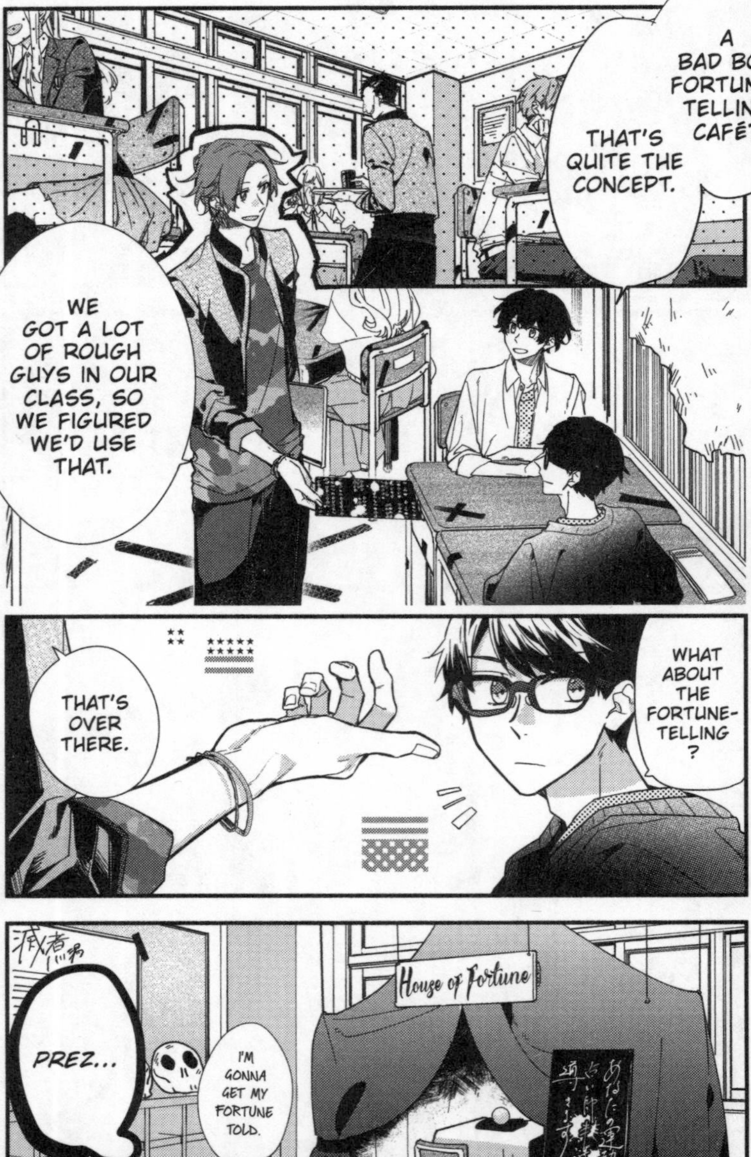
A BAD BOY FORTUNE-TELLING CAFÉ?
THAT'S QUITE THE CONCEPT.
WE GOT A LOT OF ROUGH GUYS IN OUR CLASS, SO WE FIGURED WE'D USE THAT.
WHAT ABOUT THE FORTUNE-TELLING?
THAT'S OVER THERE.
House of Fortune
I'M GONNA GET MY FORTUNE TOLD.
PREZ...

A SPACE OF SUSPICION.

PANEL SIGN: GUIDING YOU TO YOUR LUCK

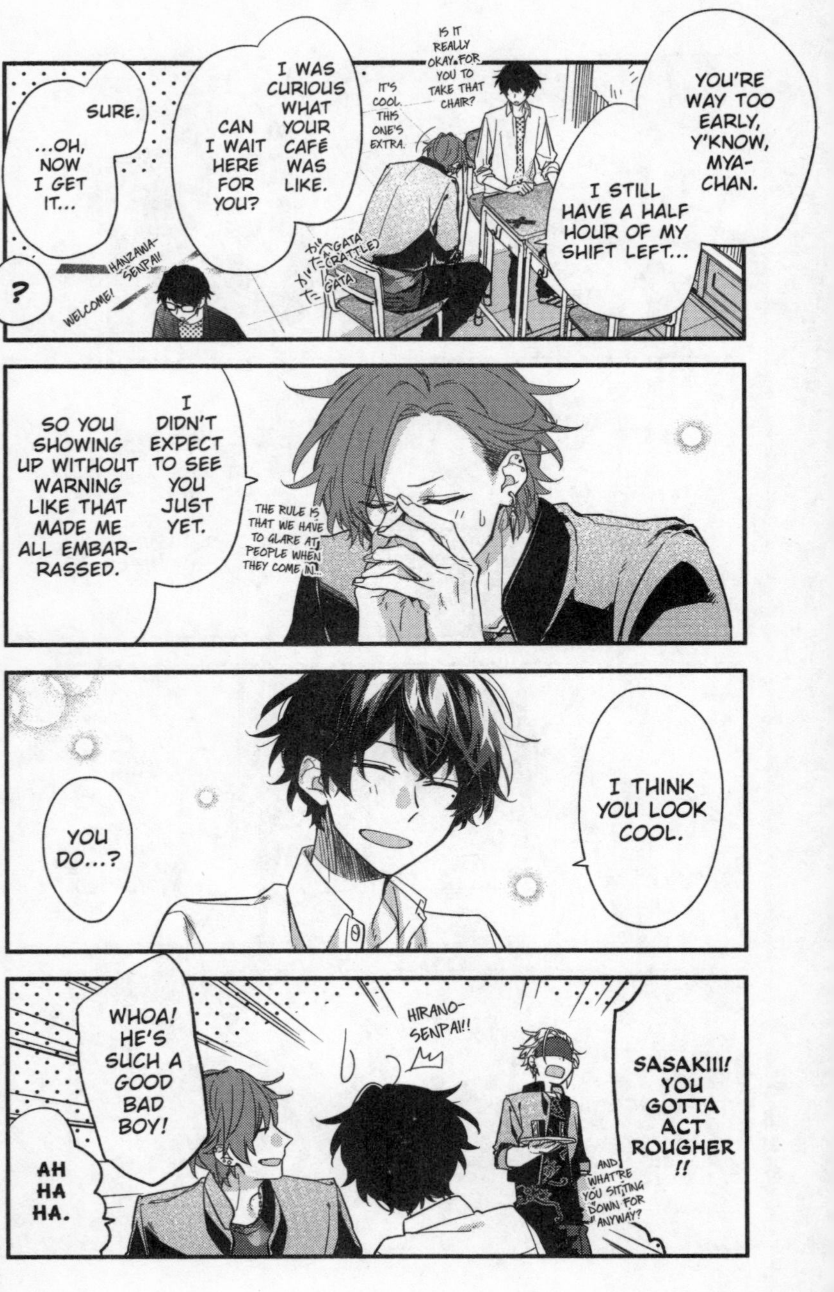
YOU'RE WAY TOO EARLY, Y'KNOW, MYA-CHAN.
I STILL HAVE A HALF HOUR OF MY SHIFT LEFT...
IS IT REALLY OKAY FOR YOU TO TAKE THAT CHAIR?
IT'S COOL. THIS ONE'S EXTRA.
I WAS CURIOUS WHAT YOUR CAFÉ WAS LIKE.
CAN I WAIT HERE FOR YOU?
GATA GATA (RATTLE)
SURE.
...OH, NOW I GET IT...
HANZAWA-SENPAI!
WELCOME!
?
I DIDN'T EXPECT TO SEE YOU JUST YET.
SO YOU SHOWING UP WITHOUT WARNING LIKE THAT MADE ME ALL EMBARRASSED.
THE RULE IS THAT WE HAVE TO GLARE AT PEOPLE WHEN THEY COME IN...
I THINK YOU LOOK COOL.
YOU DO...?
SASAKIII! YOU GOTTA ACT ROUGHER!!
AND WHAT'RE YOU SITTING DOWN FOR ANYWAY?
HIRANO-SENPAI!!
WHOA! HE'S SUCH A GOOD BAD BOY!
AH HA HA.

IT TOTALLY WORKS.

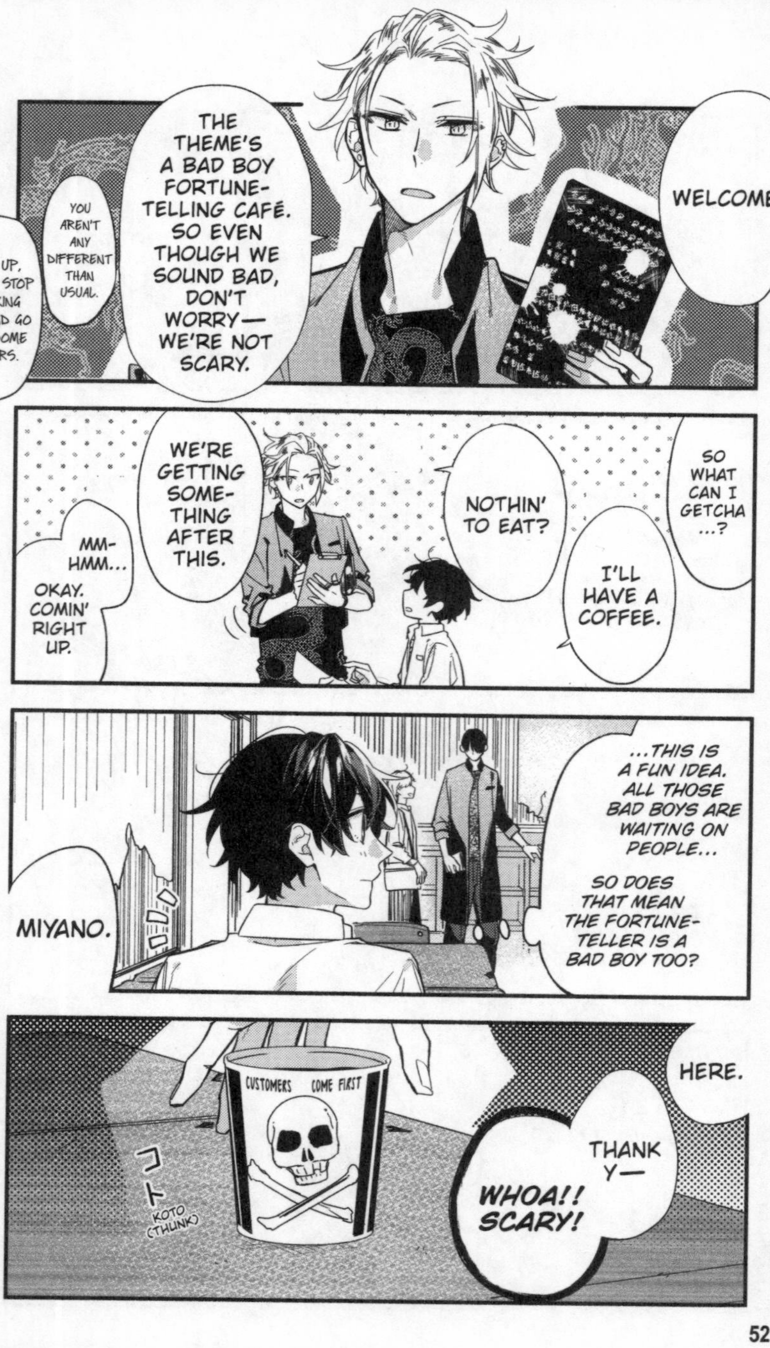
WELCOME!
THE THEME'S A BAD BOY FORTUNE-TELLING CAFÉ. SO EVEN THOUGH WE SOUND BAD, DON'T WORRY—WE'RE NOT SCARY.
YOU AREN'T ANY DIFFERENT THAN USUAL.
SHUT UP, SASAKI. STOP SLACKING OFF AND GO TAKE SOME ORDERS.
SO WHAT CAN I GETCHA...?
I'LL HAVE A COFFEE.
NOTHIN' TO EAT?
WE'RE GETTING SOMETHING AFTER THIS.
MM-HMM... OKAY. COMIN' RIGHT UP.
...THIS IS A FUN IDEA. ALL THOSE BAD BOYS ARE WAITING ON PEOPLE...
SO DOES THAT MEAN THE FORTUNE-TELLER IS A BAD BOY TOO?
MIYANO.
HERE.
CUSTOMERS COME FIRST
コト
KOTO (THUNK)
THANK Y—
WHOA!! SCARY!

PAPER CUP, BAD BOY STYLE.

HOW TO USE YOUR FORTUNE.

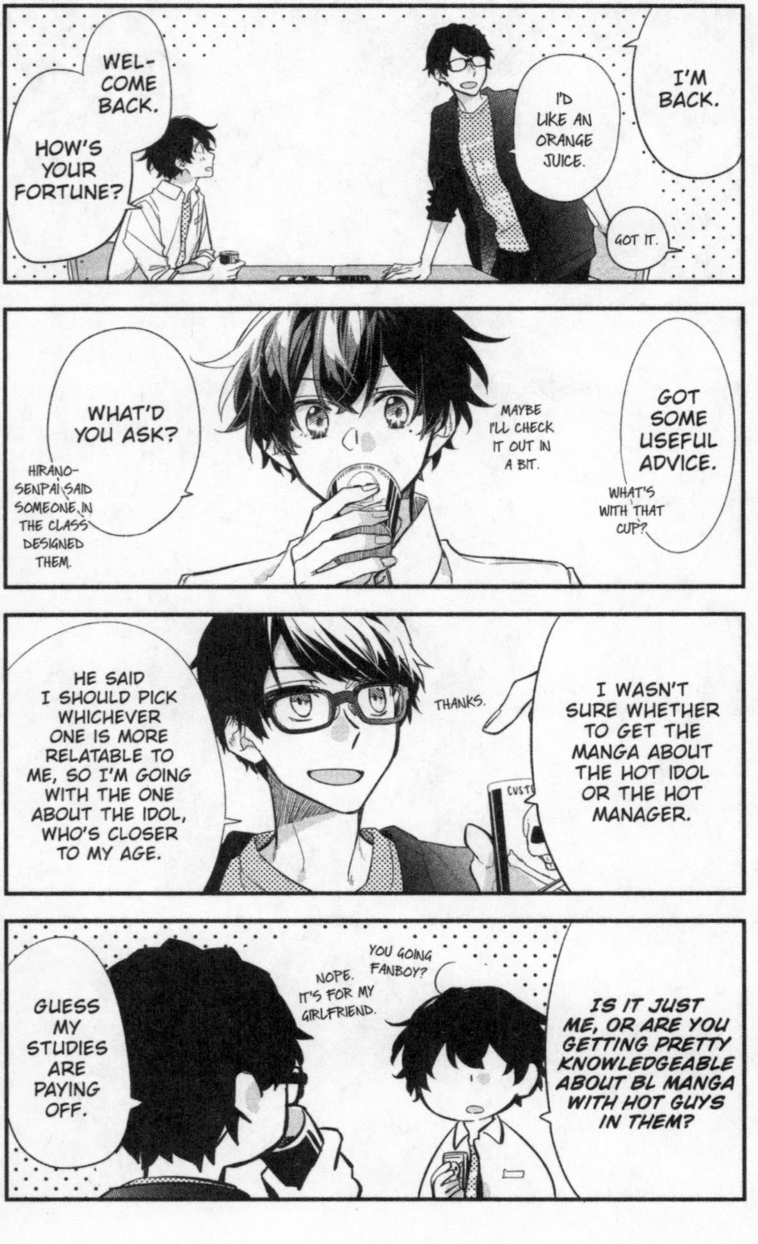
I'M BACK.
I'D LIKE AN ORANGE JUICE.
GOT IT.
WEL-COME BACK. HOW'S YOUR FORTUNE?
GOT SOME USEFUL ADVICE.
WHAT'S WITH THAT CUP?
MAYBE I'LL CHECK IT OUT IN A BIT.
WHAT'D YOU ASK?
HIRANO-SENPAI SAID SOMEONE IN THE CLASS DESIGNED THEM.
I WASN'T SURE WHETHER TO GET THE MANGA ABOUT THE HOT IDOL OR THE HOT MANAGER.
THANKS.
HE SAID I SHOULD PICK WHICHEVER ONE IS MORE RELATABLE TO ME, SO I'M GOING WITH THE ONE ABOUT THE IDOL, WHO'S CLOSER TO MY AGE.
IS IT JUST ME, OR ARE YOU GETTING PRETTY KNOWLEDGEABLE ABOUT BL MANGA WITH HOT GUYS IN THEM?
YOU GOING FANBOY?
NOPE. IT'S FOR MY GIRLFRIEND.
GUESS MY STUDIES ARE PAYING OFF.

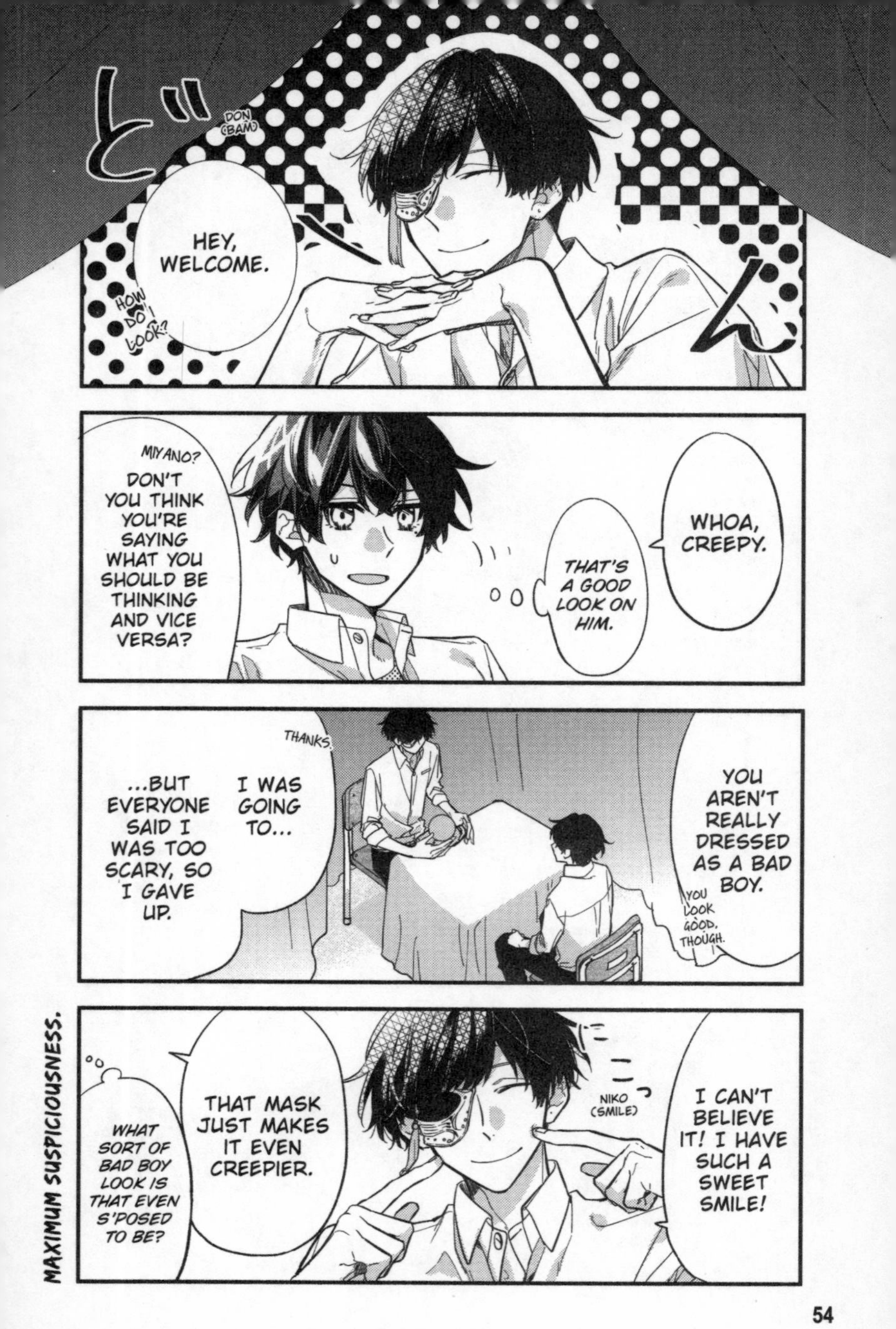
どん
DON (BAM)
HEY, WELCOME.
HOW DO I LOOK?
WHOA, CREEPY.
THAT'S A GOOD LOOK ON HIM.
MIYANO?
DON'T YOU THINK YOU'RE SAYING WHAT YOU SHOULD BE THINKING AND VICE VERSA?
YOU AREN'T REALLY DRESSED AS A BAD BOY.
YOU LOOK GOOD, THOUGH.
I WAS GOING TO...
...BUT EVERYONE SAID I WAS TOO SCARY, SO I GAVE UP.
THANKS.
I CAN'T BELIEVE IT! I HAVE SUCH A SWEET SMILE!
NIKO (SMILE)
THAT MASK JUST MAKES IT EVEN CREEPIER.
WHAT SORT OF BAD BOY LOOK IS THAT EVEN S'POSED TO BE?

MAXIMUM SUSPICIOUSNESS.

A MAN WITH NO HESITATION.

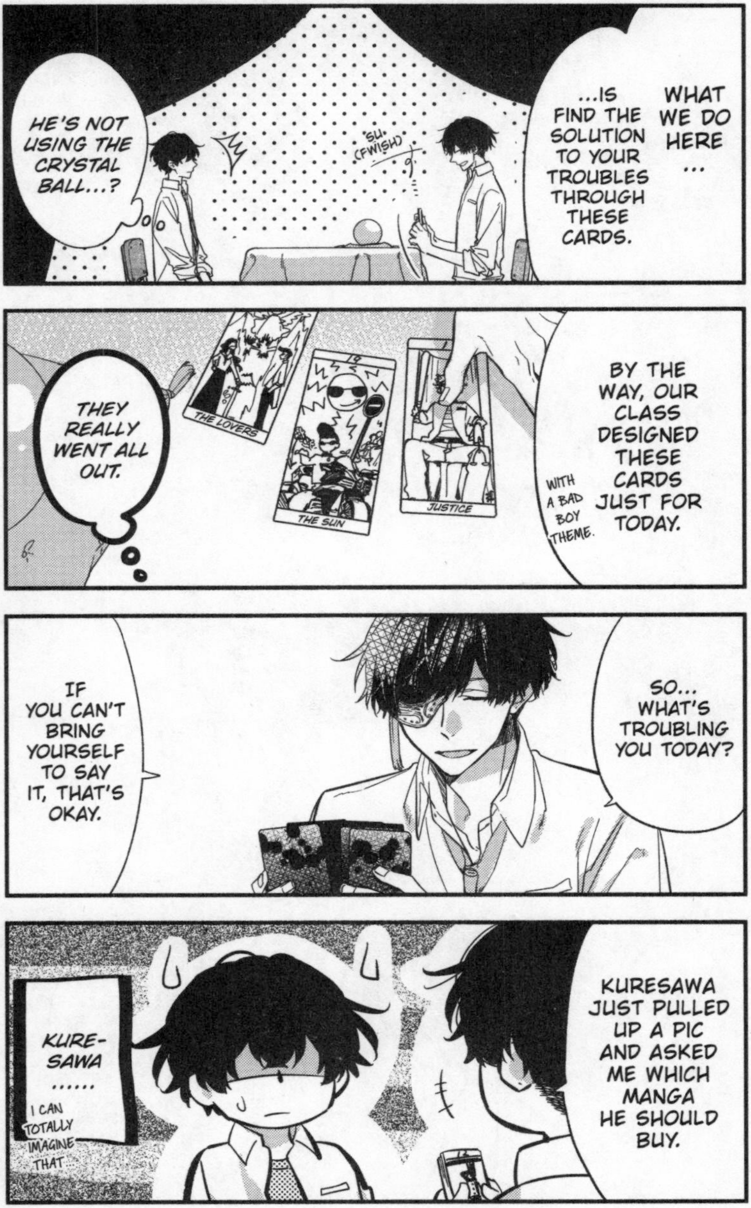
WHAT WE DO HERE ...
...IS FIND THE SOLUTION TO YOUR TROUBLES THROUGH THESE CARDS.
SU (FWISH)
HE'S NOT USING THE CRYSTAL BALL...?
BY THE WAY, OUR CLASS DESIGNED THESE CARDS JUST FOR TODAY.
WITH A BAD BOY THEME.
JUSTICE
THE SUN
THE LOVERS
THEY REALLY WENT ALL OUT.
SO... WHAT'S TROUBLING YOU TODAY?
IF YOU CAN'T BRING YOURSELF TO SAY IT, THAT'S OKAY.
KURESAWA JUST PULLED UP A PIC AND ASKED ME WHICH MANGA HE SHOULD BUY.
KURE-SAWA ......
I CAN TOTALLY IMAGINE THAT...

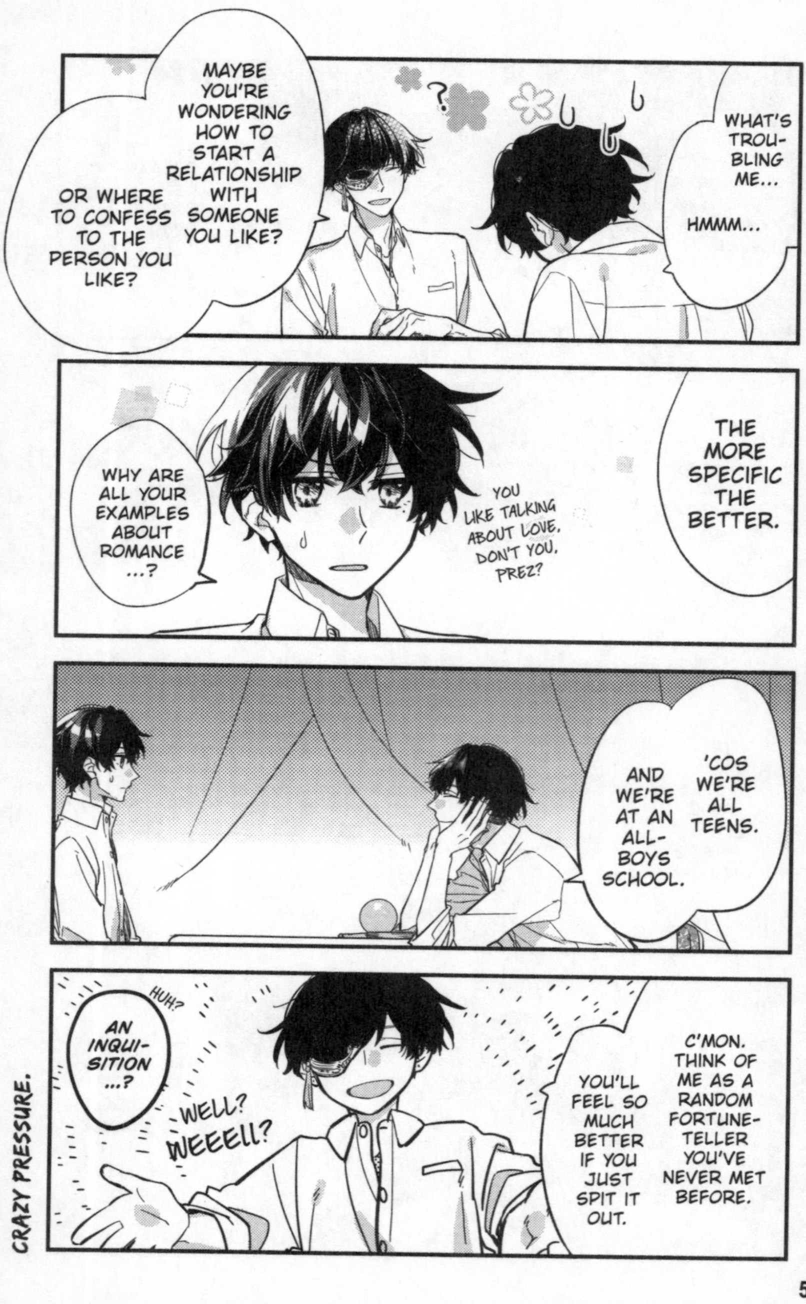
WHAT'S TROUBLING ME... HMMM...
MAYBE YOU'RE WONDERING HOW TO START A RELATIONSHIP WITH SOMEONE YOU LIKE?
OR WHERE TO CONFESS TO THE PERSON YOU LIKE?
THE MORE SPECIFIC THE BETTER.
YOU LIKE TALKING ABOUT LOVE, DON'T YOU, PREZ?
WHY ARE ALL YOUR EXAMPLES ABOUT ROMANCE ...?
'COS WE'RE ALL TEENS.
AND WE'RE AT AN ALL-BOYS SCHOOL.
C'MON. THINK OF ME AS A RANDOM FORTUNE-TELLER YOU'VE NEVER MET BEFORE.
YOU'LL FEEL SO MUCH BETTER IF YOU JUST SPIT IT OUT.
WELL? WEEEll?
HUH?
AN INQUISITION ...?

CRAZY PRESSURE.

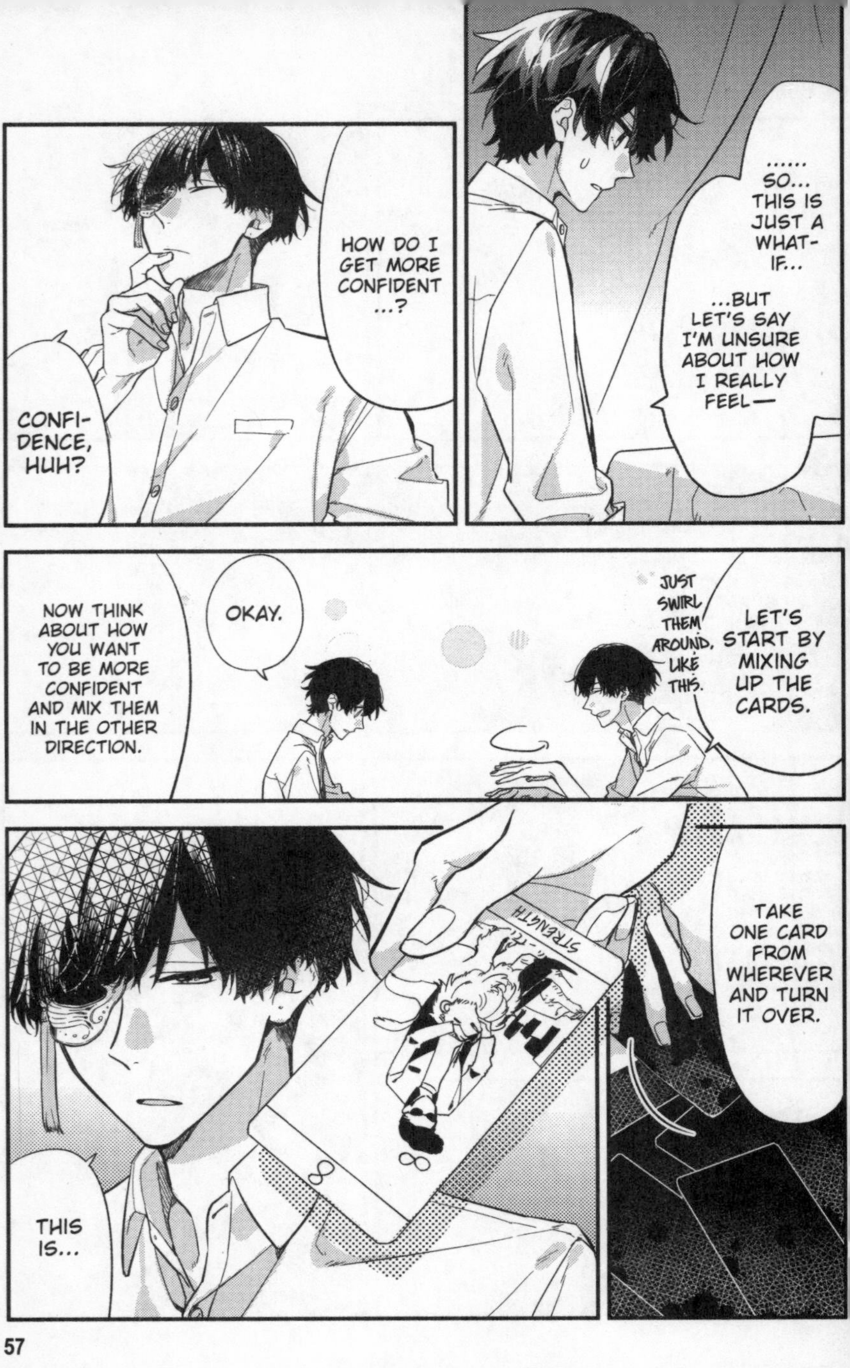

......
SO... THIS IS JUST A WHAT-IF...
...BUT LET'S SAY I'M UNSURE ABOUT HOW I REALLY FEEL—
HOW DO I GET MORE CONFIDENT ...?
CONFIDENCE, HUH?
LET'S START BY MIXING UP THE CARDS.
JUST SWIRL THEM AROUND, LIKE THIS.
OKAY.
NOW THINK ABOUT HOW YOU WANT TO BE MORE CONFIDENT AND MIX THEM IN THE OTHER DIRECTION.
TAKE ONE CARD FROM WHEREVER AND TURN IT OVER.
STRENGTH
THIS IS...

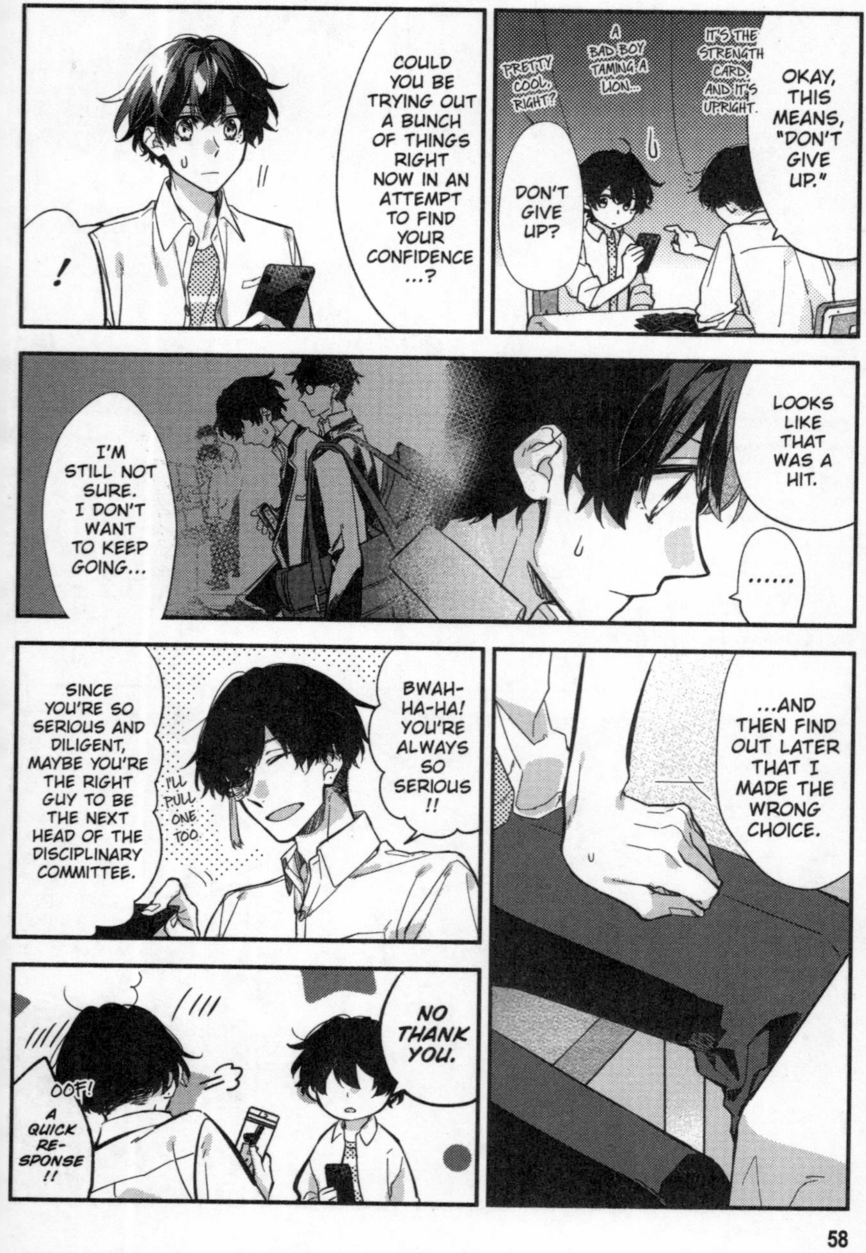
OKAY, THIS MEANS, "DON'T GIVE UP."
IT'S THE STRENGTH CARD, AND IT'S UPRIGHT.
A BAD BOY TAMING A LION...
PRETTY COOL, RIGHT?
DON'T GIVE UP?
COULD YOU BE TRYING OUT A BUNCH OF THINGS RIGHT NOW IN AN ATTEMPT TO FIND YOUR CONFIDENCE ...?
LOOKS LIKE THAT WAS A HIT.
......
I'M STILL NOT SURE. I DON'T WANT TO KEEP GOING...
...AND THEN FIND OUT LATER THAT I MADE THE WRONG CHOICE.
BWAH-HA-HA! YOU'RE ALWAYS SO SERIOUS!!
I'LL PULL ONE TOO.
SINCE YOU'RE SO SERIOUS AND DILIGENT, MAYBE YOU'RE THE RIGHT GUY TO BE THE NEXT HEAD OF THE DISCIPLINARY COMMITTEE.
NO THANK YOU.
OOF! A QUICK RE-SPONSE!!

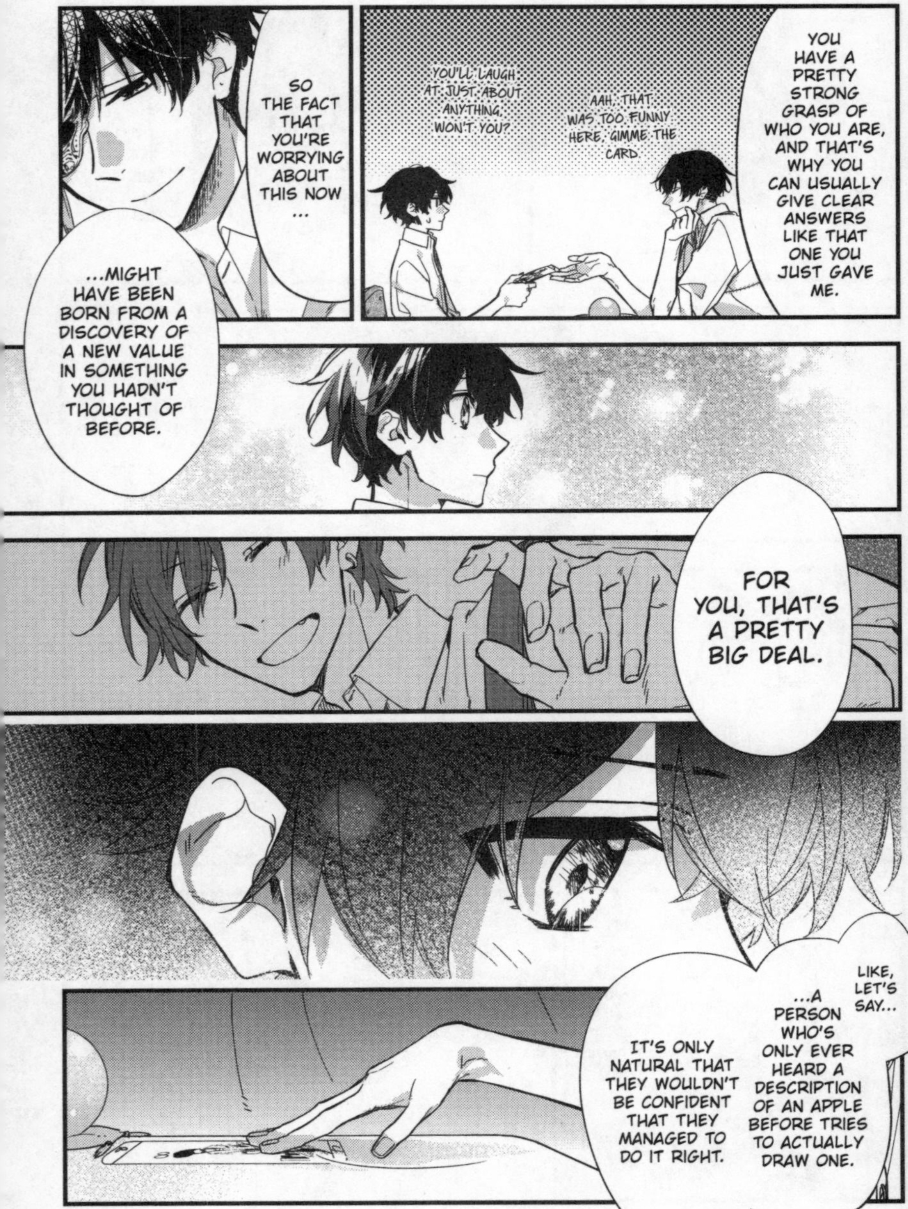
YOU HAVE A PRETTY STRONG GRASP OF WHO YOU ARE, AND THAT'S WHY YOU CAN USUALLY GIVE CLEAR ANSWERS LIKE THAT ONE YOU JUST GAVE ME.
AAH, THAT WAS TOO FUNNY HERE, GIMME THE CARD
YOU'LL LAUGH AT JUST ABOUT ANYTHING, WON'T YOU?
SO THE FACT THAT YOU'RE WORRYING ABOUT THIS NOW ...
...MIGHT HAVE BEEN BORN FROM A DISCOVERY OF A NEW VALUE IN SOMETHING YOU HADN'T THOUGHT OF BEFORE.
FOR YOU, THAT'S A PRETTY BIG DEAL.
LIKE, LET'S SAY...
...A PERSON WHO'S ONLY EVER HEARD A DESCRIPTION OF AN APPLE BEFORE TRIES TO ACTUALLY DRAW ONE.
IT'S ONLY NATURAL THAT THEY WOULDN'T BE CONFIDENT THAT THEY MANAGED TO DO IT RIGHT.

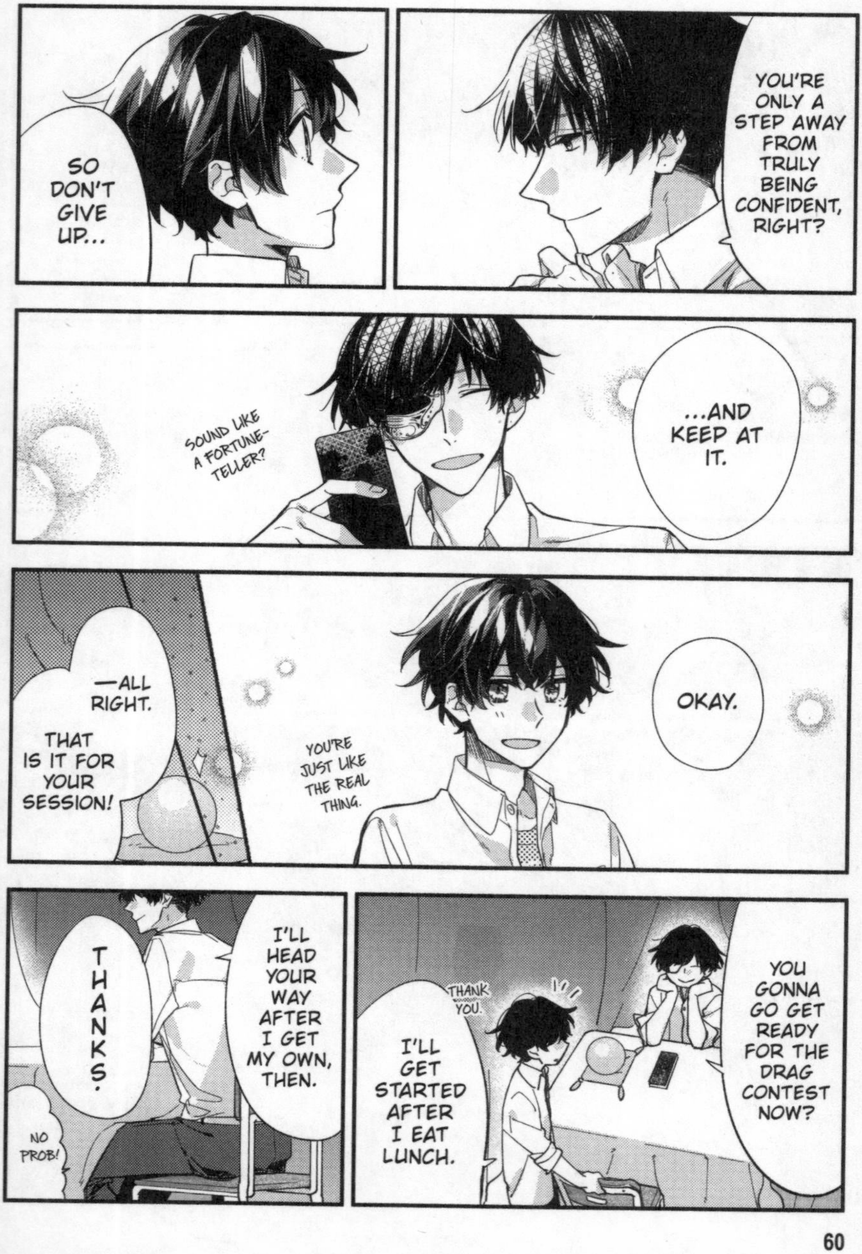
YOU'RE ONLY A STEP AWAY FROM TRULY BEING CONFIDENT, RIGHT?
SO DON'T GIVE UP...
...AND KEEP AT IT.
SOUND LIKE A FORTUNE-TELLER?
OKAY.
YOU'RE JUST LIKE THE REAL THING.
—ALL RIGHT.
THAT IS IT FOR YOUR SESSION!
YOU GONNA GO GET READY FOR THE DRAG CONTEST NOW?
THANK YOU.
I'LL GET STARTED AFTER I EAT LUNCH.
I'LL HEAD YOUR WAY AFTER I GET MY OWN, THEN.
THANKS.
NO PROB!

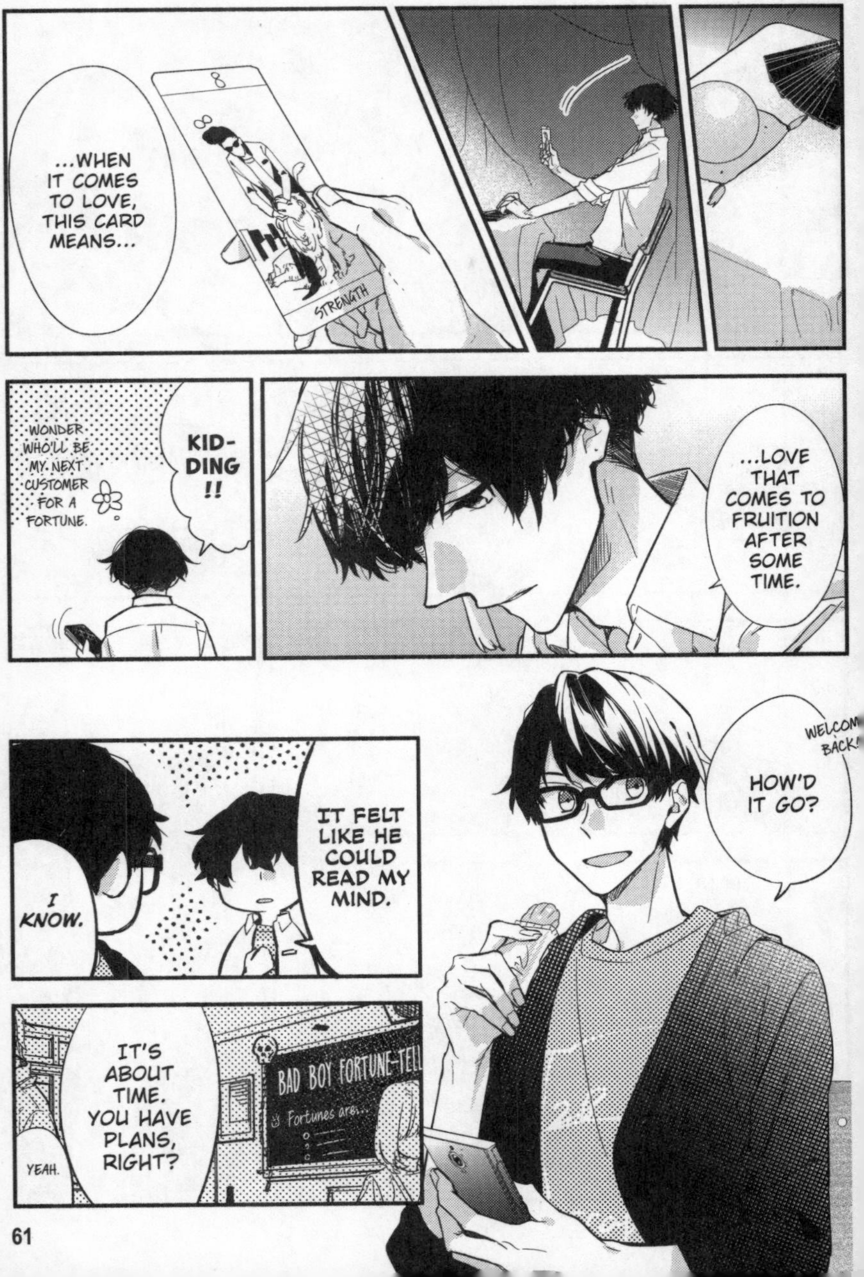
...WHEN IT COMES TO LOVE, THIS CARD MEANS...
STRENGTH
...LOVE THAT COMES TO FRUITION AFTER SOME TIME.
KID-DING!!
WONDER WHO'LL BE MY NEXT CUSTOMER FOR A FORTUNE.
WELCOM BACK!
HOW'D IT GO?
IT FELT LIKE HE COULD READ MY MIND.
I KNOW.
IT'S ABOUT TIME. YOU HAVE PLANS, RIGHT?
BAD BOY FORTUNE-TELL
Fortunes are...
YEAH.

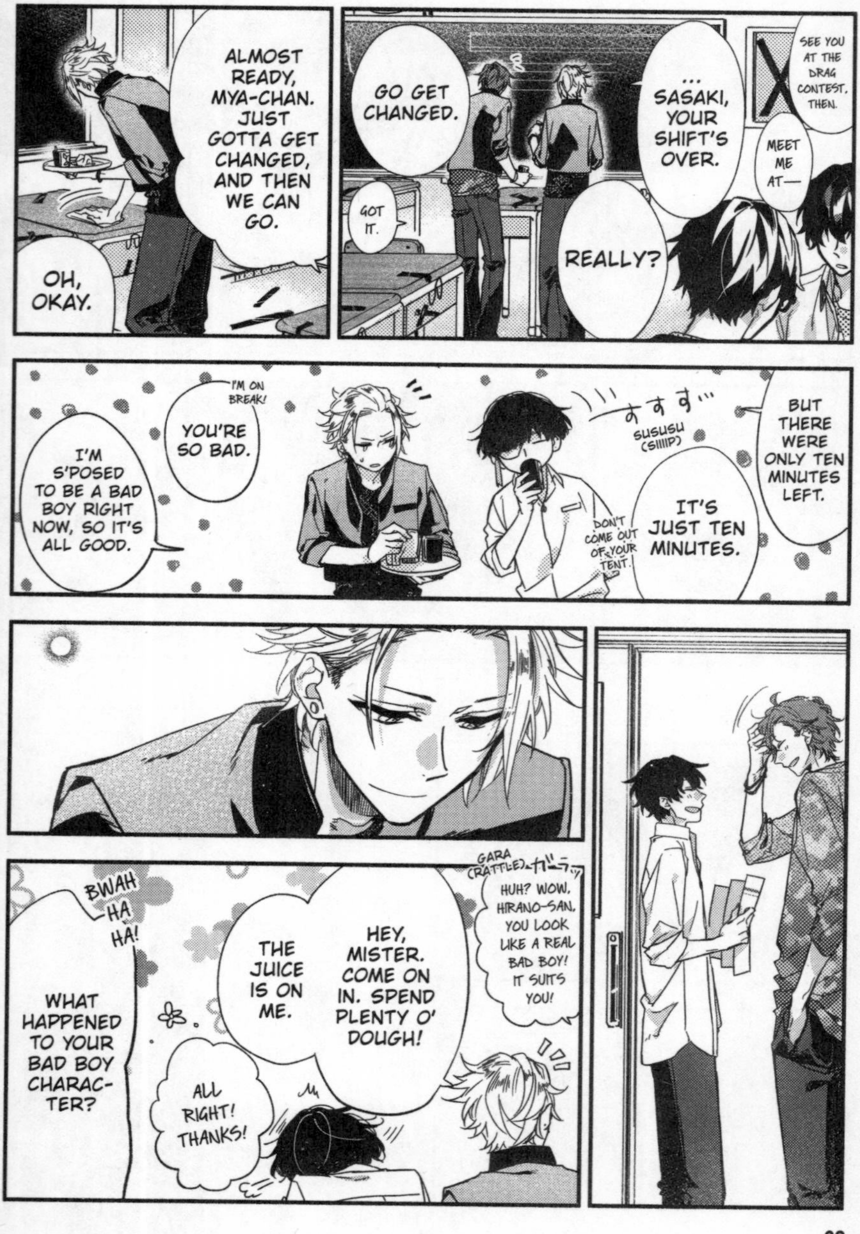
SEE YOU AT THE DRAG CONTEST, THEN.
MEET ME AT—
... SASAKI, YOUR SHIFT'S OVER.
REALLY?
GO GET CHANGED.
GOT IT.
ALMOST READY, MYA-CHAN. JUST GOTTA GET CHANGED, AND THEN WE CAN GO.
OH, OKAY.
BUT THERE WERE ONLY TEN MINUTES LEFT.
すすす
SUSUSU (SIIIIP)
IT'S JUST TEN MINUTES.
DON'T COME OUT OF YOUR TENT.
I'M ON BREAK!
YOU'RE SO BAD.
I'M S'POSED TO BE A BAD BOY RIGHT NOW, SO IT'S ALL GOOD.
ガラ
GARA (RATTLE)
HUH? WOW, HIRANO-SAN, YOU LOOK LIKE A REAL BAD BOY! IT SUITS YOU!
HEY, MISTER. COME ON IN. SPEND PLENTY O' DOUGH!
THE JUICE IS ON ME.
ALL RIGHT! THANKS!
BWAH HA HA!
WHAT HAPPENED TO YOUR BAD BOY CHARACTER?

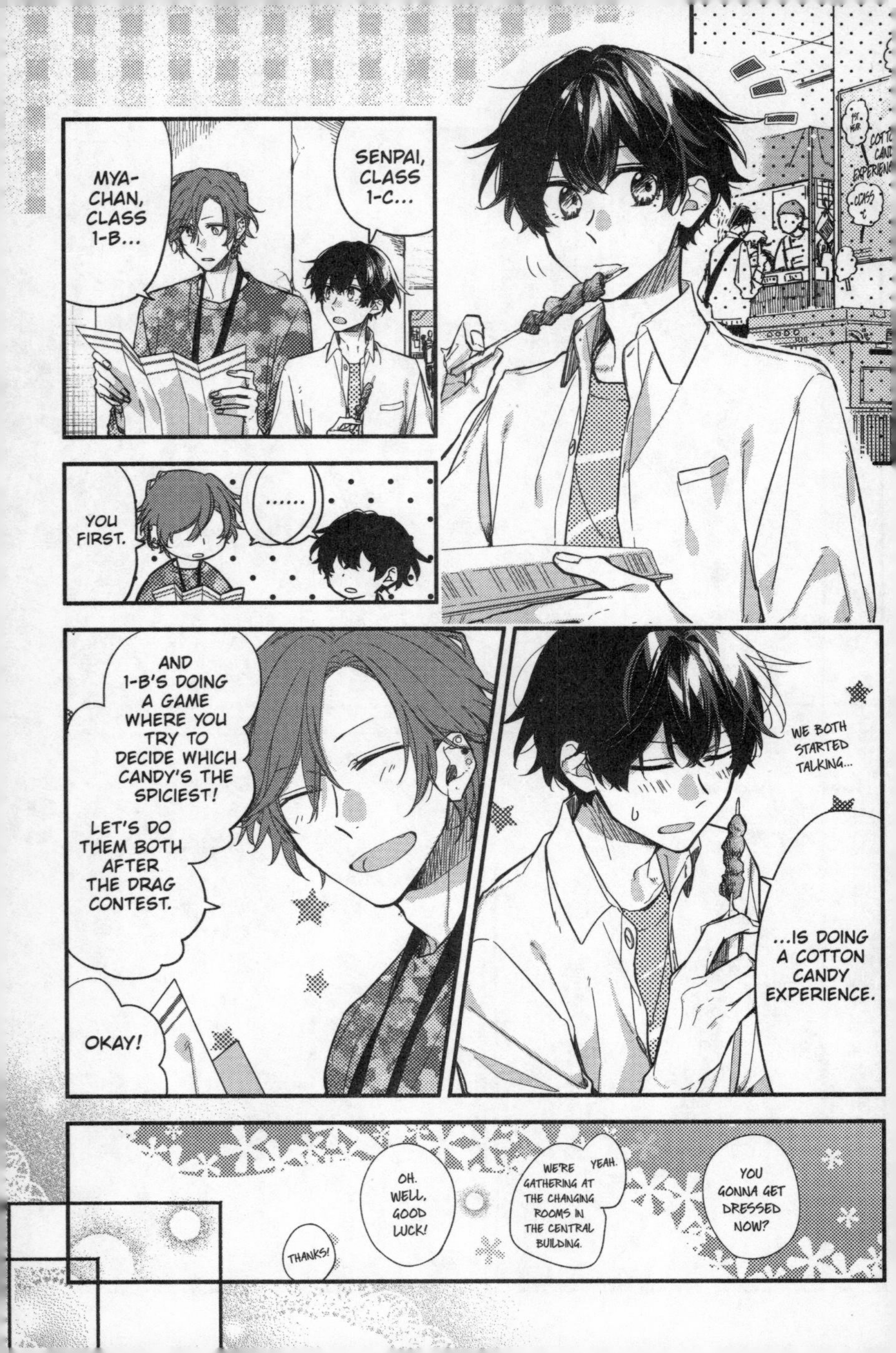
1st YEAR
CLASS 1-C
SENPAI, CLASS 1-C...
MYA-CHAN, CLASS 1-B...
......
YOU FIRST.
WE BOTH STARTED TALKING...
...IS DOING A COTTON CANDY EXPERIENCE.
AND 1-B'S DOING A GAME WHERE YOU TRY TO DECIDE WHICH CANDY'S THE SPICIEST!
LET'S DO THEM BOTH AFTER THE DRAG CONTEST.
OKAY!
YOU GONNA GET DRESSED NOW?
YEAH.
WE'RE GATHERING AT THE CHANGING ROOMS IN THE CENTRAL BUILDING.
OH. WELL, GOOD LUCK!
THANKS!

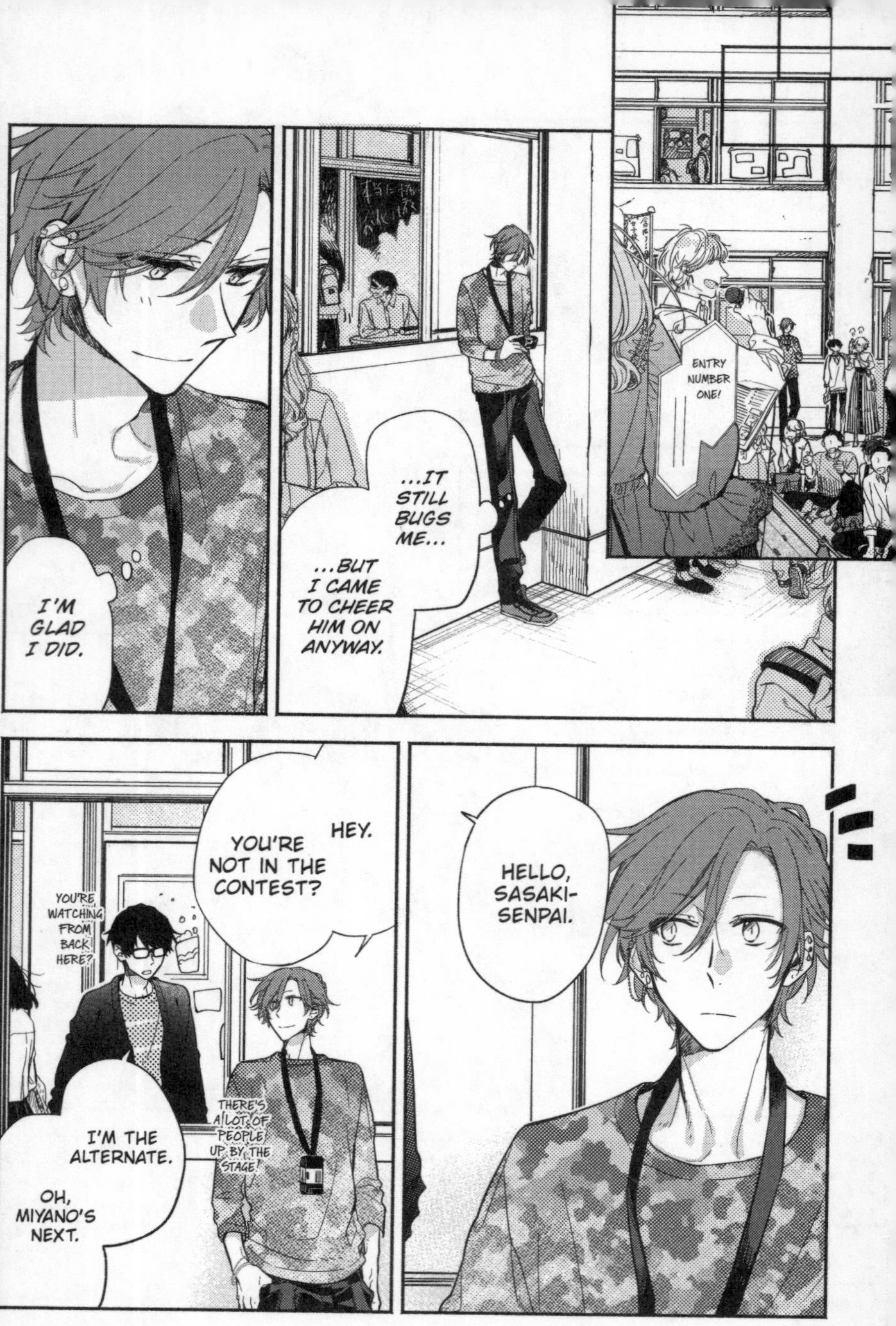

ENTRY NUMBER ONE!
...IT STILL BUGS ME...
...BUT I CAME TO CHEER HIM ON ANYWAY.
I'M GLAD I DID.
HELLO, SASAKI-SENPAI.
HEY.
YOU'RE NOT IN THE CONTEST?
YOU'RE WATCHING FROM BACK HERE?
THERE'S A LOT OF PEOPLE UP BY THE STAGE.
I'M THE ALTERNATE.
OH, MIYANO'S NEXT.

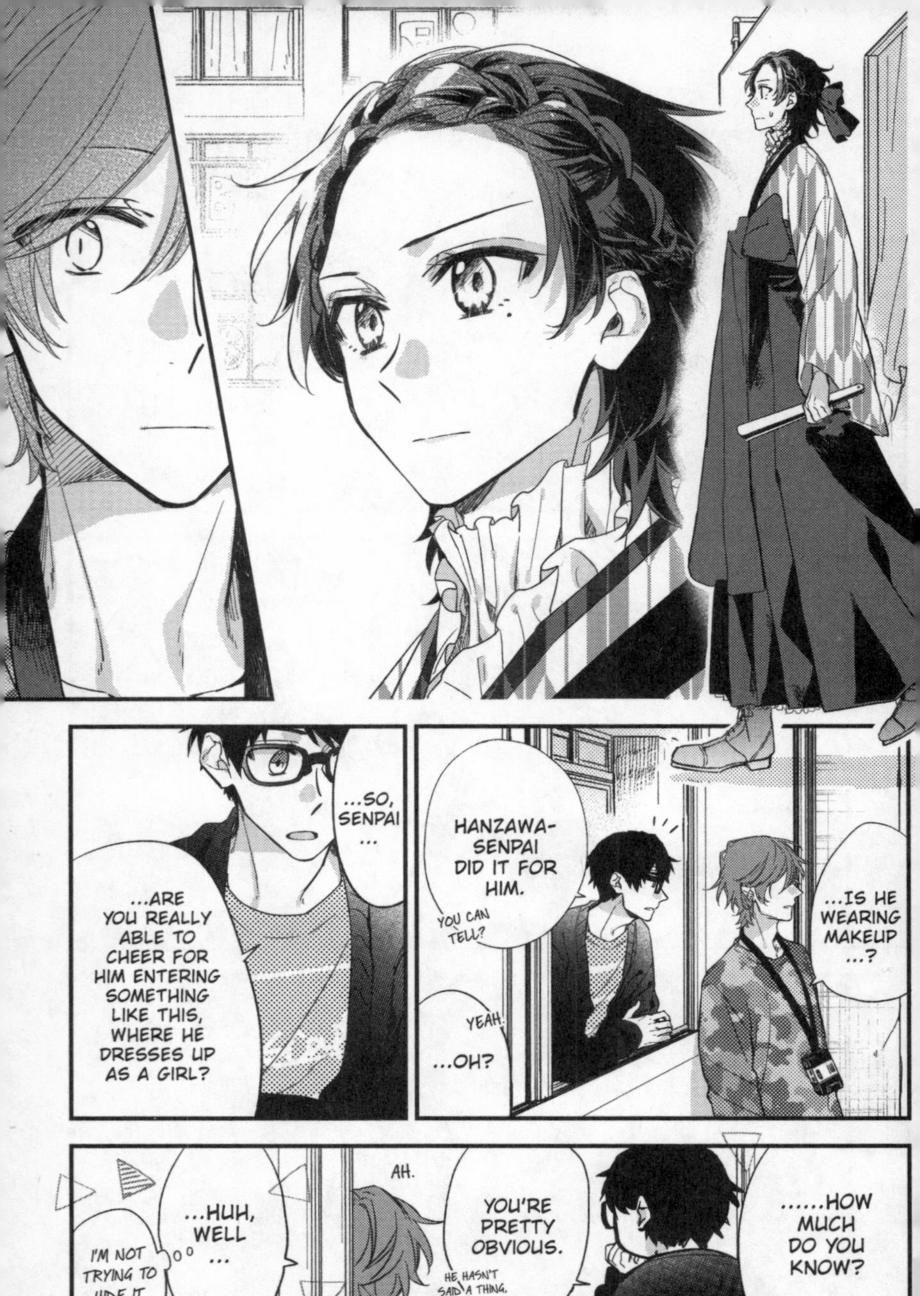
...IS HE WEARING MAKEUP ...?
HANZAWA-SENPAI DID IT FOR HIM.
YOU CAN TELL?
YEAH.
...OH?
...SO, SENPAI ...
...ARE YOU REALLY ABLE TO CHEER FOR HIM ENTERING SOMETHING LIKE THIS, WHERE HE DRESSES UP AS A GIRL?
......HOW MUCH DO YOU KNOW?
AH.
YOU'RE PRETTY OBVIOUS.
HE HASN'T SAID A THING, THOUGH.
...HUH, WELL ...
I'M NOT TRYING TO HIDE IT.

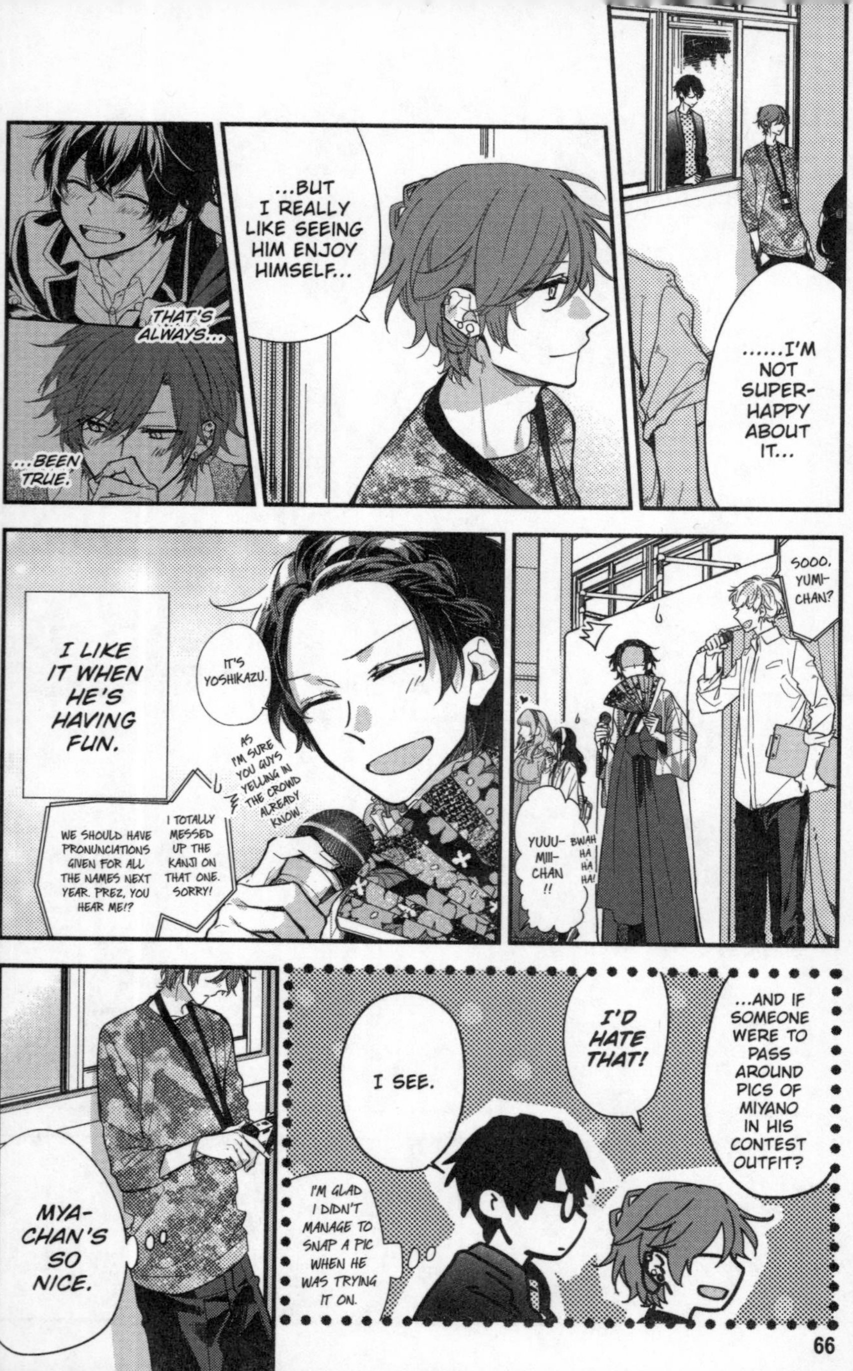
......I'M NOT SUPER-HAPPY ABOUT IT...
...BUT I REALLY LIKE SEEING HIM ENJOY HIMSELF...
THAT'S ALWAYS...
...BEEN TRUE.
SOOO, YUMI-CHAN?
YUUU-MIII-CHAN!!
BWAH HA HA HA!
IT'S YOSHIKAZU.
AS I'M SURE YOU GUYS YELLING IN THE CROWD ALREADY KNOW.
I TOTALLY MESSED UP THE KANJI ON THAT ONE. SORRY!
WE SHOULD HAVE PRONUNCIATIONS GIVEN FOR ALL THE NAMES NEXT YEAR. PREZ, YOU HEAR ME!?
I LIKE IT WHEN HE'S HAVING FUN.
...AND IF SOMEONE WERE TO PASS AROUND PICS OF MIYANO IN HIS CONTEST OUTFIT?
I'D HATE THAT!
I SEE.
I'M GLAD I DIDN'T MANAGE TO SNAP A PIC WHEN HE WAS TRYING IT ON.
MYA-CHAN'S SO NICE.

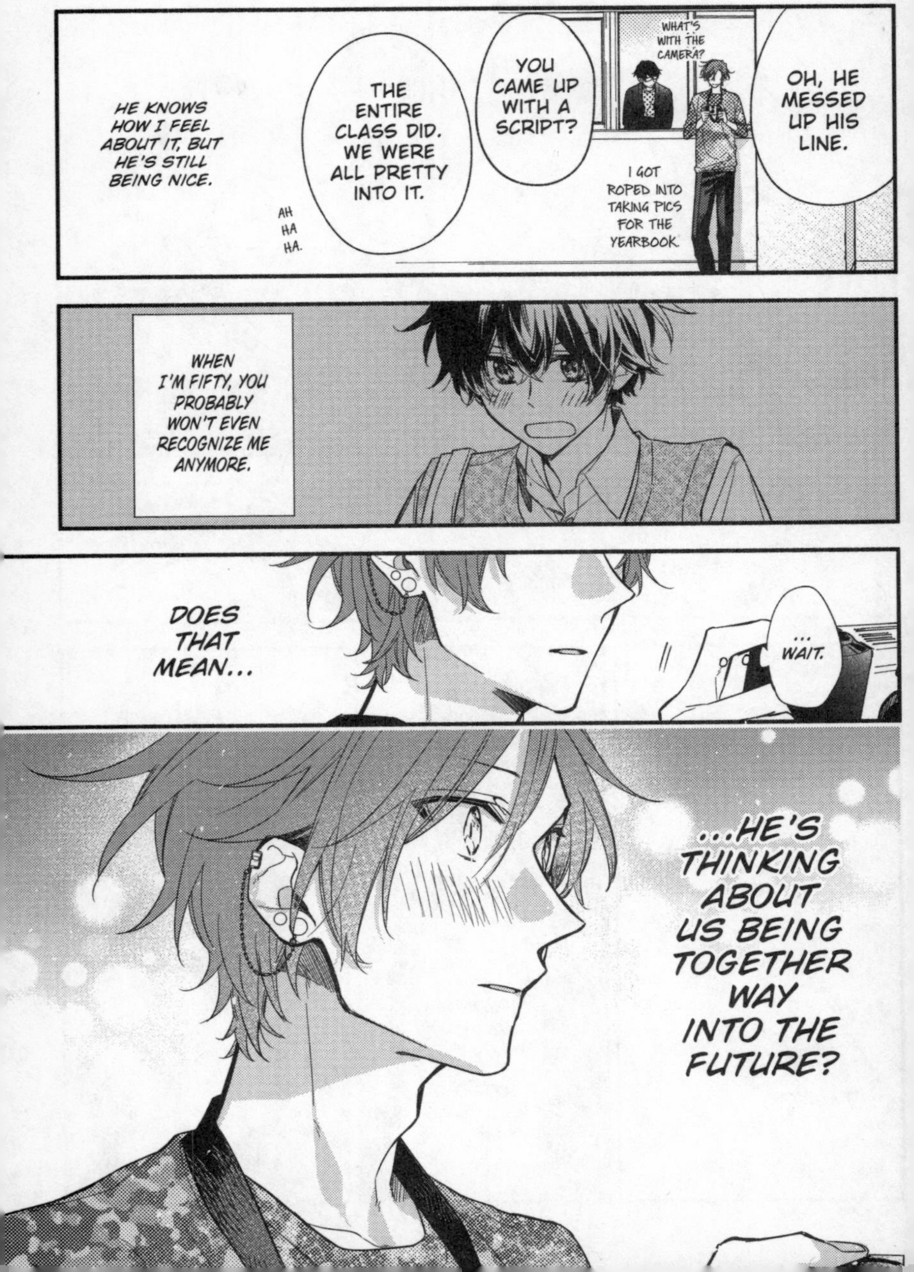
OH, HE MESSED UP HIS LINE.
WHAT'S WITH THE CAMERA?
I GOT ROPED INTO TAKING PICS FOR THE YEARBOOK.
YOU CAME UP WITH A SCRIPT?
THE ENTIRE CLASS DID. WE WERE ALL PRETTY INTO IT.
AH HA HA.
HE KNOWS HOW I FEEL ABOUT IT, BUT HE'S STILL BEING NICE.
WHEN I'M FIFTY, YOU PROBABLY WON'T EVEN RECOGNIZE ME ANYMORE.
...WAIT.
DOES THAT MEAN...
...HE'S THINKING ABOUT US BEING TOGETHER WAY INTO THE FUTURE?

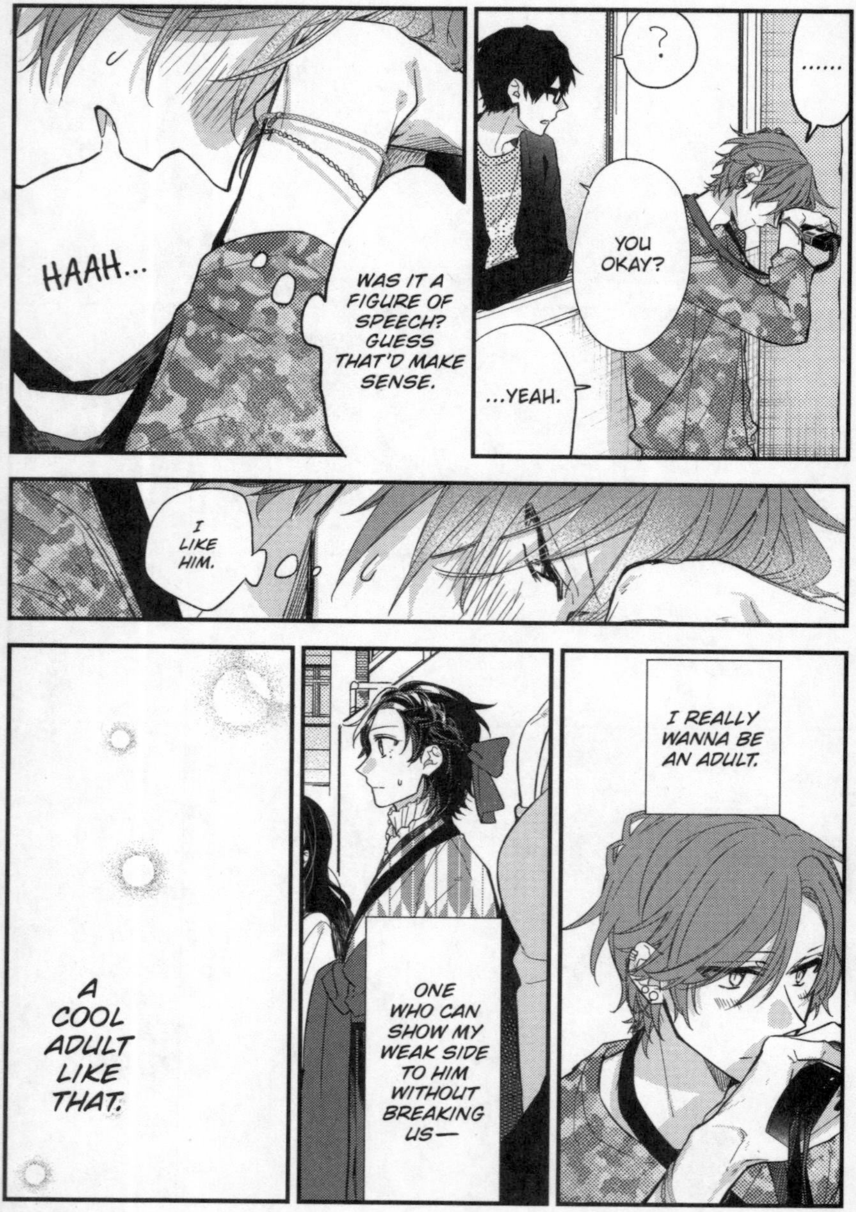
......
?
YOU OKAY?
...YEAH.
WAS IT A FIGURE OF SPEECH? GUESS THAT'D MAKE SENSE.
HAAH...
I LIKE HIM.
I REALLY WANNA BE AN ADULT.
ONE WHO CAN SHOW MY WEAK SIDE TO HIM WITHOUT BREAKING US—
A COOL ADULT LIKE THAT.

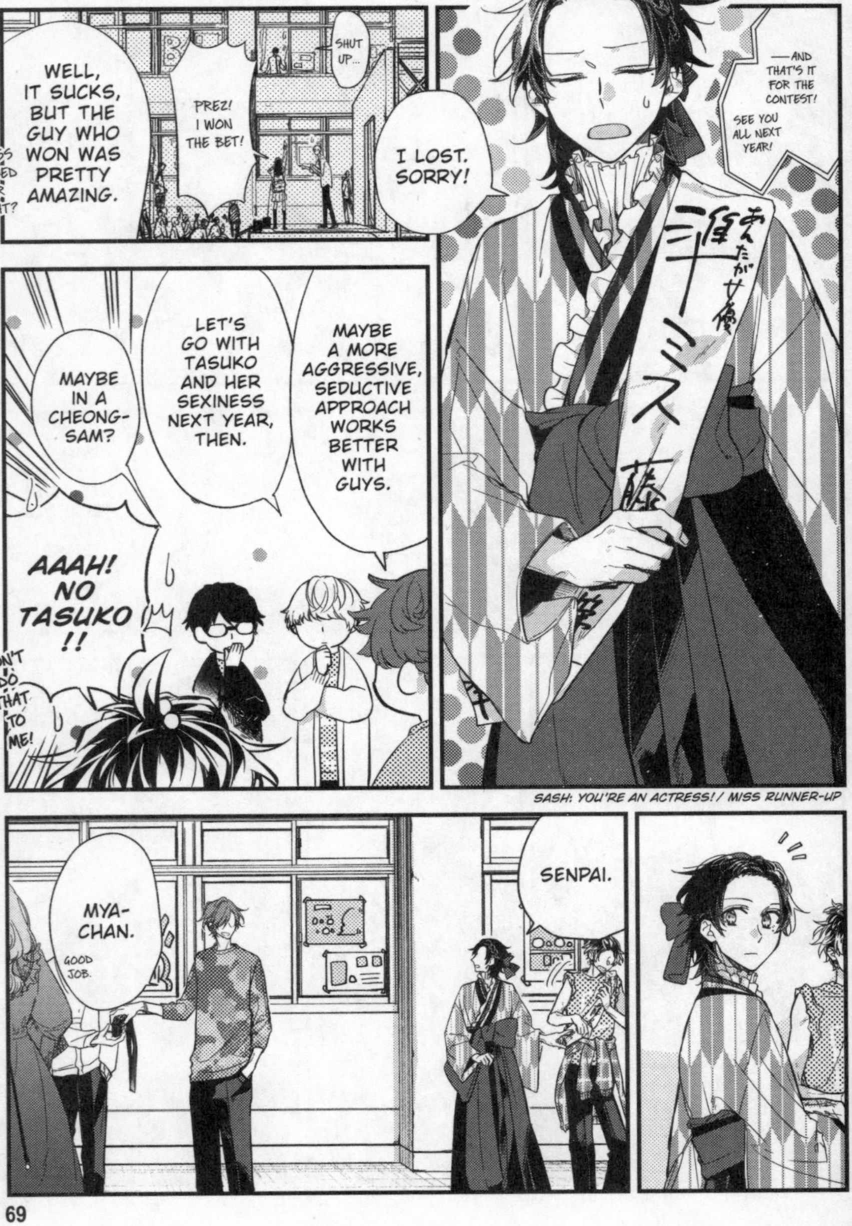
—AND THAT'S IT FOR THE CONTEST! SEE YOU ALL NEXT YEAR!
I LOST. SORRY!
あんたが女優
準ミス
SASH: YOU'RE AN ACTRESS! / MISS RUNNER-UP
SHUT UP...
PREZ! I WON THE BET!
WELL, IT SUCKS, BUT THE GUY WHO WON WAS PRETTY AMAZING.
IS CLASS A COED OR WHAT?
MAYBE A MORE AGGRESSIVE, SEDUCTIVE APPROACH WORKS BETTER WITH GUYS.
LET'S GO WITH TASUKO AND HER SEXINESS NEXT YEAR, THEN.
MAYBE IN A CHEONG-SAM?
AAAH! NO TASUKO!!
DON'T DO THAT TO ME!
SENPAI.
MYA-CHAN.
GOOD JOB.

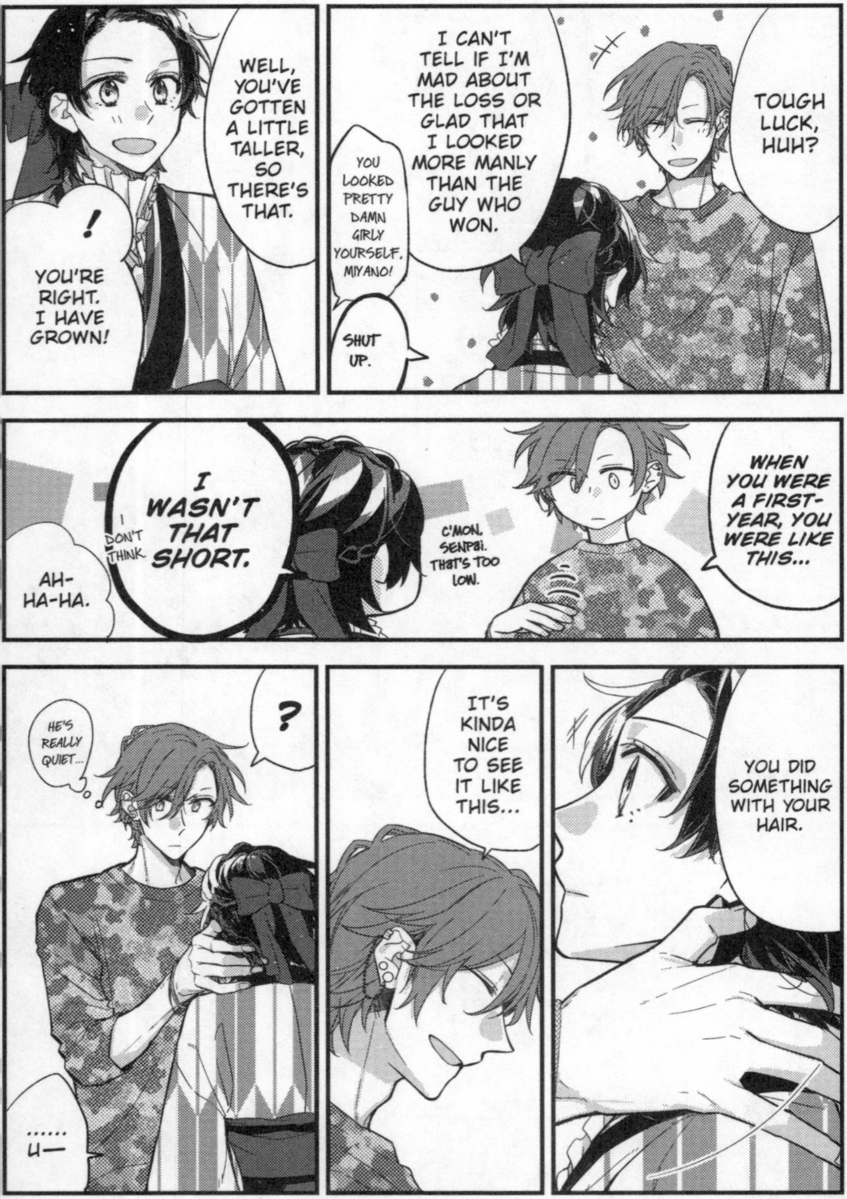
TOUGH LUCK, HUH?
I CAN'T TELL IF I'M MAD ABOUT THE LOSS OR GLAD THAT I LOOKED MORE MANLY THAN THE GUY WHO WON.
YOU LOOKED PRETTY DAMN GIRLY YOURSELF, MIYANO!
SHUT UP.
WELL, YOU'VE GOTTEN A LITTLE TALLER, SO THERE'S THAT.
!
YOU'RE RIGHT. I HAVE GROWN!
WHEN YOU WERE A FIRST-YEAR, YOU WERE LIKE THIS...
C'MON, SENPAI. THAT'S TOO LOW.
I WASN'T THAT SHORT.
I DON'T THINK.
AH-HA-HA.
YOU DID SOMETHING WITH YOUR HAIR.
IT'S KINDA NICE TO SEE IT LIKE THIS...
?
HE'S REALLY QUIET...
......
U—

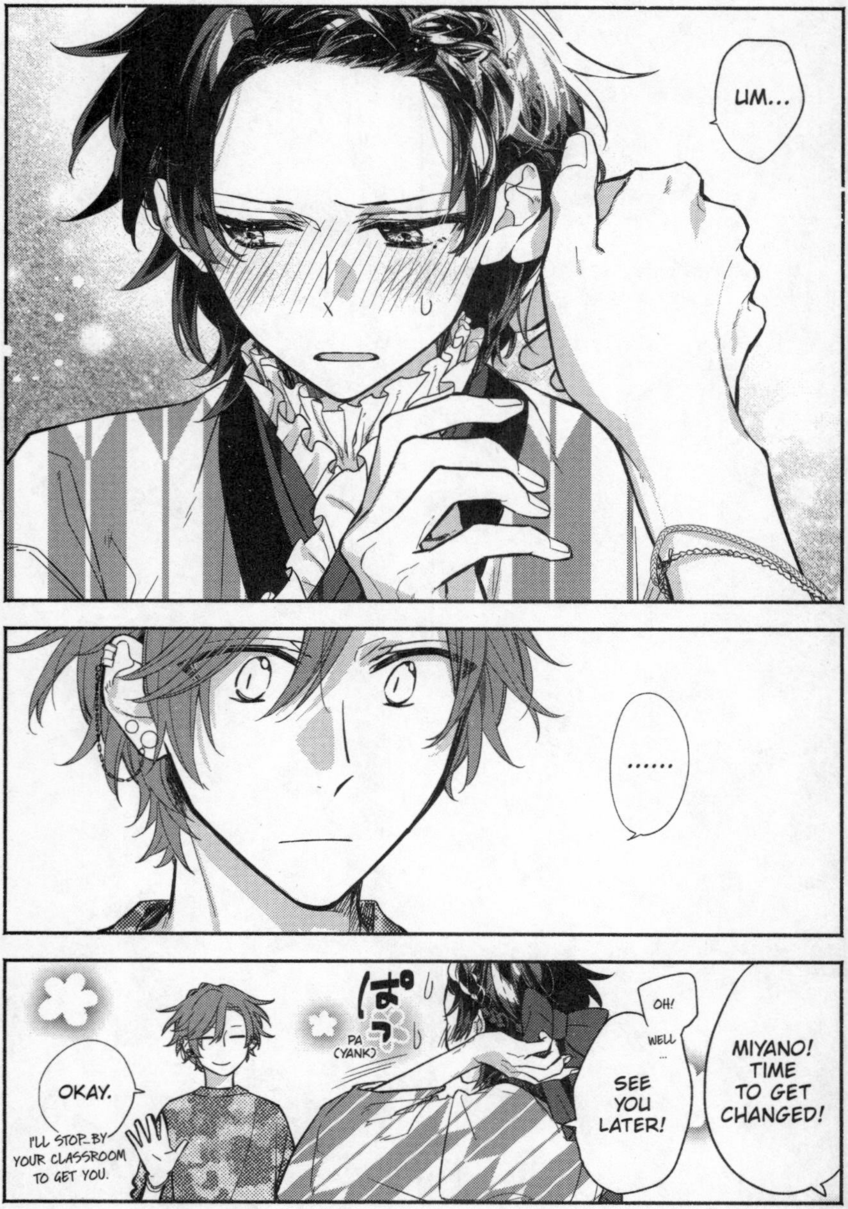
UM...
......
MIYANO! TIME TO GET CHANGED!
OH!
WELL ...
SEE YOU LATER!
ぱっ
PA (YANK)
OKAY.
I'LL STOP BY YOUR CLASSROOM TO GET YOU.

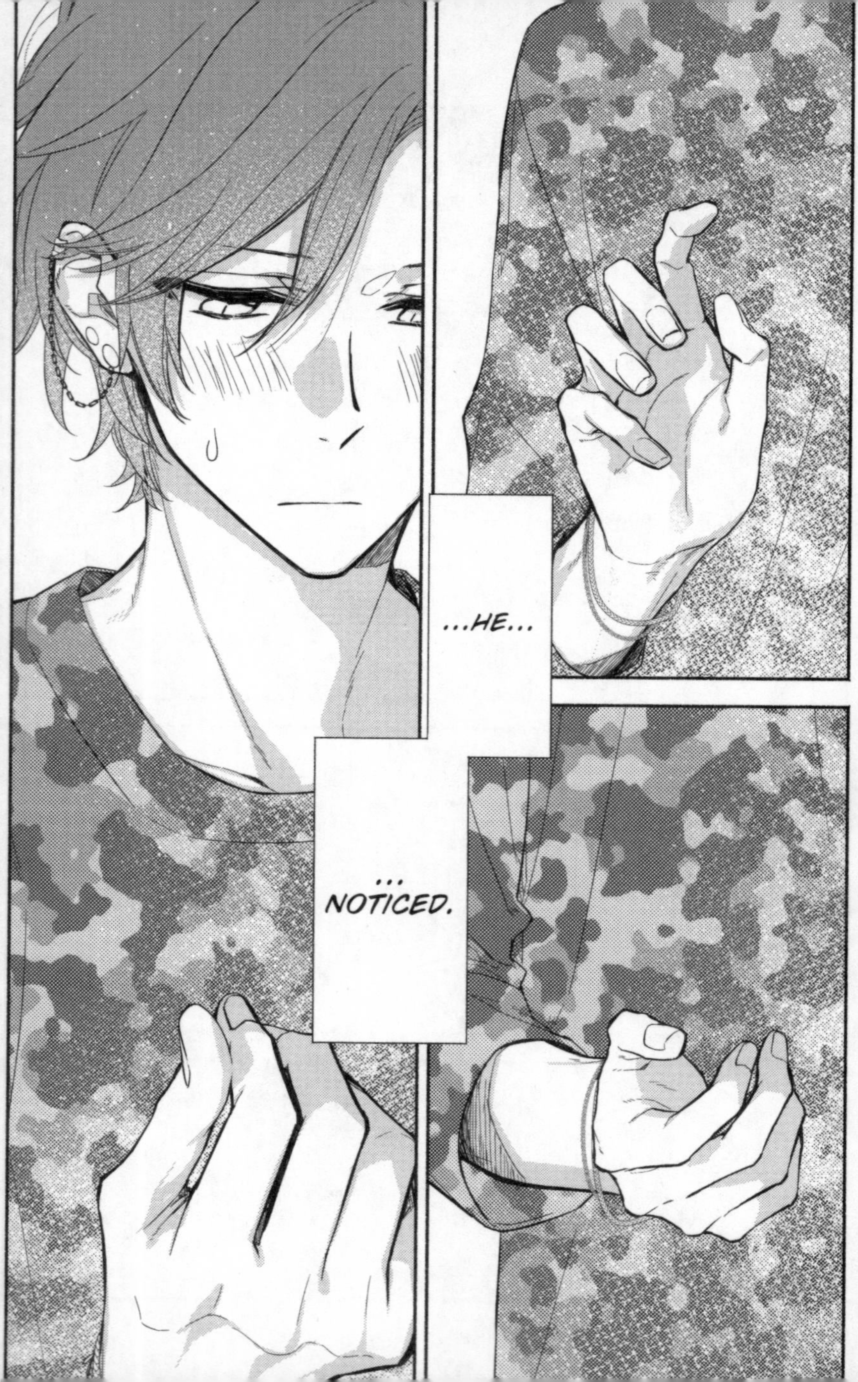
...HE...
...
NOTICED.

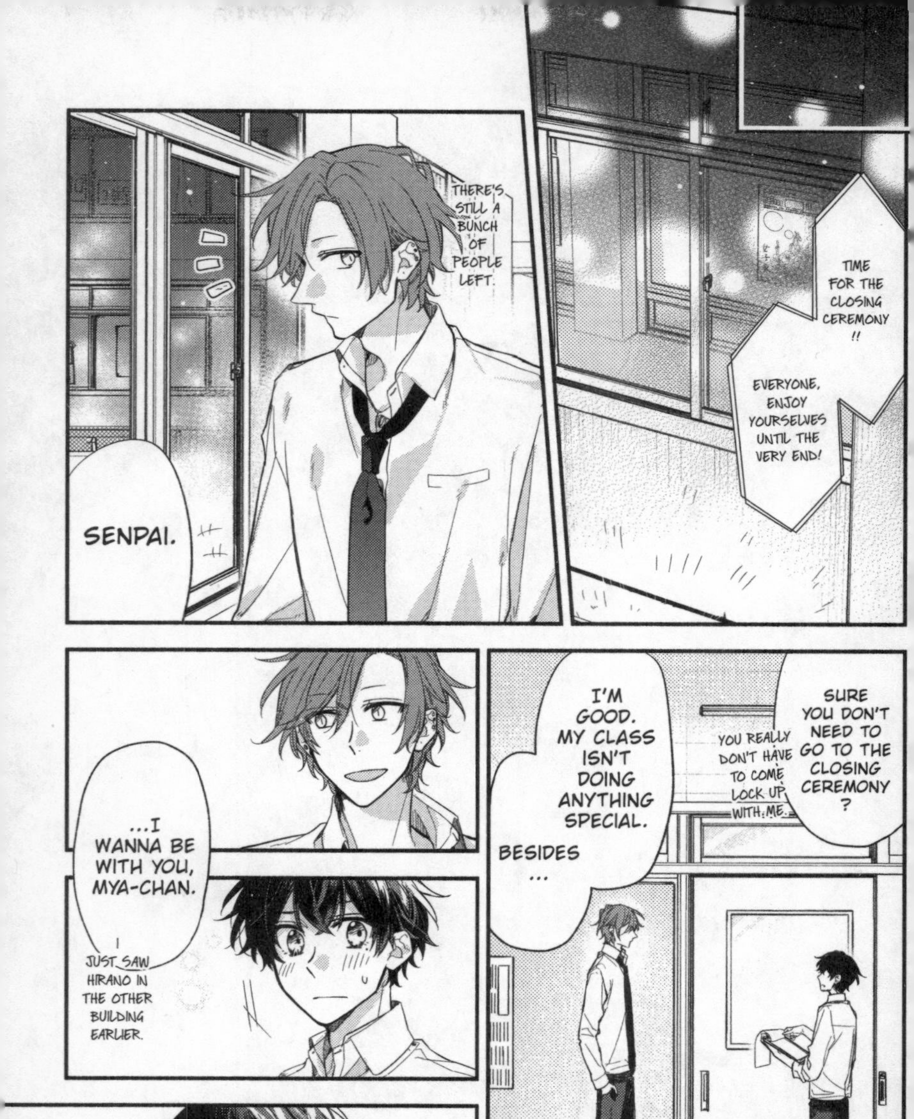
TIME FOR THE CLOSING CEREMONY !!
EVERYONE, ENJOY YOURSELVES UNTIL THE VERY END!
THERE'S STILL A BUNCH OF PEOPLE LEFT.
SENPAI.
SURE YOU DON'T NEED TO GO TO THE CLOSING CEREMONY ?
YOU REALLY DON'T HAVE TO COME LOCK UP WITH ME.
I'M GOOD. MY CLASS ISN'T DOING ANYTHING SPECIAL.
BESIDES ...
...I WANNA BE WITH YOU, MYA-CHAN.
I JUST SAW HIRANO IN THE OTHER BUILDING EARLIER.
S-SO, UM...

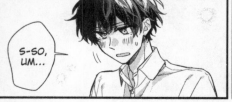

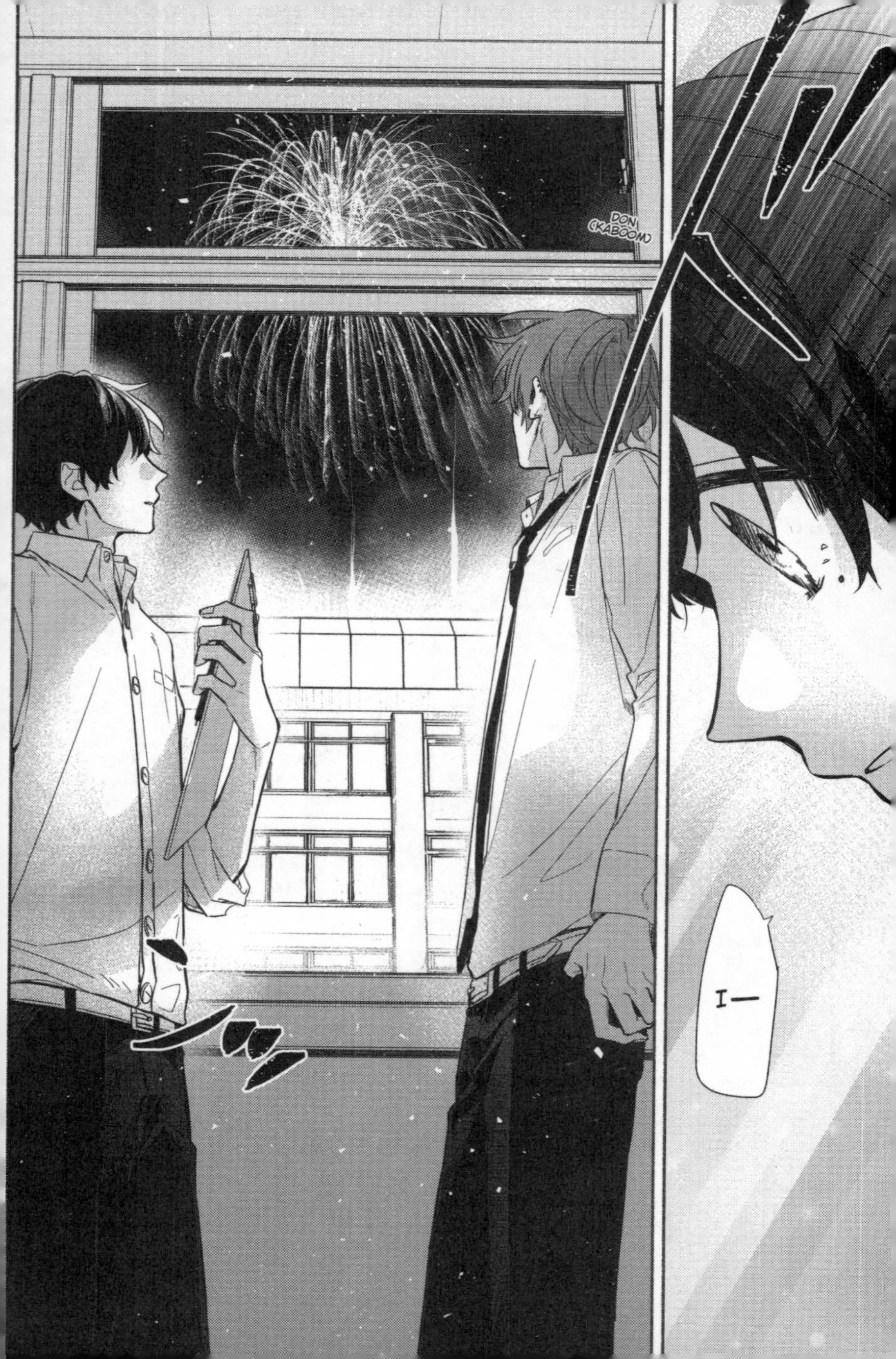
I—
DON
(KABOOM)

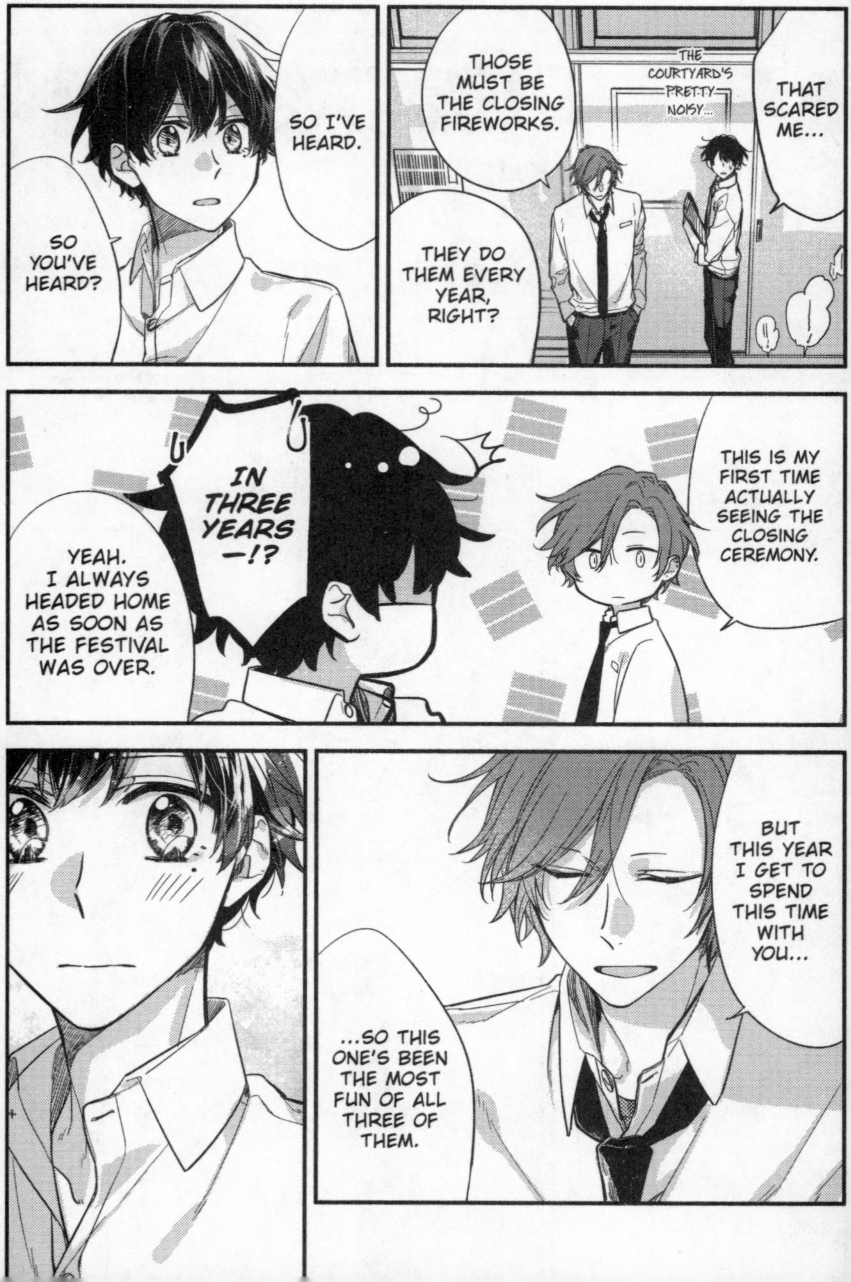
THAT SCARED ME...
THE COURTYARD'S PRETTY NOISY...
THOSE MUST BE THE CLOSING FIREWORKS.
THEY DO THEM EVERY YEAR, RIGHT?
SO I'VE HEARD.
SO YOU'VE HEARD?
THIS IS MY FIRST TIME ACTUALLY SEEING THE CLOSING CEREMONY.
IN THREE YEARS—!?
YEAH. I ALWAYS HEADED HOME AS SOON AS THE FESTIVAL WAS OVER.
BUT THIS YEAR I GET TO SPEND THIS TIME WITH YOU...
...SO THIS ONE'S BEEN THE MOST FUN OF ALL THREE OF THEM.

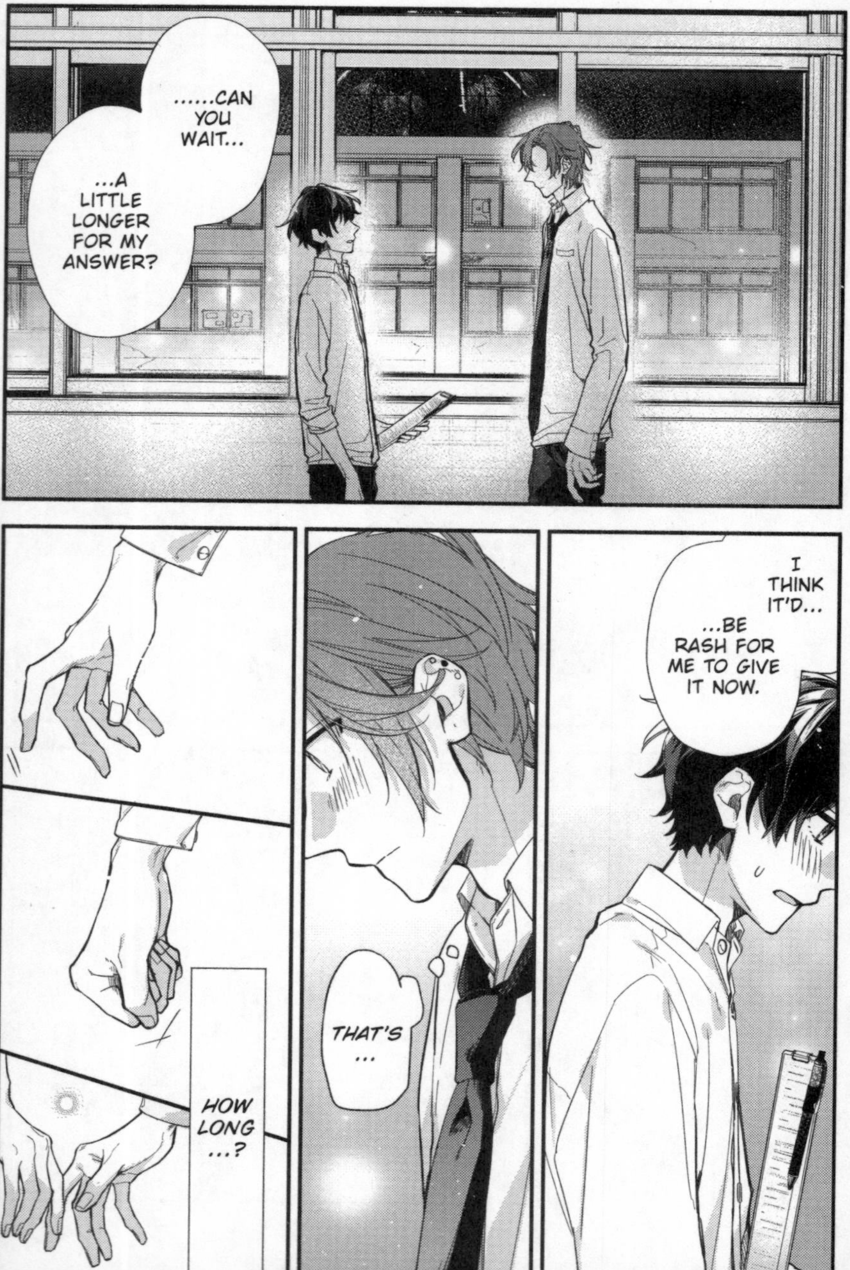
......CAN YOU WAIT...
...A LITTLE LONGER FOR MY ANSWER?
I THINK IT'D...
...BE RASH FOR ME TO GIVE IT NOW.
THAT'S ...
HOW LONG ...?

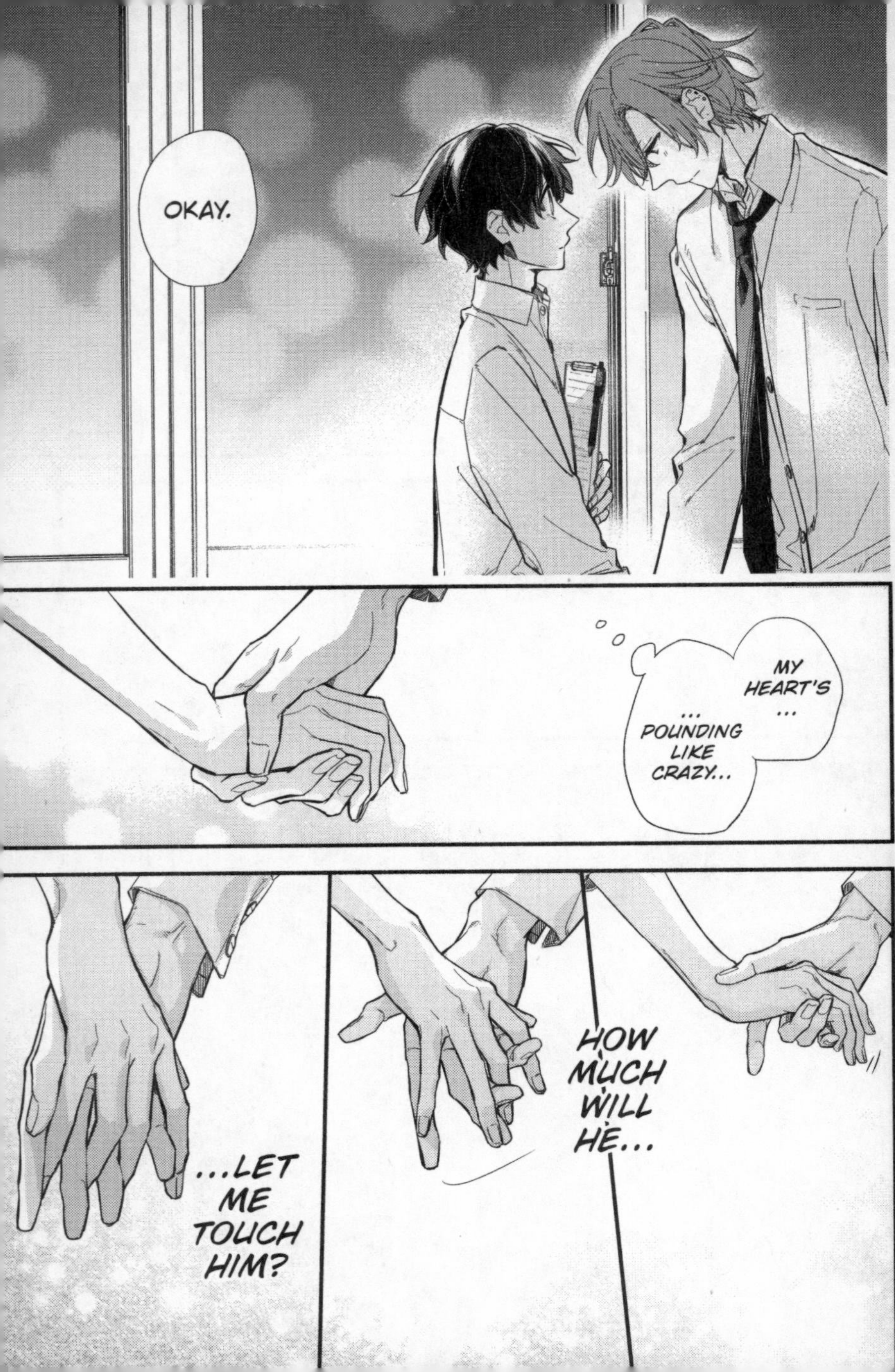
OKAY.
MY HEART'S ... ... POUNDING LIKE CRAZY...
HOW MUCH WILL HE...
...LET ME TOUCH HIM?

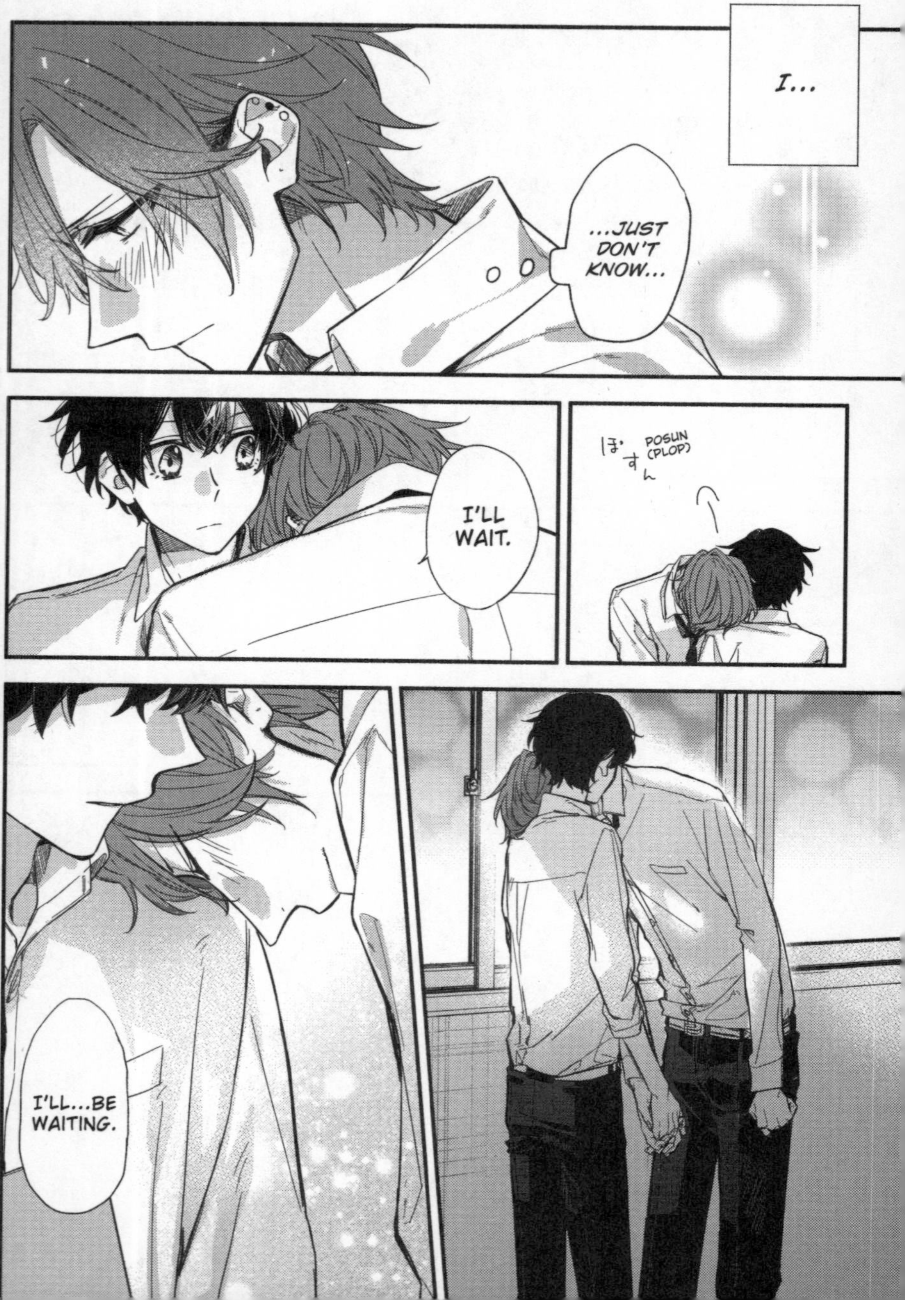
I...
...JUST DON'T KNOW...
ほすん
POSUN (PLOP)
I'LL WAIT.
I'LL...BE WAITING.

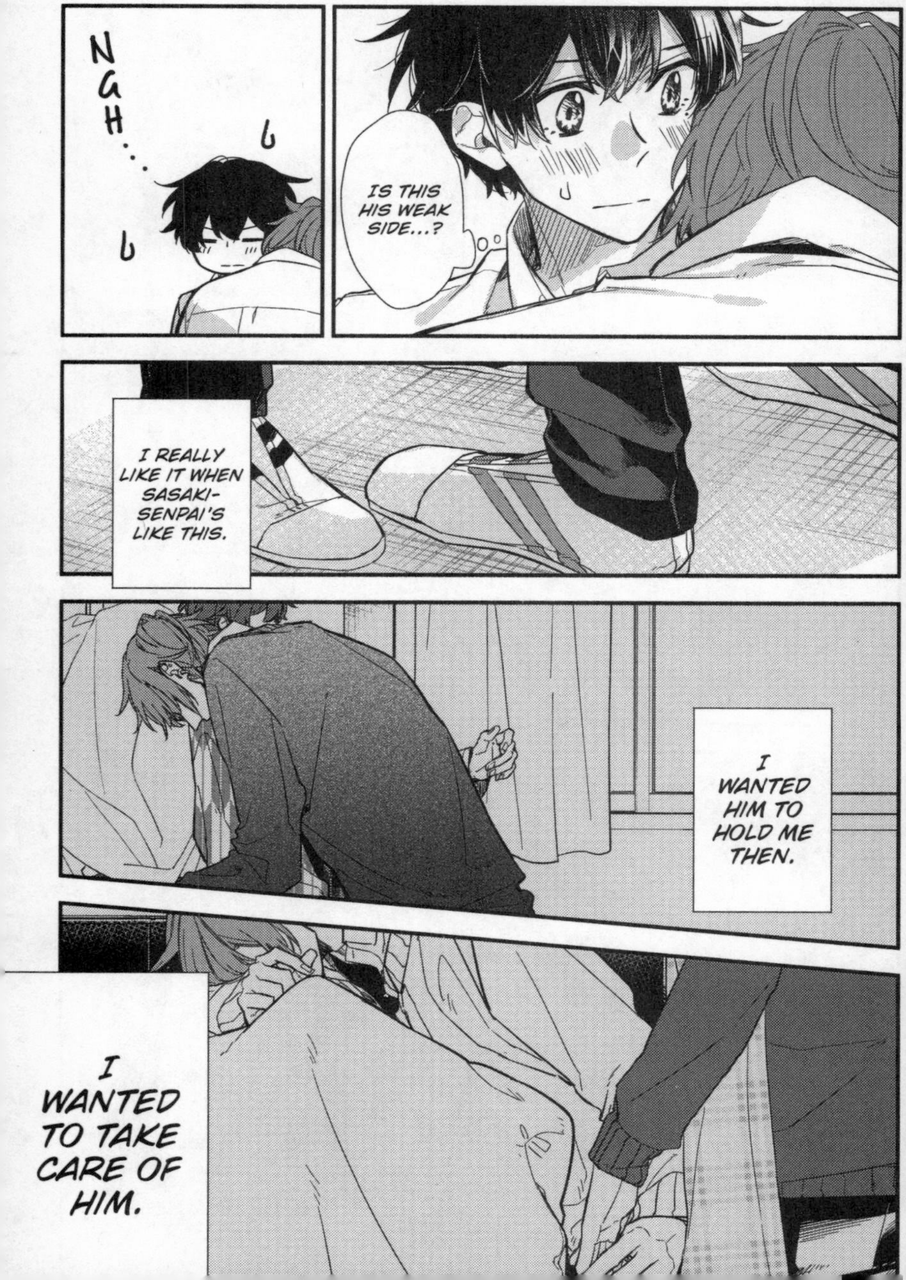
IS THIS HIS WEAK SIDE...?
NGH...
I REALLY LIKE IT WHEN SASAKI-SENPAI'S LIKE THIS.
I WANTED HIM TO HOLD ME THEN.
I WANTED TO TAKE CARE OF HIM.

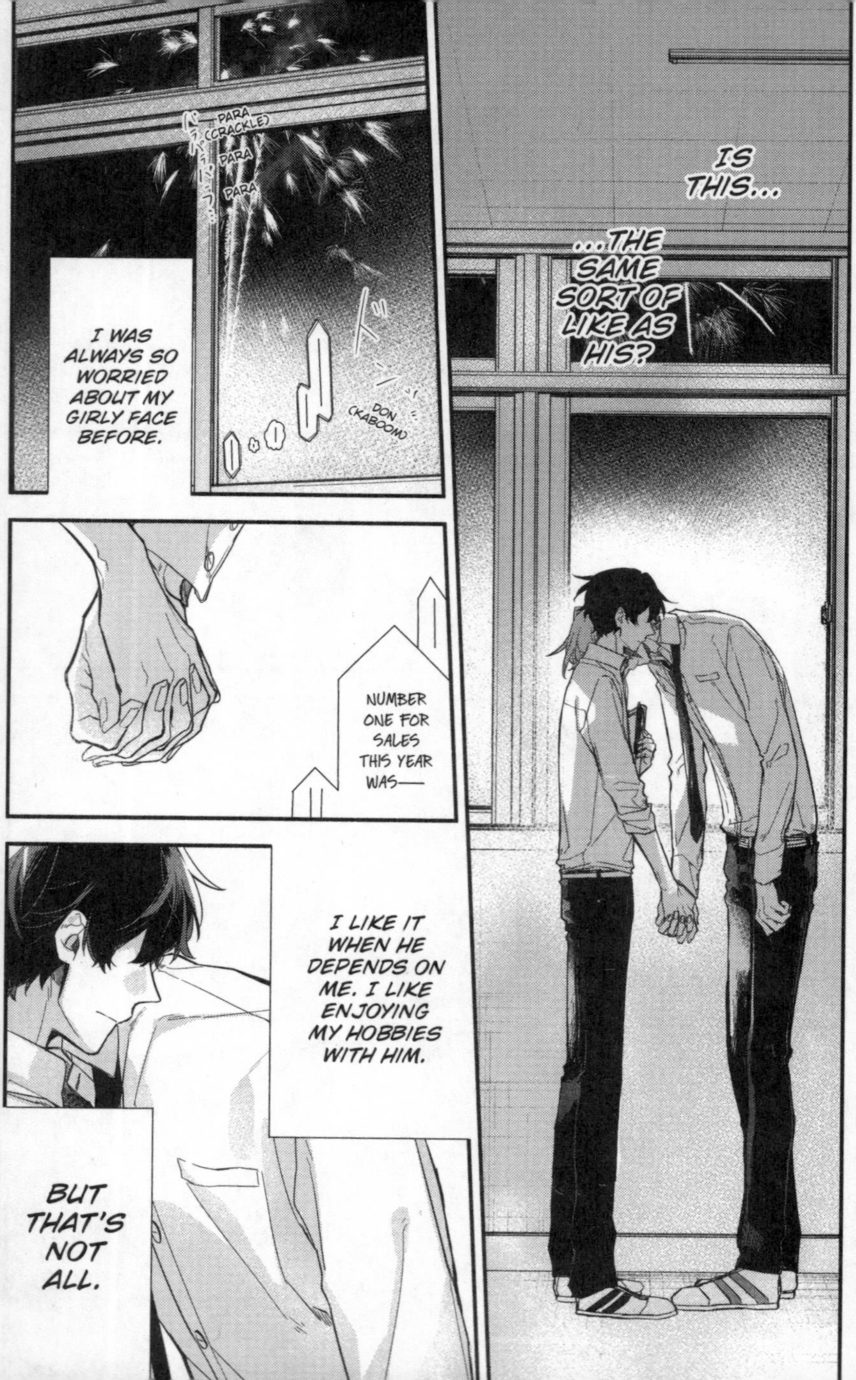
IS THIS...
...THE SAME SORT OF LIKE AS HIS?
PARA (CRACKLE) PARA PARA
DON (KABOOM)
I WAS ALWAYS SO WORRIED ABOUT MY GIRLY FACE BEFORE.
NUMBER ONE FOR SALES THIS YEAR WAS—
I LIKE IT WHEN HE DEPENDS ON ME. I LIKE ENJOYING MY HOBBIES WITH HIM.
BUT THAT'S NOT ALL.

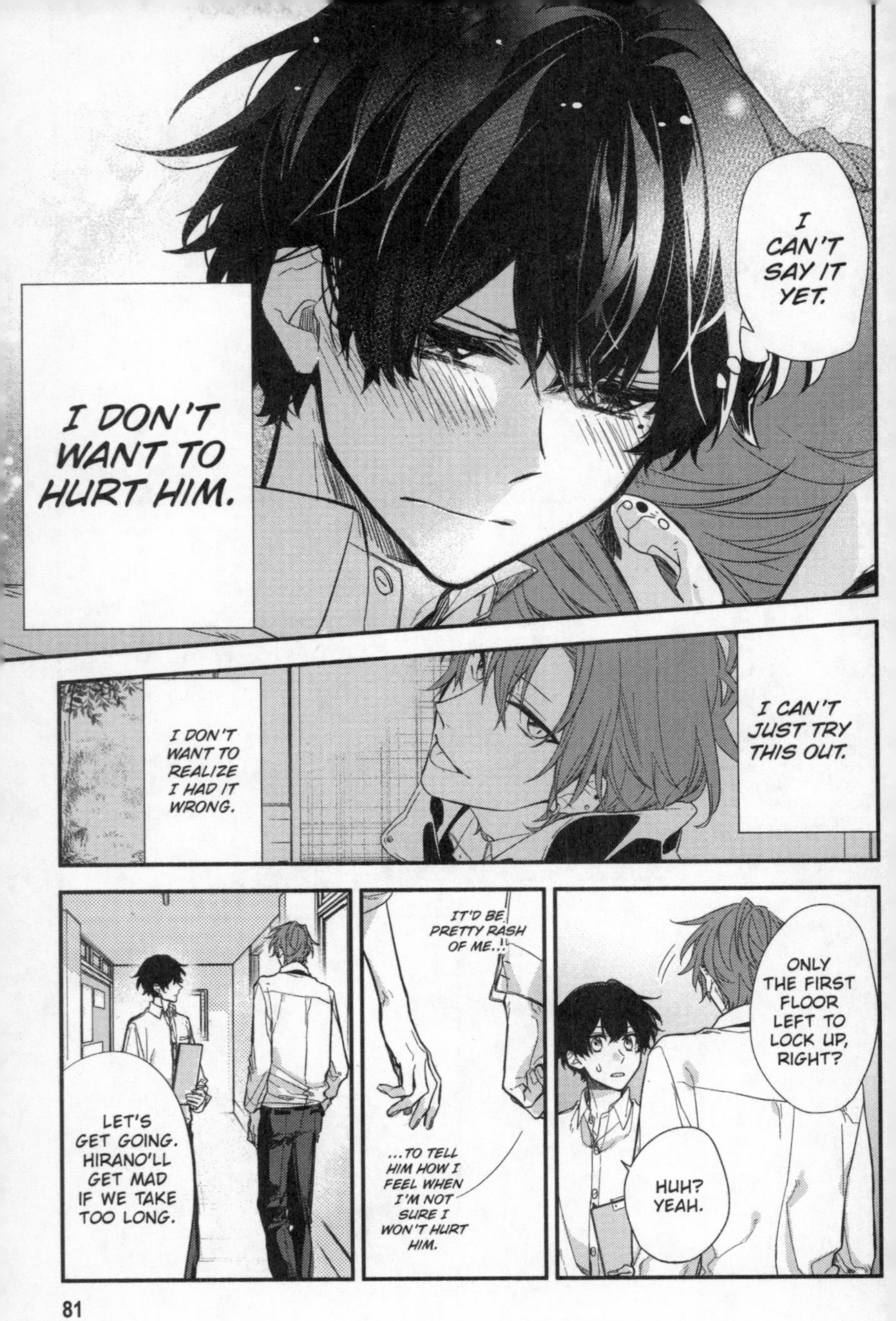
I CAN'T SAY IT YET.
I DON'T WANT TO HURT HIM.
I CAN'T JUST TRY THIS OUT.
I DON'T WANT TO REALIZE I HAD IT WRONG.
ONLY THE FIRST FLOOR LEFT TO LOCK UP, RIGHT?
HUH? YEAH.
IT'D BE PRETTY RASH OF ME...
...TO TELL HIM HOW I FEEL WHEN I'M NOT SURE I WON'T HURT HIM.
LET'S GET GOING. HIRANO'LL GET MAD IF WE TAKE TOO LONG.

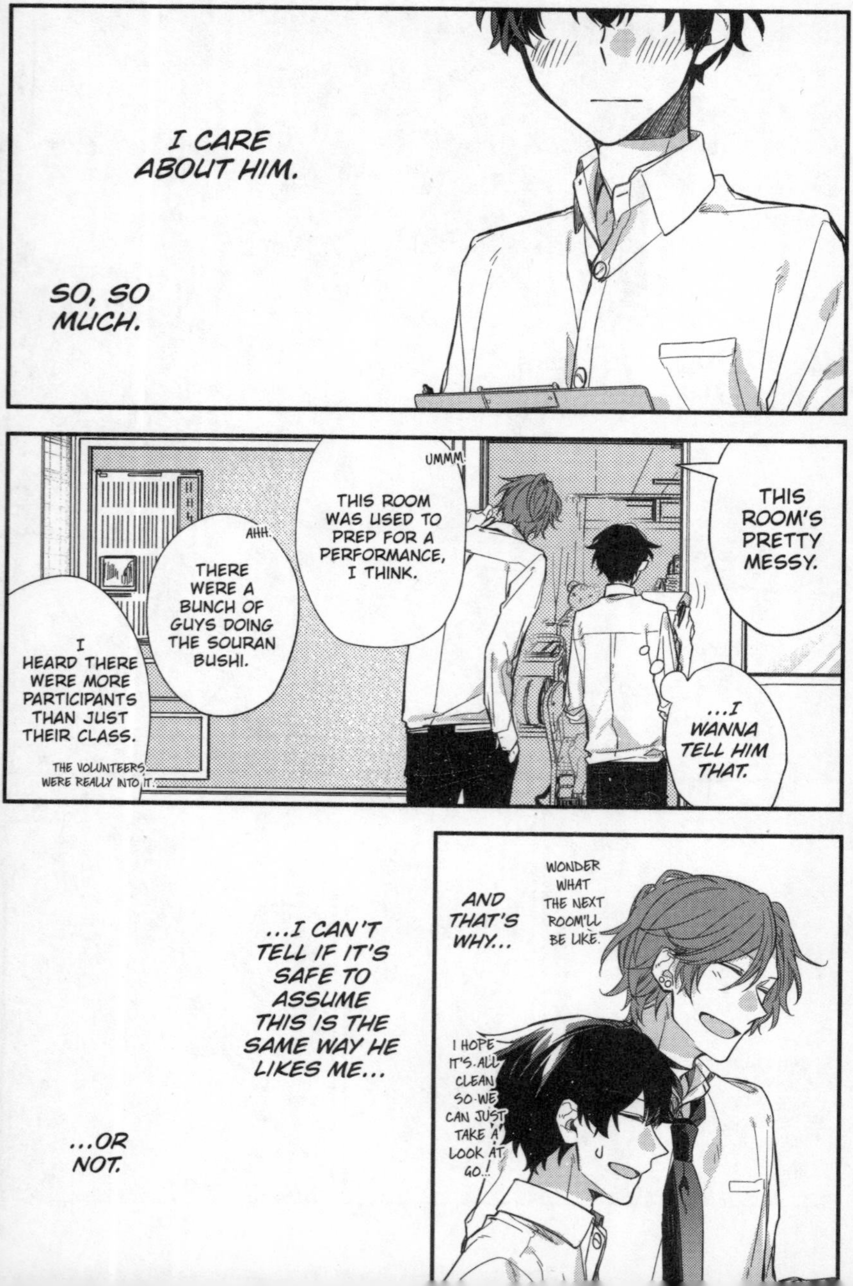
I CARE ABOUT HIM.
SO, SO MUCH.
THIS ROOM'S PRETTY MESSY.
...I WANNA TELL HIM THAT.
UMMM!
THIS ROOM WAS USED TO PREP FOR A PERFORMANCE, I THINK.
AHH.
THERE WERE A BUNCH OF GUYS DOING THE SOURAN BUSHI.
I HEARD THERE WERE MORE PARTICIPANTS THAN JUST THEIR CLASS.
THE VOLUNTEERS WERE REALLY INTO IT.
WONDER WHAT THE NEXT ROOM'LL BE LIKE.
AND THAT'S WHY...
I HOPE IT'S ALL CLEAN SO WE CAN JUST TAKE A LOOK AT GO..!
...I CAN'T TELL IF IT'S SAFE TO ASSUME THIS IS THE SAME WAY HE LIKES ME...
...OR NOT.

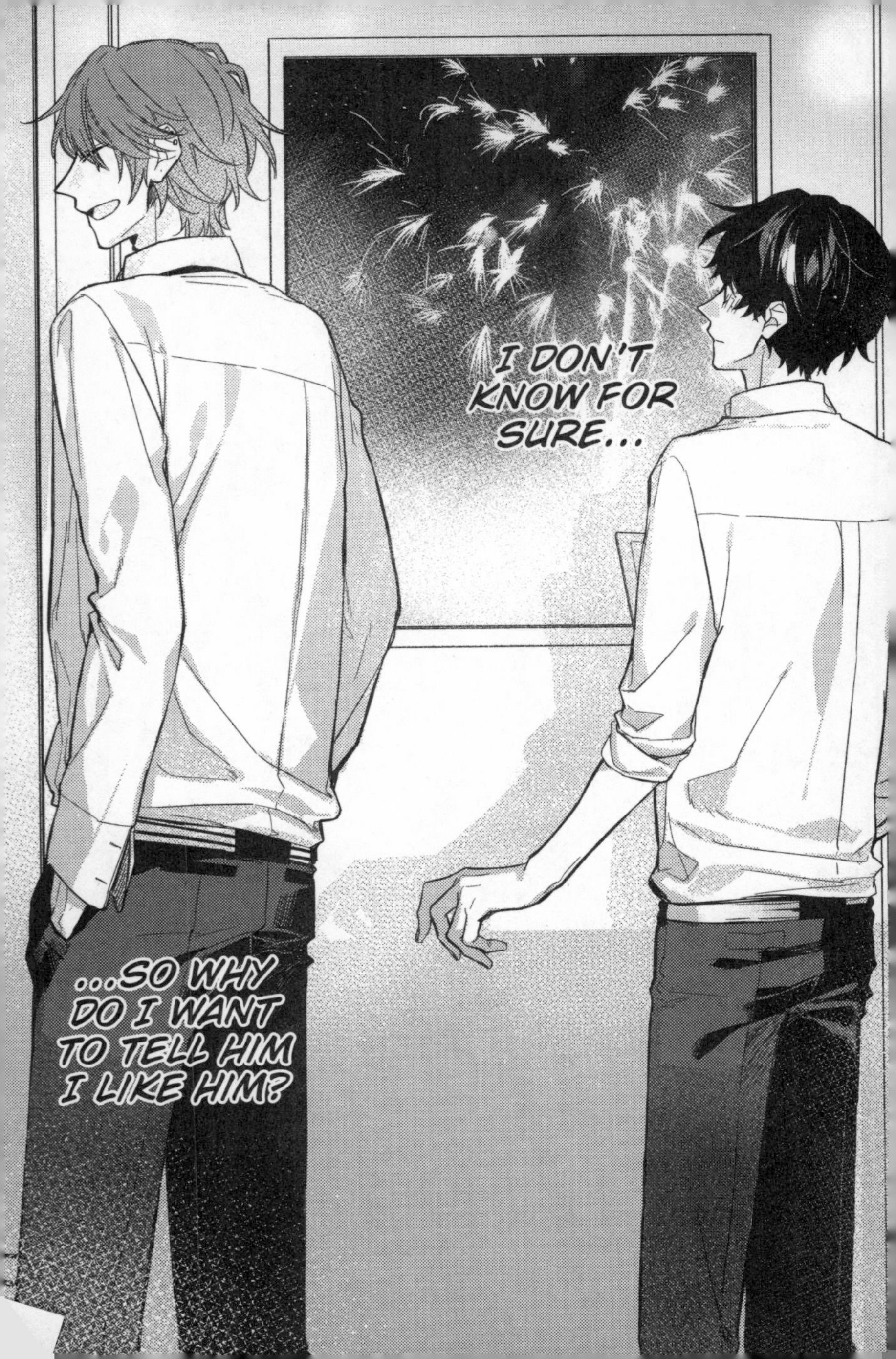
I DON'T KNOW FOR SURE...
...SO WHY DO I WANT TO TELL HIM I LIKE HIM?

Sasaki and Miyano

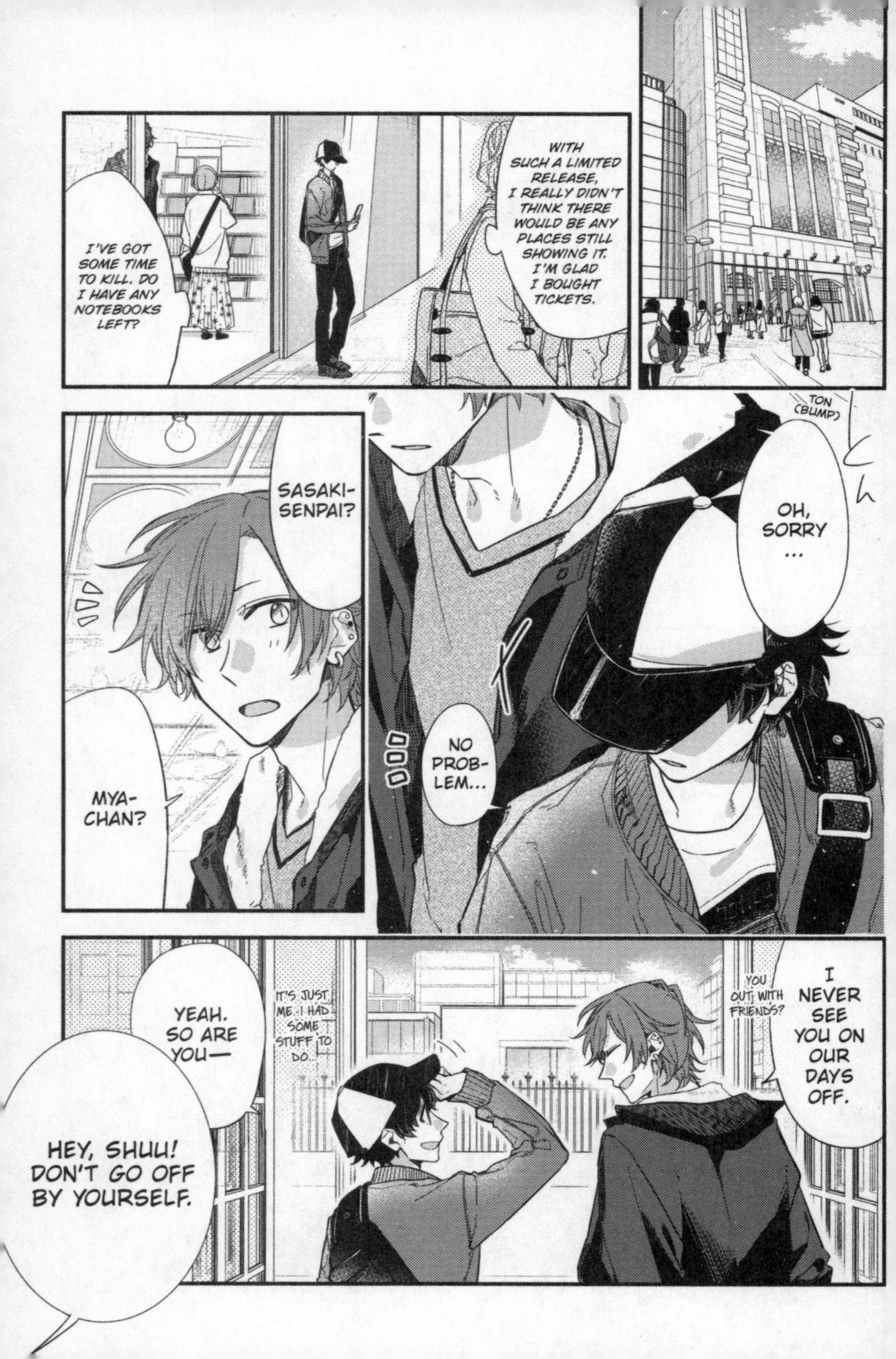
WITH SUCH A LIMITED RELEASE, I REALLY DIDN'T THINK THERE WOULD BE ANY PLACES STILL SHOWING IT. I'M GLAD I BOUGHT TICKETS.
I'VE GOT SOME TIME TO KILL. DO I HAVE ANY NOTEBOOKS LEFT?
とん
TON (BUMP)
OH, SORRY ...
NO PROB-LEM...
SASAKI-SENPAI?
MYA-CHAN?
I NEVER SEE YOU ON OUR DAYS OFF.
YOU OUT WITH FRIENDS?
IT'S JUST ME. I HAD SOME STUFF TO DO...
YEAH. SO ARE YOU—
HEY, SHUU! DON'T GO OFF BY YOURSELF.

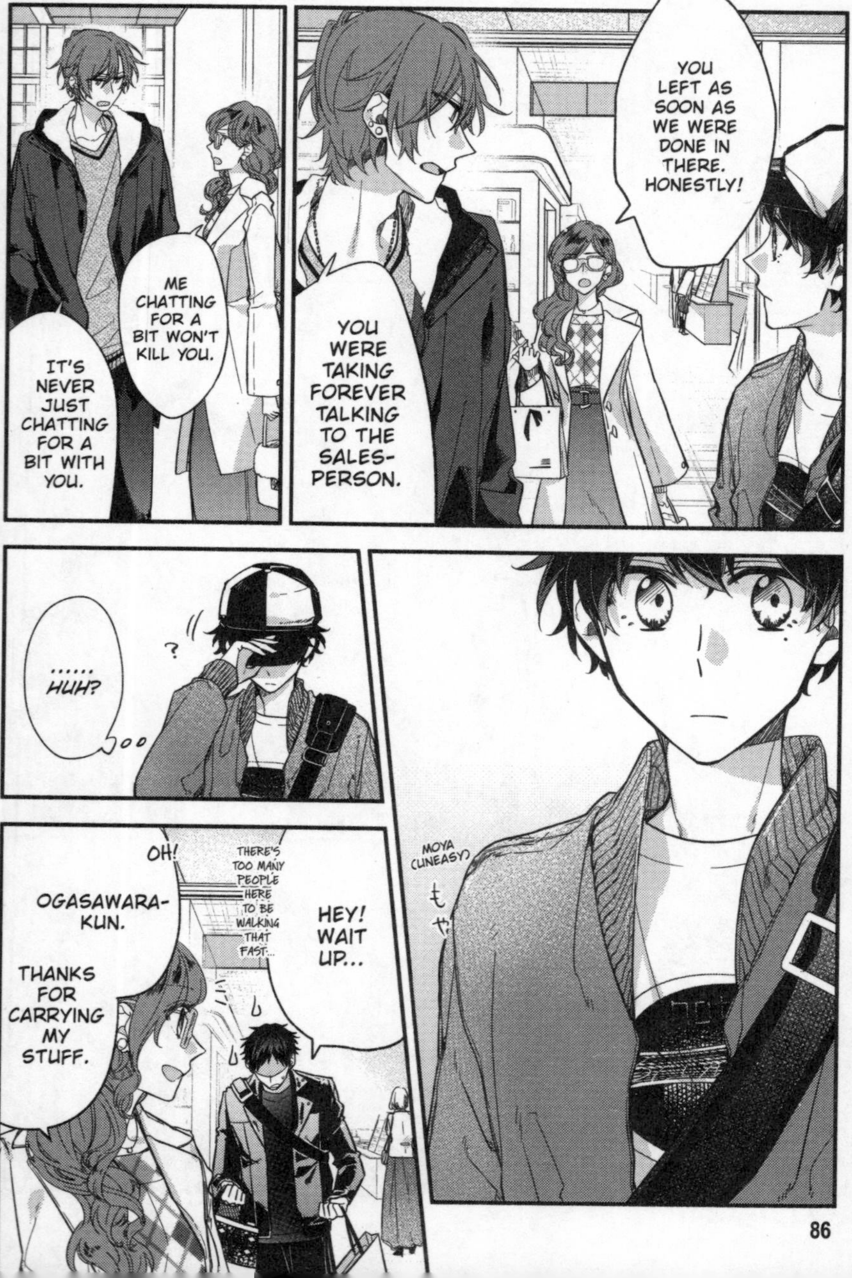
YOU LEFT AS SOON AS WE WERE DONE IN THERE. HONESTLY!
YOU WERE TAKING FOREVER TALKING TO THE SALES-PERSON.
ME CHATTING FOR A BIT WON'T KILL YOU.
IT'S NEVER JUST CHATTING FOR A BIT WITH YOU.
MOYA (UNEASY)
もや
......HUH?
?
HEY! WAIT UP...
THERE'S TOO MANY PEOPLE HERE TO BE WALKING THAT FAST...
OH!
OGASAWARA-KUN.
THANKS FOR CARRYING MY STUFF.

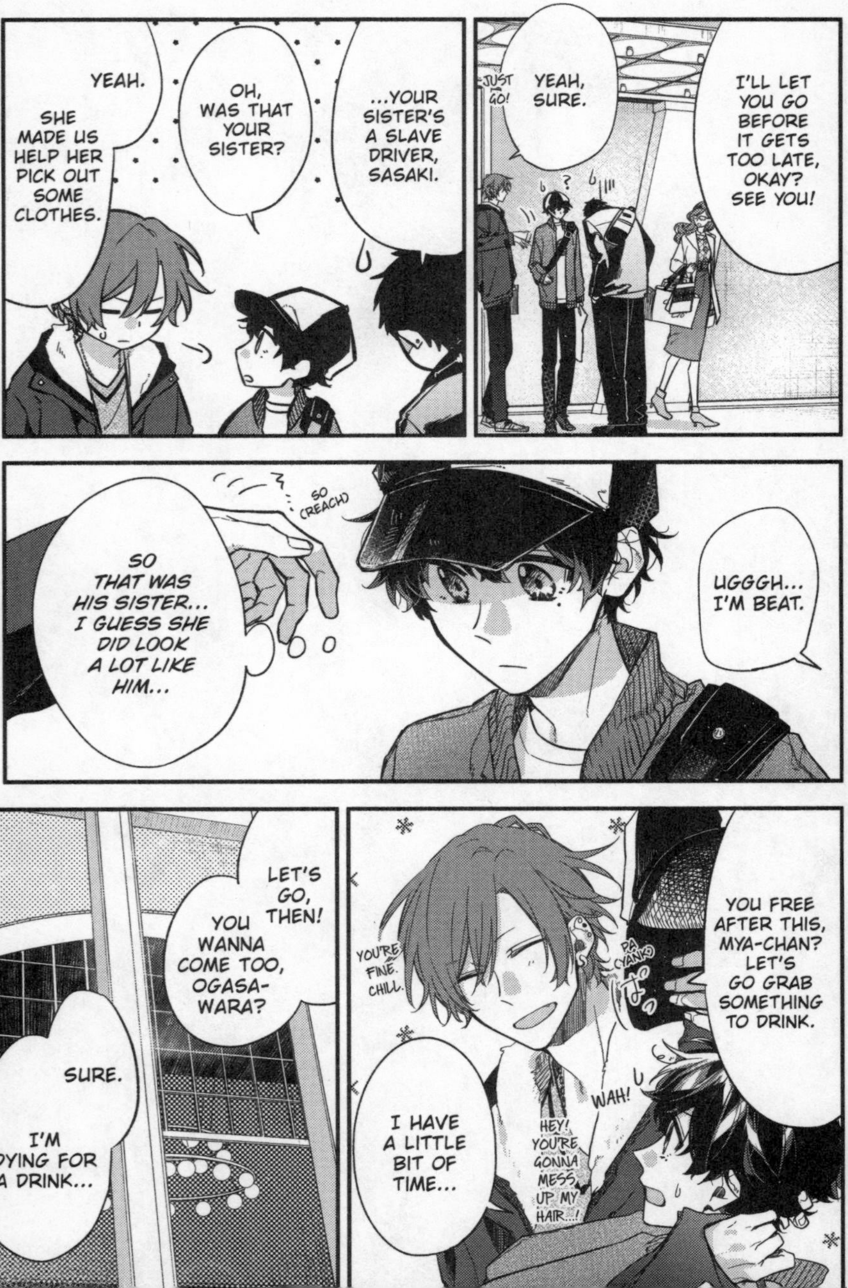
I'LL LET YOU GO BEFORE IT GETS TOO LATE, OKAY? SEE YOU!
YEAH, SURE.
JUST GO!
...YOUR SISTER'S A SLAVE DRIVER, SASAKI.
OH, WAS THAT YOUR SISTER?
YEAH.
SHE MADE US HELP HER PICK OUT SOME CLOTHES.
UGGGH... I'M BEAT.
SO (REACH)
SO THAT WAS HIS SISTER... I GUESS SHE DID LOOK A LOT LIKE HIM...
YOU FREE AFTER THIS, MYA-CHAN? LET'S GO GRAB SOMETHING TO DRINK.
PA CYANK
YOU'RE FINE. CHILL.
WAH!
HEY! YOU'RE GONNA MESS UP MY HAIR...
I HAVE A LITTLE BIT OF TIME...
LET'S GO, THEN!
YOU WANNA COME TOO, OGASAWARA?
SURE.
I'M DYING FOR A DRINK...

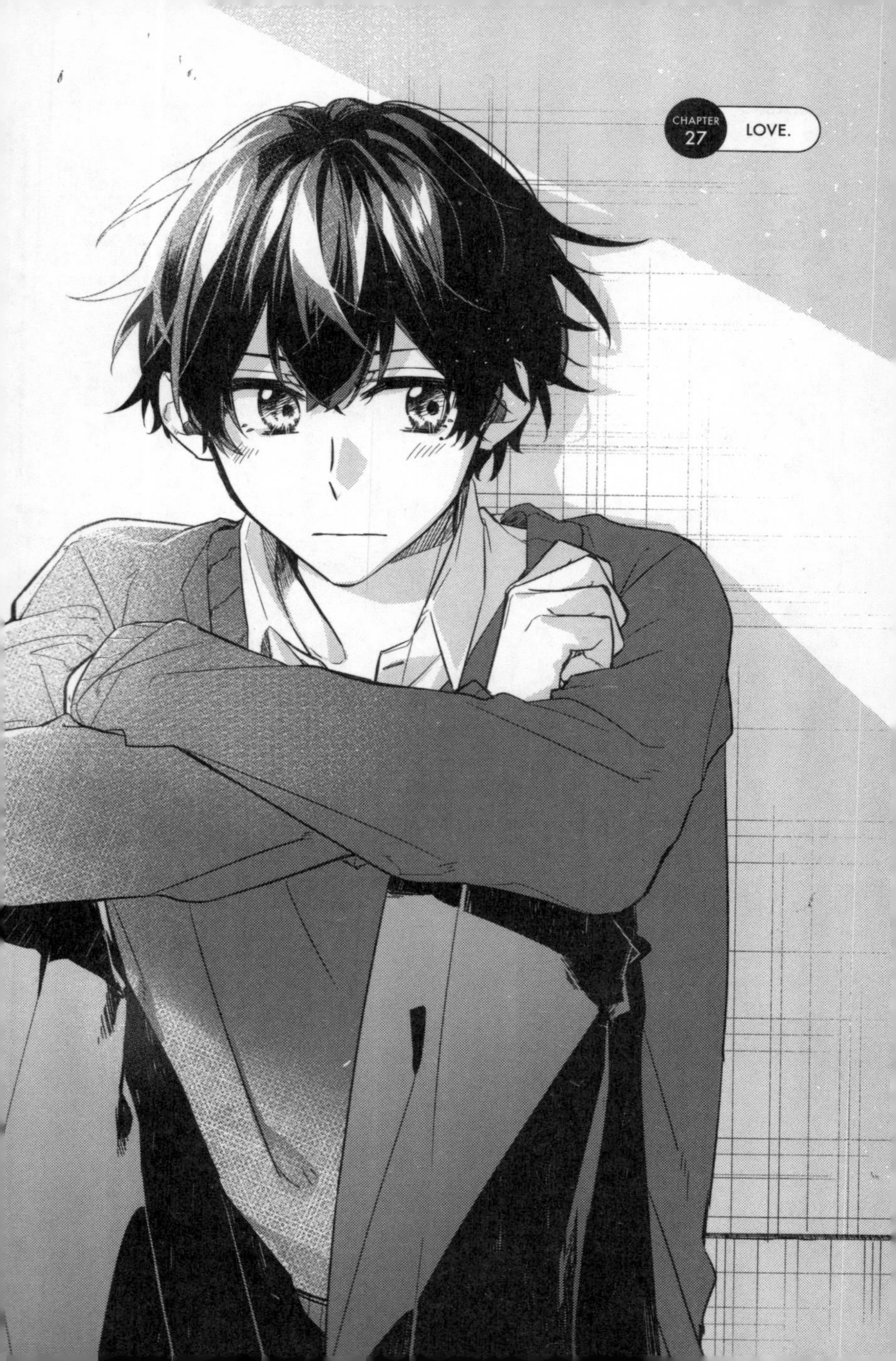
CHAPTER 27
LOVE.

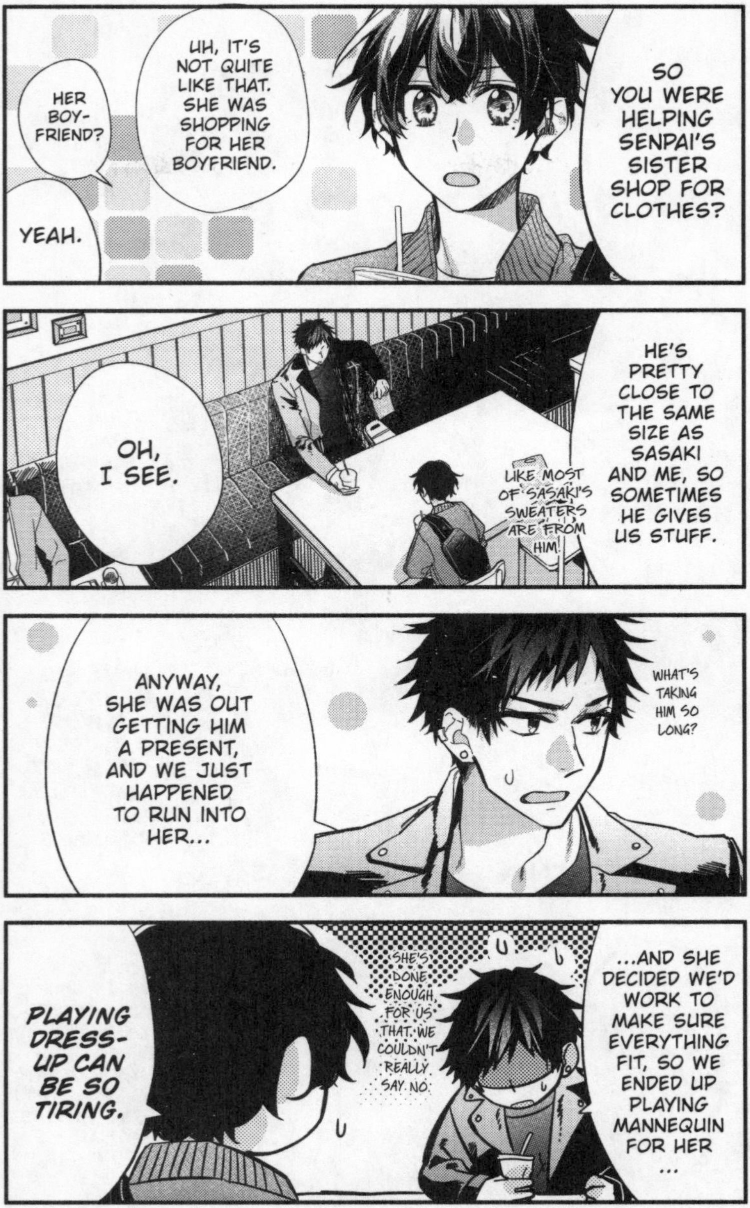
SO YOU WERE HELPING SENPAI'S SISTER SHOP FOR CLOTHES?
UH, IT'S NOT QUITE LIKE THAT. SHE WAS SHOPPING FOR HER BOYFRIEND.
HER BOY-FRIEND?
YEAH.
HE'S PRETTY CLOSE TO THE SAME SIZE AS SASAKI AND ME, SO SOMETIMES HE GIVES US STUFF.
LIKE MOST OF SASAKI'S SWEATERS ARE FROM HIM.
OH, I SEE.
WHAT'S TAKING HIM SO LONG?
ANYWAY, SHE WAS OUT GETTING HIM A PRESENT, AND WE JUST HAPPENED TO RUN INTO HER...
...AND SHE DECIDED WE'D WORK TO MAKE SURE EVERYTHING FIT, SO WE ENDED UP PLAYING MANNEQUIN FOR HER ...
SHE'S DONE ENOUGH FOR US THAT WE COULDN'T REALLY SAY NO.
PLAYING DRESS-UP CAN BE SO TIRING.

ANY FORMER PARTICIPANT IN THE DRAG CONTEST WOULD AGREE.

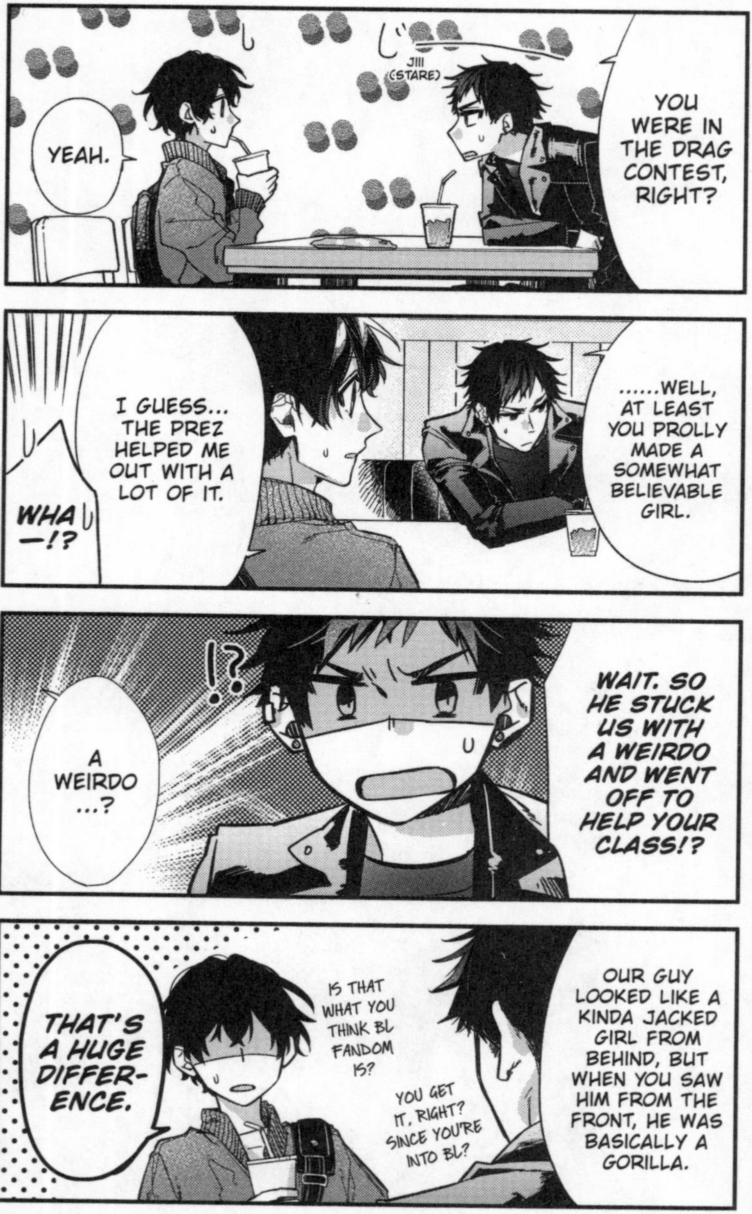
じ
JIII (STARE)
YOU WERE IN THE DRAG CONTEST, RIGHT?
YEAH.
......WELL, AT LEAST YOU PROLLY MADE A SOMEWHAT BELIEVABLE GIRL.
I GUESS... THE PREZ HELPED ME OUT WITH A LOT OF IT.
WHA—!?
WAIT. SO HE STUCK US WITH A WEIRDO AND WENT OFF TO HELP YOUR CLASS!?
!?
A WEIRDO ...?
OUR GUY LOOKED LIKE A KINDA JACKED GIRL FROM BEHIND, BUT WHEN YOU SAW HIM FROM THE FRONT, HE WAS BASICALLY A GORILLA.
YOU GET IT, RIGHT? SINCE YOU'RE INTO BL?
IS THAT WHAT YOU THINK BL FANDOM IS?
THAT'S A HUGE DIFFERENCE.

A PAINFUL PLEA.

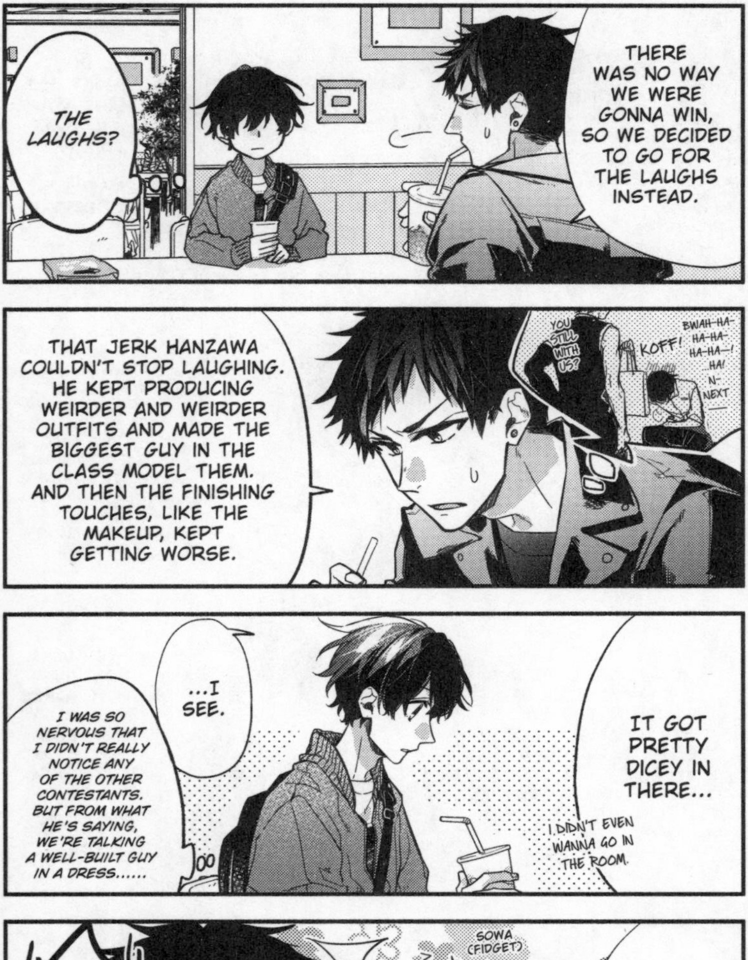
THERE WAS NO WAY WE WERE GONNA WIN, SO WE DECIDED TO GO FOR THE LAUGHS INSTEAD.
THE LAUGHS?
BWAH-HA-HA-HA-HA—! ...HA! N-NEXT—
KOFF!
YOU STILL WITH US?
THAT JERK HANZAWA COULDN'T STOP LAUGHING. HE KEPT PRODUCING WEIRDER AND WEIRDER OUTFITS AND MADE THE BIGGEST GUY IN THE CLASS MODEL THEM. AND THEN THE FINISHING TOUCHES, LIKE THE MAKEUP, KEPT GETTING WORSE.
IT GOT PRETTY DICEY IN THERE...
I DIDN'T EVEN WANNA GO IN THE ROOM.
...I SEE.
I WAS SO NERVOUS THAT I DIDN'T REALLY NOTICE ANY OF THE OTHER CONTESTANTS. BUT FROM WHAT HE'S SAYING, WE'RE TALKING A WELL-BUILT GUY IN A DRESS......
I KIND OF WISH I'D SEEN IT.
SOWA (FIDGET)
YOU WANNA SEE THAT!?

HE SHOULD HAVE PAID ATTENTION.

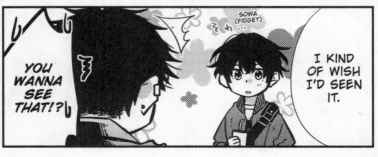

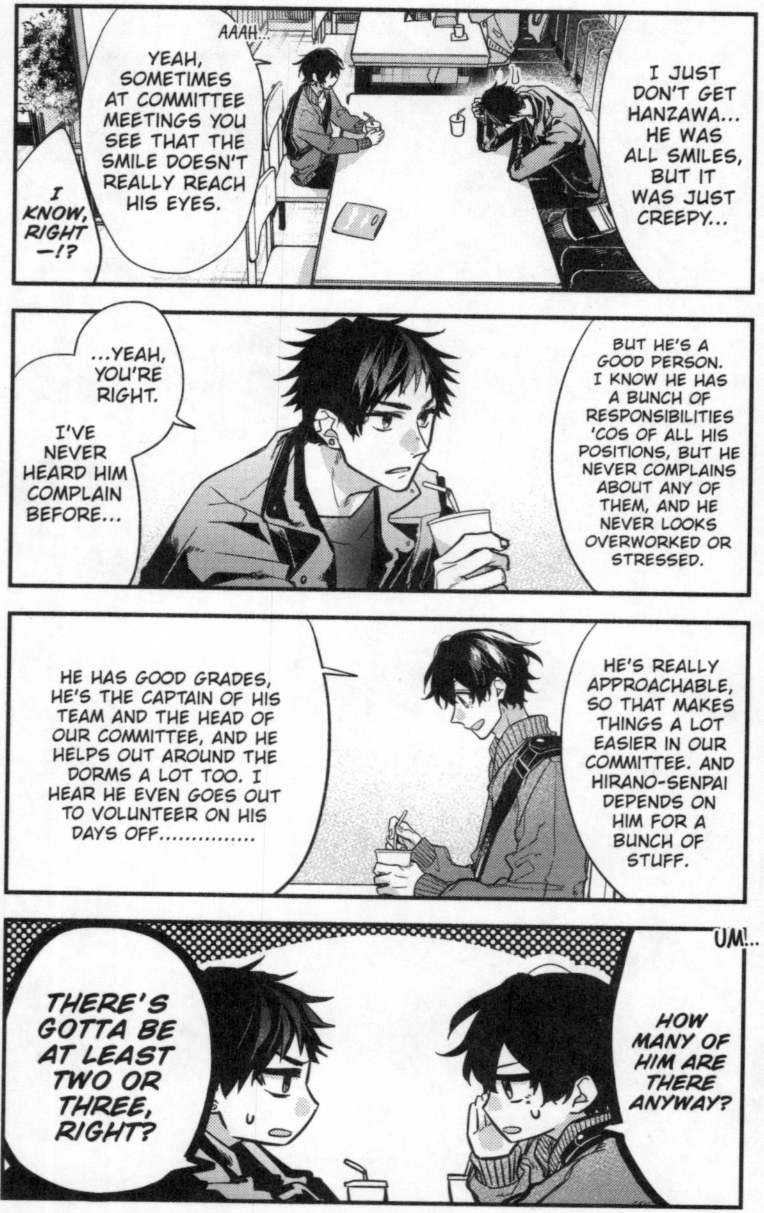
I JUST DON'T GET HANZAWA... HE WAS ALL SMILES, BUT IT WAS JUST CREEPY...
AAAH...
YEAH, SOMETIMES AT COMMITTEE MEETINGS YOU SEE THAT THE SMILE DOESN'T REALLY REACH HIS EYES.
I KNOW, RIGHT—!?
BUT HE'S A GOOD PERSON. I KNOW HE HAS A BUNCH OF RESPONSIBILITIES 'COS OF ALL HIS POSITIONS, BUT HE NEVER COMPLAINS ABOUT ANY OF THEM, AND HE NEVER LOOKS OVERWORKED OR STRESSED.
...YEAH, YOU'RE RIGHT.
I'VE NEVER HEARD HIM COMPLAIN BEFORE...
HE'S REALLY APPROACHABLE, SO THAT MAKES THINGS A LOT EASIER IN OUR COMMITTEE. AND HIRANO-SENPAI DEPENDS ON HIM FOR A BUNCH OF STUFF.
HE HAS GOOD GRADES, HE'S THE CAPTAIN OF HIS TEAM AND THE HEAD OF OUR COMMITTEE, AND HE HELPS OUT AROUND THE DORMS A LOT TOO. I HEAR HE EVEN GOES OUT TO VOLUNTEER ON HIS DAYS OFF...............
UM!...
HOW MANY OF HIM ARE THERE ANYWAY?
THERE'S GOTTA BE AT LEAST TWO OR THREE, RIGHT?

MASATO HANZAWA. MAN OF MYSTERY.

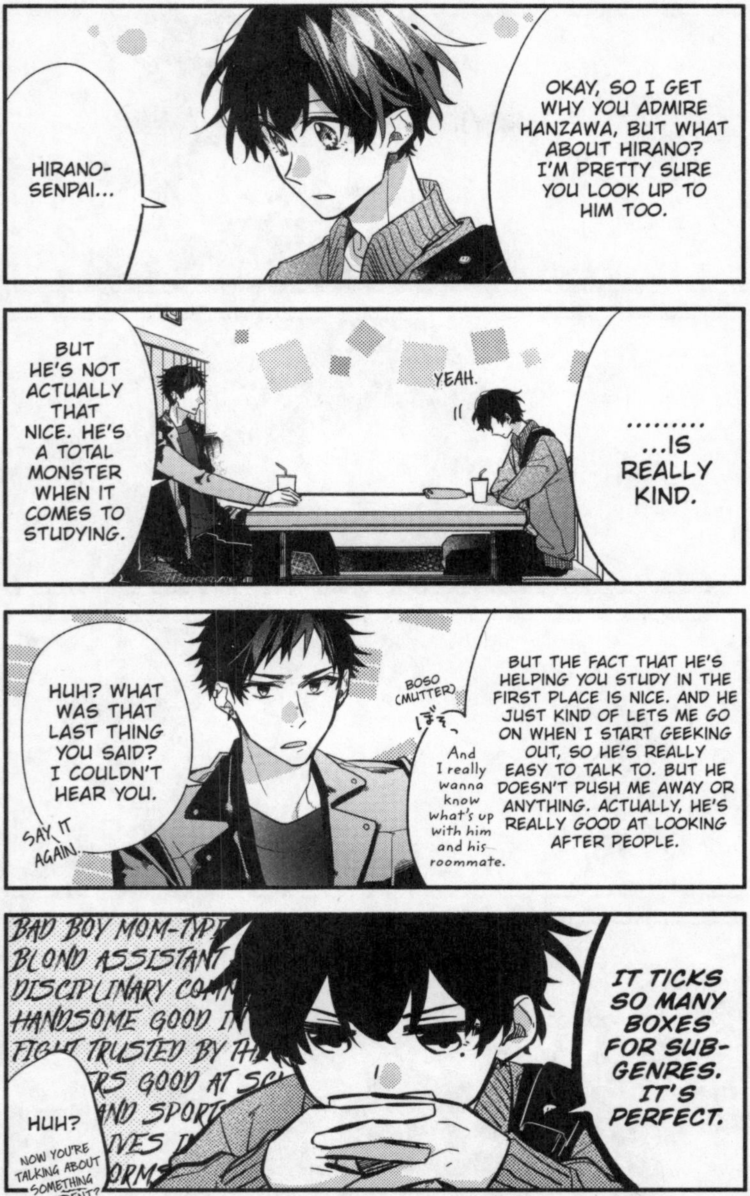
OKAY, SO I GET WHY YOU ADMIRE HANZAWA, BUT WHAT ABOUT HIRANO? I'M PRETTY SURE YOU LOOK UP TO HIM TOO.
HIRANO-SENPAI...
....
...IS REALLY KIND.
YEAH.
BUT HE'S NOT ACTUALLY THAT NICE. HE'S A TOTAL MONSTER WHEN IT COMES TO STUDYING.
ALL HE DOES IS GET MAD.
BUT THE FACT THAT HE'S HELPING YOU STUDY IN THE FIRST PLACE IS NICE. AND HE JUST KIND OF LETS ME GO ON WHEN I START GEEKING OUT, SO HE'S REALLY EASY TO TALK TO. BUT HE DOESN'T PUSH ME AWAY OR ANYTHING. ACTUALLY, HE'S REALLY GOOD AT LOOKING AFTER PEOPLE.
BOSO (MUTTER)
ぼそ
And I really wanna know what's up with him and his roommate.
HUH? WHAT WAS THAT LAST THING YOU SAID? I COULDN'T HEAR YOU.
SAY IT AGAIN.
IT TICKS SO MANY BOXES FOR SUB-GENRES. IT'S PERFECT.
HUH?
NOW YOU'RE TALKING ABOUT SOMETHING DIFFERENT?

RESPECT AND WHAT GETS HIM GOING.

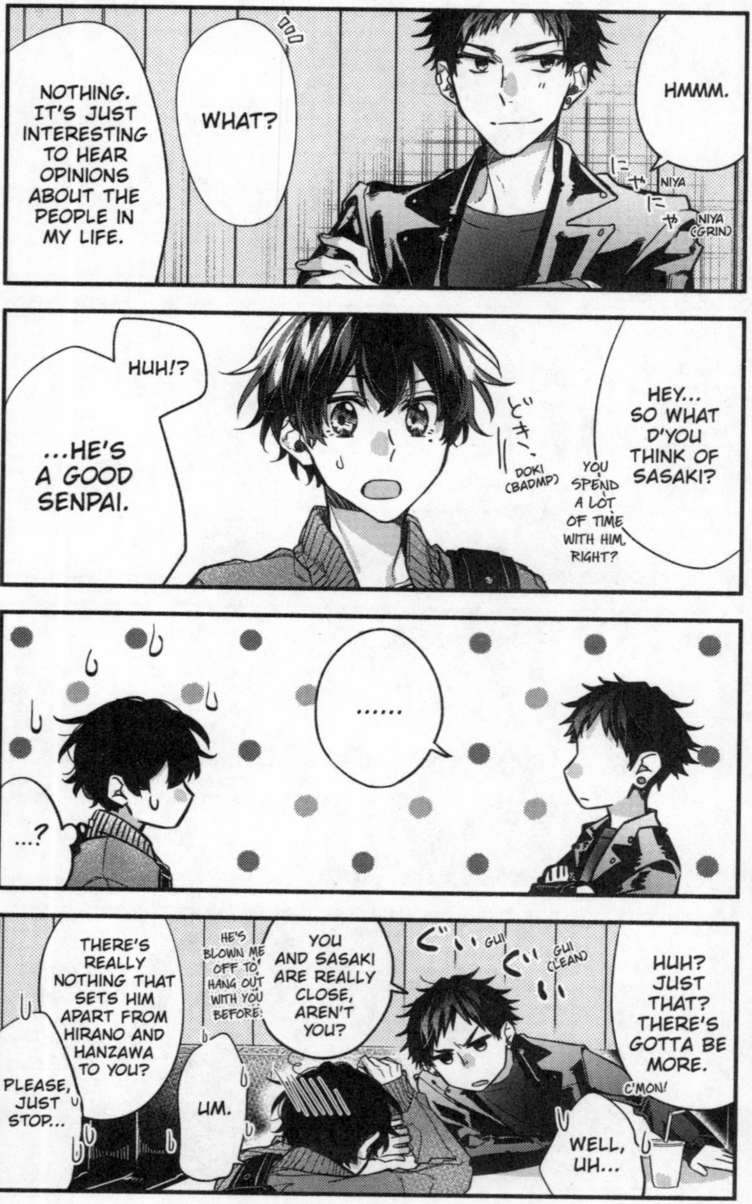
HMMM.
にやにや
NIYA NIYA (GRIN)
WHAT?
NOTHING. IT'S JUST INTERESTING TO HEAR OPINIONS ABOUT THE PEOPLE IN MY LIFE.
HEY... SO WHAT D'YOU THINK OF SASAKI?
YOU SPEND A LOT OF TIME WITH HIM, RIGHT?
どきっ
DOKI (BADMP)
HUH!?
...HE'S A GOOD SENPAI.
......
...?
HUH? JUST THAT? THERE'S GOTTA BE MORE.
C'MON!
ぐいぐい
GUI GUI (LEAN)
WELL, UH...
YOU AND SASAKI ARE REALLY CLOSE, AREN'T YOU?
HE'S BLOWN ME OFF TO HANG OUT WITH YOU BEFORE.
UM.
THERE'S REALLY NOTHING THAT SETS HIM APART FROM HIRANO AND HANZAWA TO YOU?
PLEASE, JUST STOP...

A COMPLETELY INNOCENT BARRAGE OF QUESTIONS.

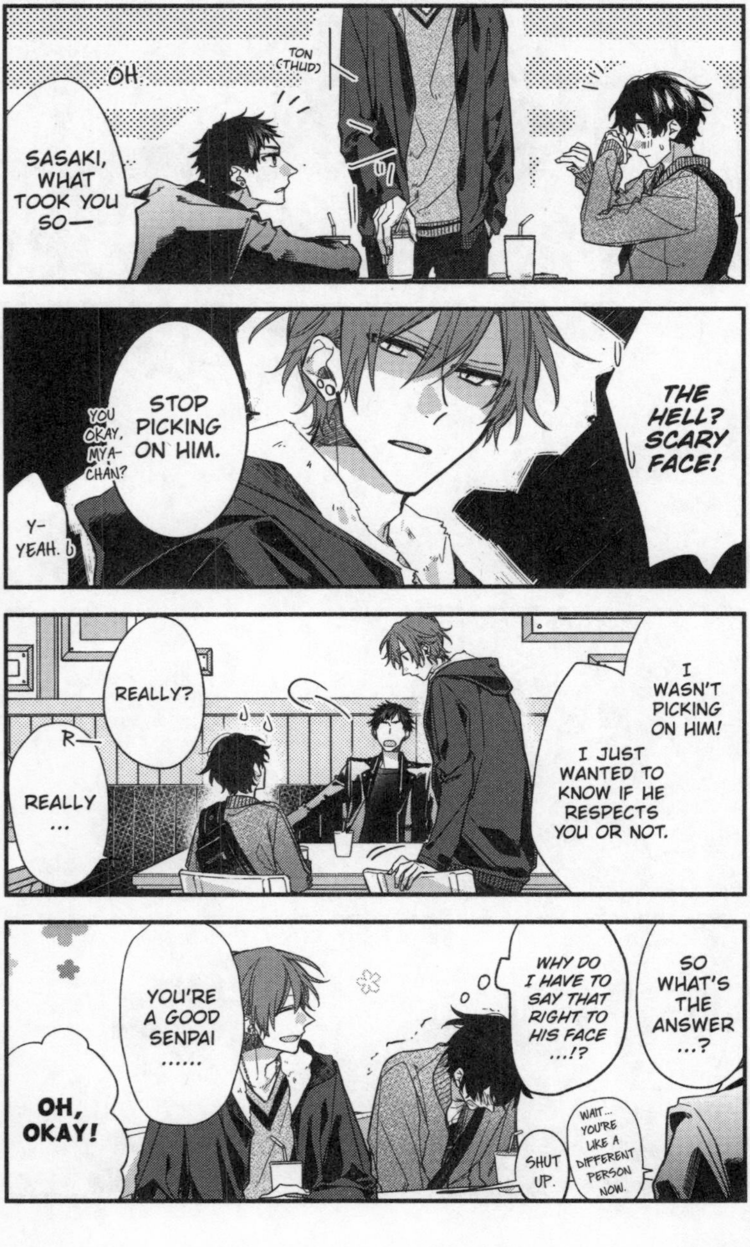
TON (THUD)
OH.
SASAKI, WHAT TOOK YOU SO—
THE HELL? SCARY FACE!
STOP PICKING ON HIM.
YOU OKAY, MYA-CHAN?
Y-YEAH.
I WASN'T PICKING ON HIM!
I JUST WANTED TO KNOW IF HE RESPECTS YOU OR NOT.
REALLY?
R— REALLY ...
SO WHAT'S THE ANSWER ...?
WHY DO I HAVE TO SAY THAT RIGHT TO HIS FACE ...!?
WAIT... YOU'RE LIKE A DIFFERENT PERSON NOW.
SHUT UP.
YOU'RE A GOOD SENPAI ......
OH, OKAY!

MOOD RESTORED.

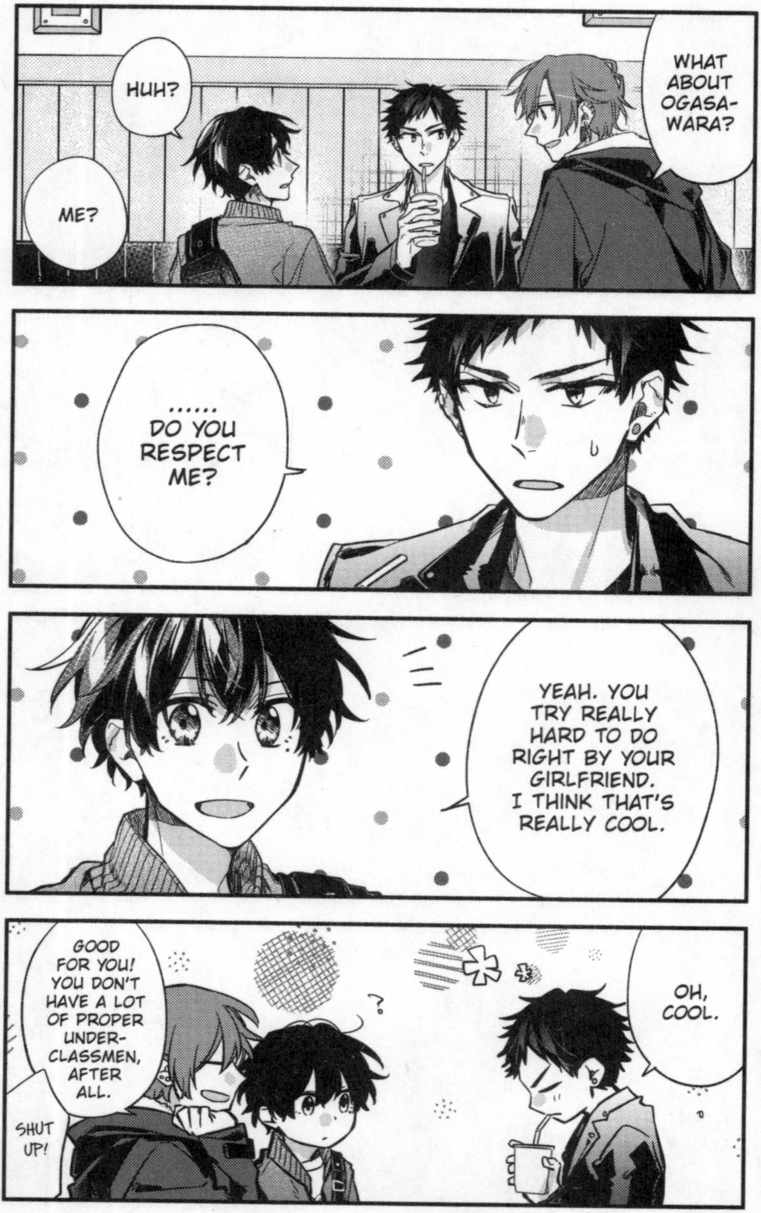
WHAT ABOUT OGASA-WARA?
HUH?
ME?
...... DO YOU RESPECT ME?
YEAH. YOU TRY REALLY HARD TO DO RIGHT BY YOUR GIRLFRIEND. I THINK THAT'S REALLY COOL.
OH, COOL.
GOOD FOR YOU! YOU DON'T HAVE A LOT OF PROPER UNDER-CLASSMEN, AFTER ALL.
SHUT UP!

A COUPLE OF RESPECTED SENPAIS.

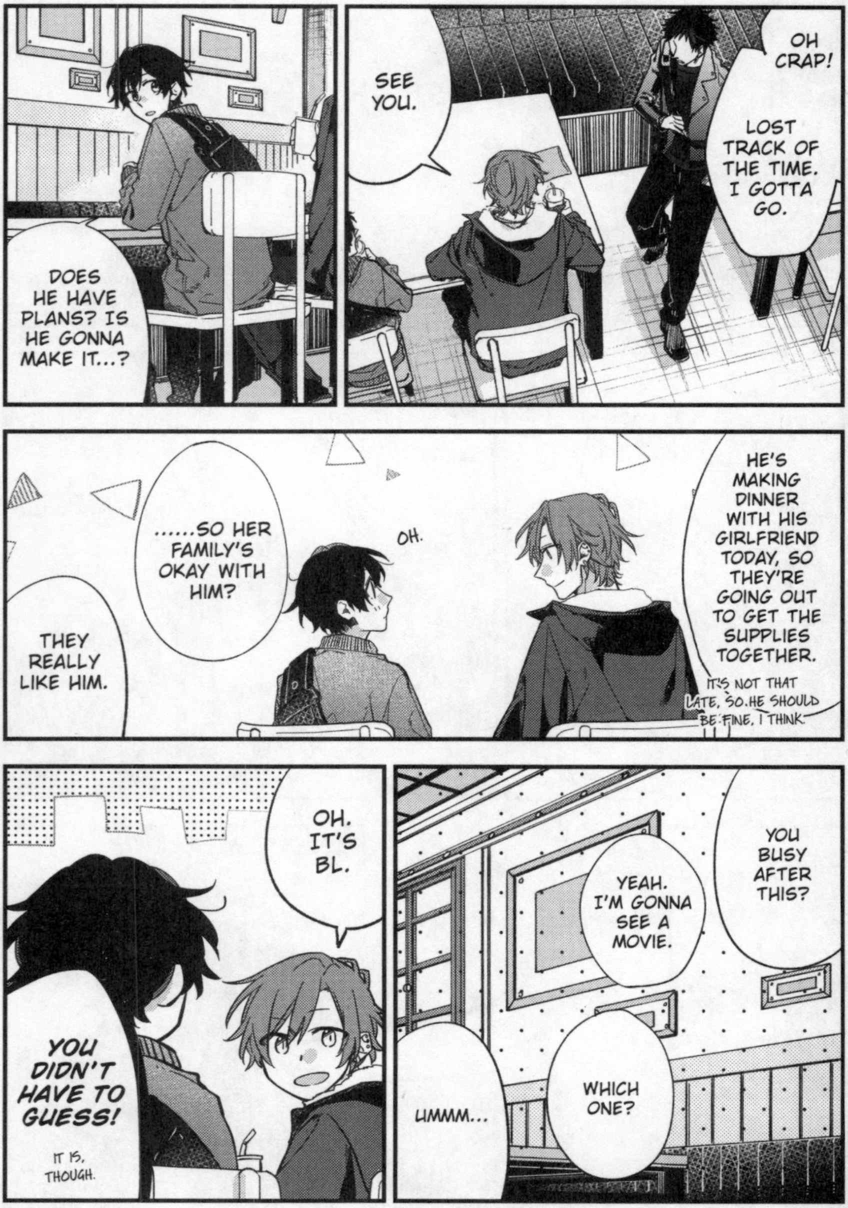
OH CRAP!
LOST TRACK OF THE TIME. I GOTTA GO.
SEE YOU.
DOES HE HAVE PLANS? IS HE GONNA MAKE IT...?
HE'S MAKING DINNER WITH HIS GIRLFRIEND TODAY, SO THEY'RE GOING OUT TO GET THE SUPPLIES TOGETHER.
IT'S NOT THAT LATE, SO HE SHOULD BE FINE, I THINK.
OH.
......SO HER FAMILY'S OKAY WITH HIM?
THEY REALLY LIKE HIM.
YOU BUSY AFTER THIS?
YEAH. I'M GONNA SEE A MOVIE.
WHICH ONE?
UMMM...
OH. IT'S BL.
YOU DIDN'T HAVE TO GUESS!
IT IS, THOUGH.

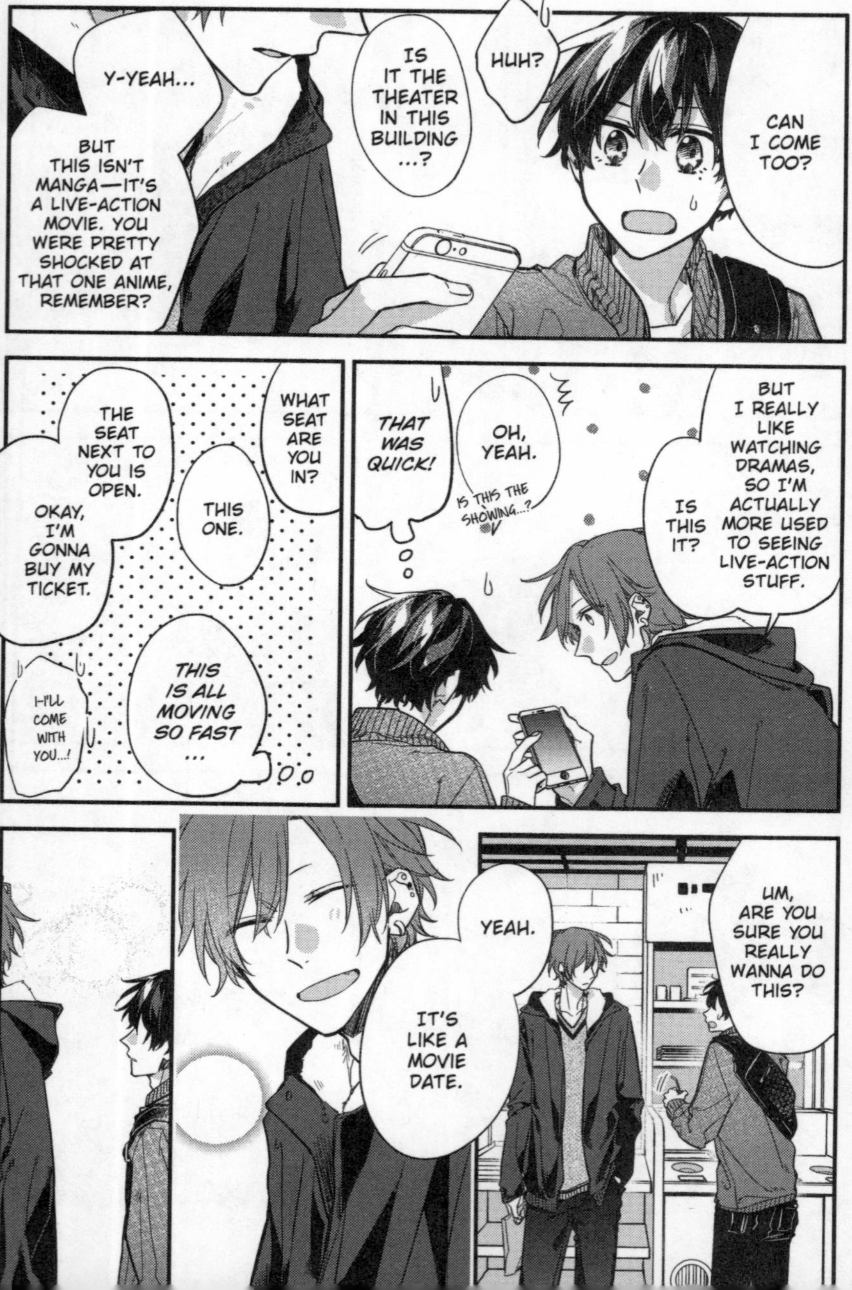
CAN I COME TOO?
HUH?
IS IT THE THEATER IN THIS BUILDING ...?
Y-YEAH...
BUT THIS ISN'T MANGA—IT'S A LIVE-ACTION MOVIE. YOU WERE PRETTY SHOCKED AT THAT ONE ANIME, REMEMBER?
BUT I REALLY LIKE WATCHING DRAMAS, SO I'M ACTUALLY MORE USED TO SEEING LIVE-ACTION STUFF.
IS THIS IT?
OH, YEAH.
IS THIS THE SHOWING...?
THAT WAS QUICK!
WHAT SEAT ARE YOU IN?
THIS ONE.
THE SEAT NEXT TO YOU IS OPEN.
OKAY, I'M GONNA BUY MY TICKET.
THIS IS ALL MOVING SO FAST ...
I-I'LL COME WITH YOU...!
UM, ARE YOU SURE YOU REALLY WANNA DO THIS?
YEAH.
IT'S LIKE A MOVIE DATE.

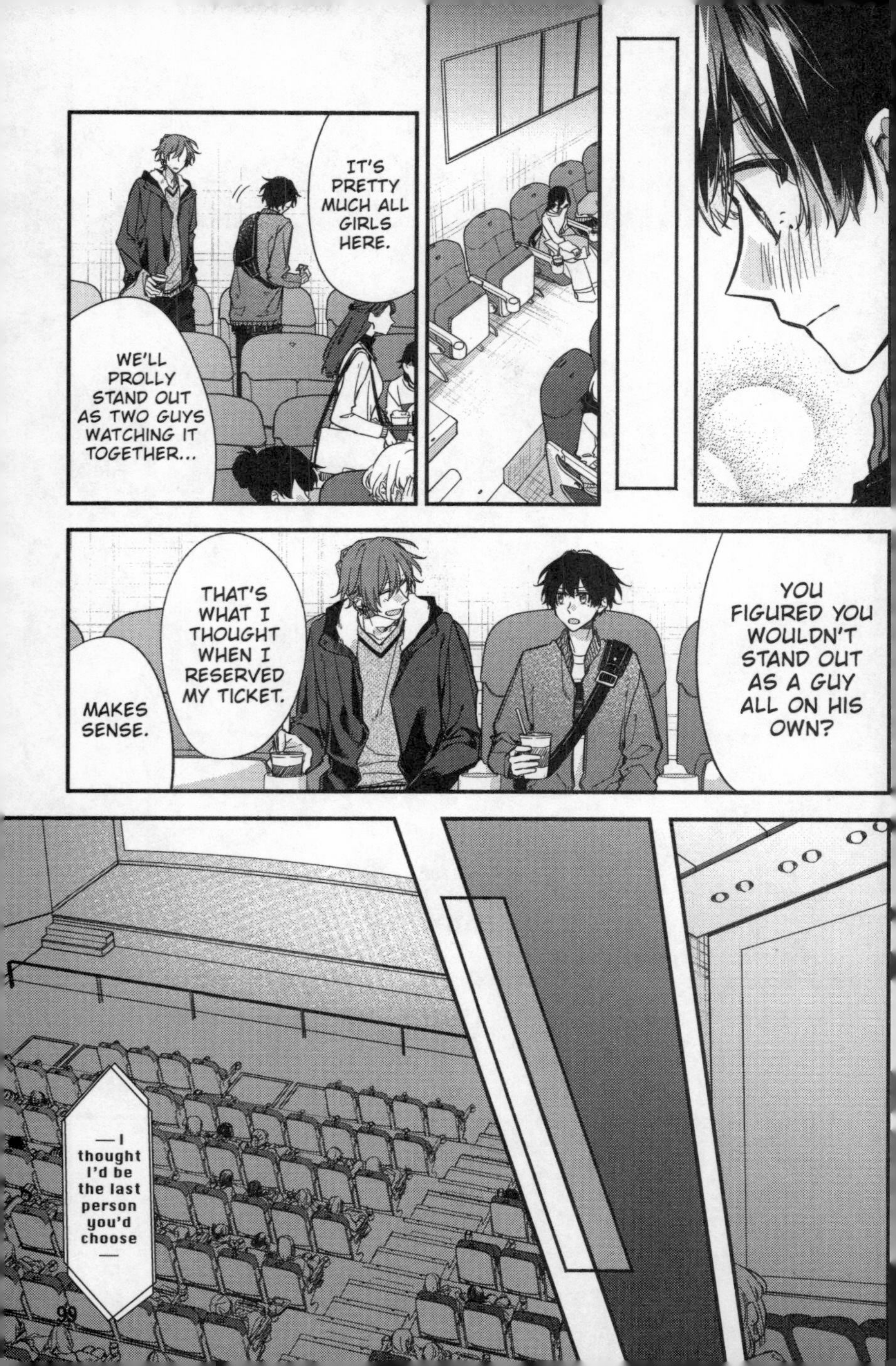
IT'S PRETTY MUCH ALL GIRLS HERE.
WE'LL PROLLY STAND OUT AS TWO GUYS WATCHING IT TOGETHER...
YOU FIGURED YOU WOULDN'T STAND OUT AS A GUY ALL ON HIS OWN?
THAT'S WHAT I THOUGHT WHEN I RESERVED MY TICKET.
MAKES SENSE.
—I thought I'd be the last person you'd choose—

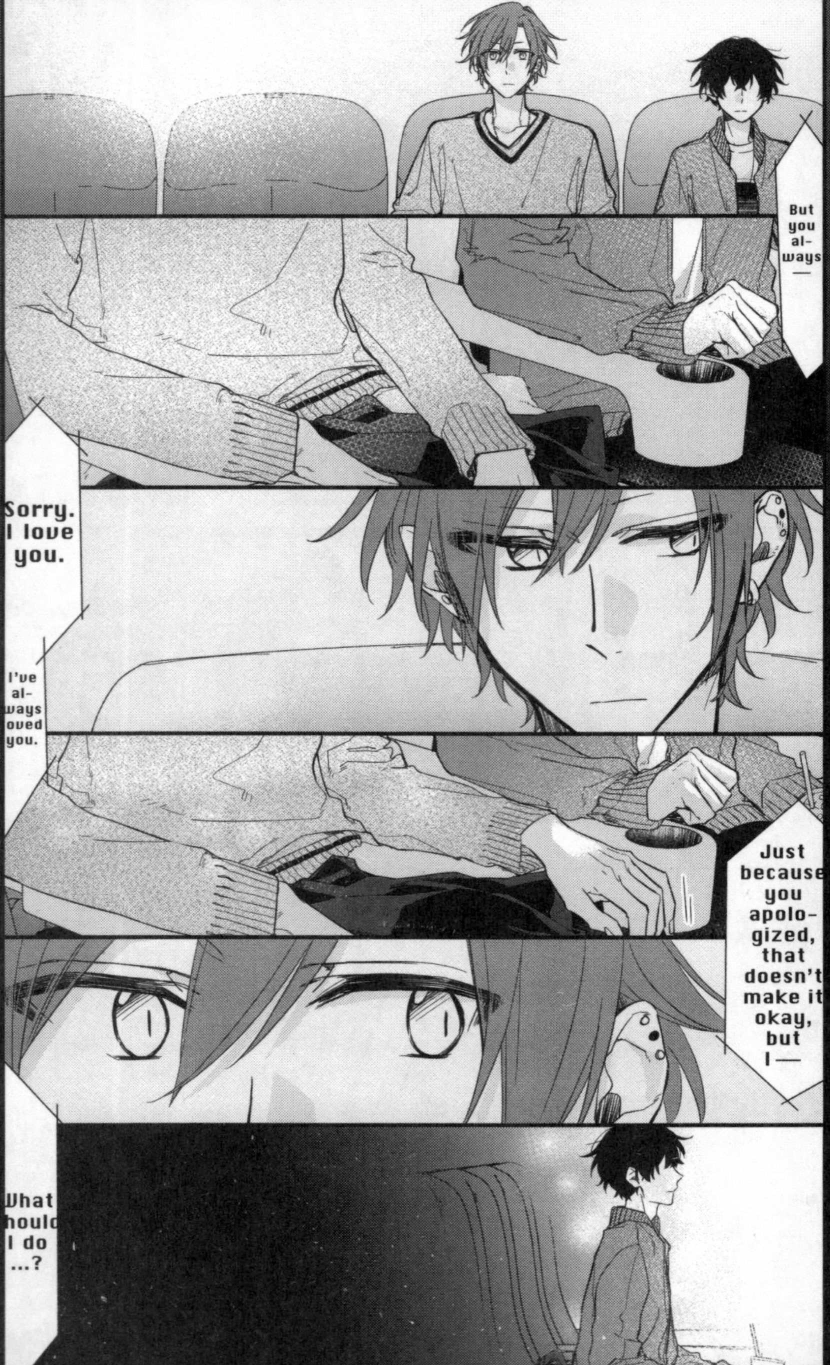
But you al-ways—
Sorry. I love you.
I've al-ways oved you.
Just because you apolo-gized, that doesn't make it okay, but I—
What hould I do ...?

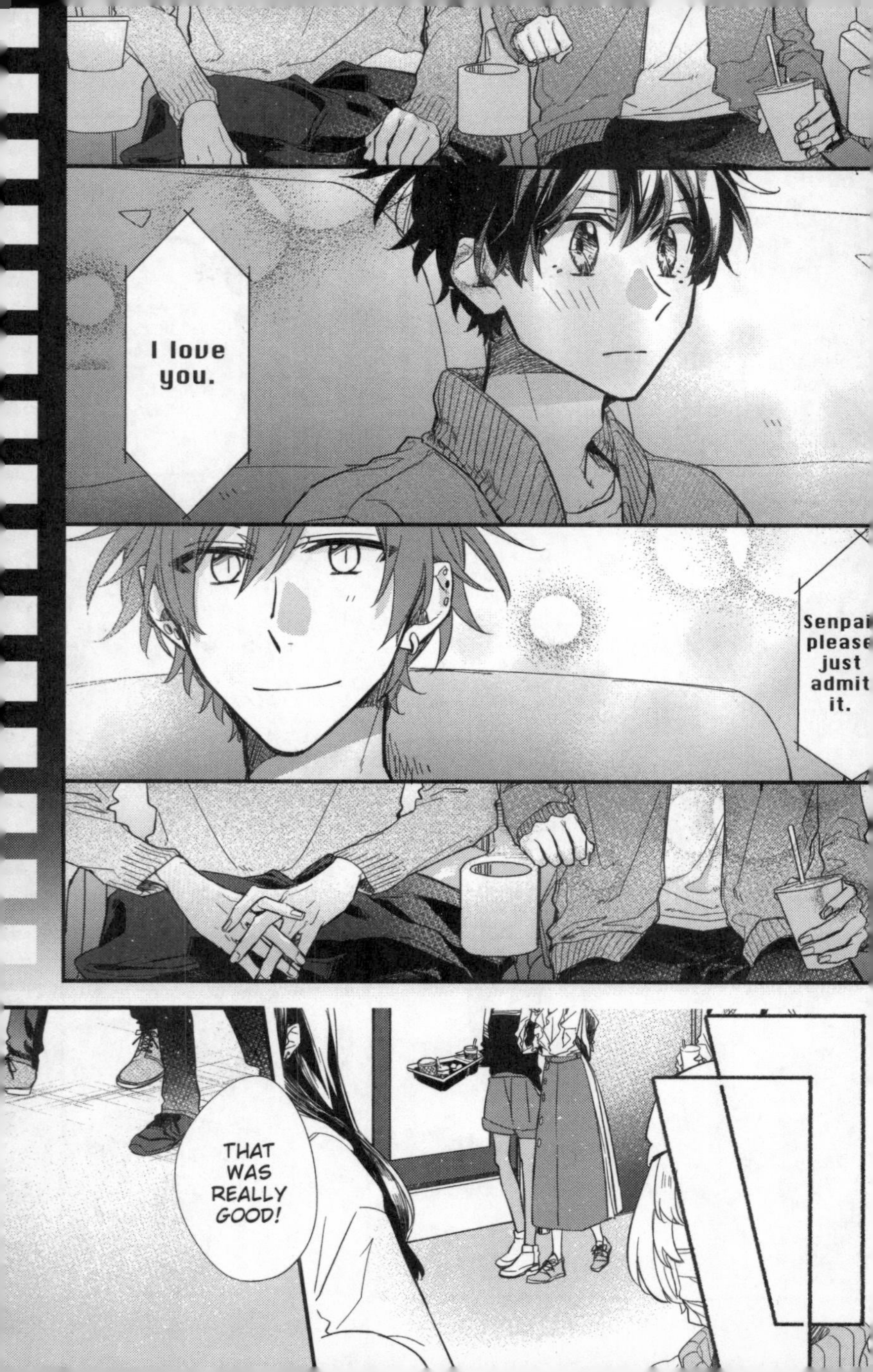
I love you.
Senpai please just admit it.
THAT WAS REALLY GOOD!

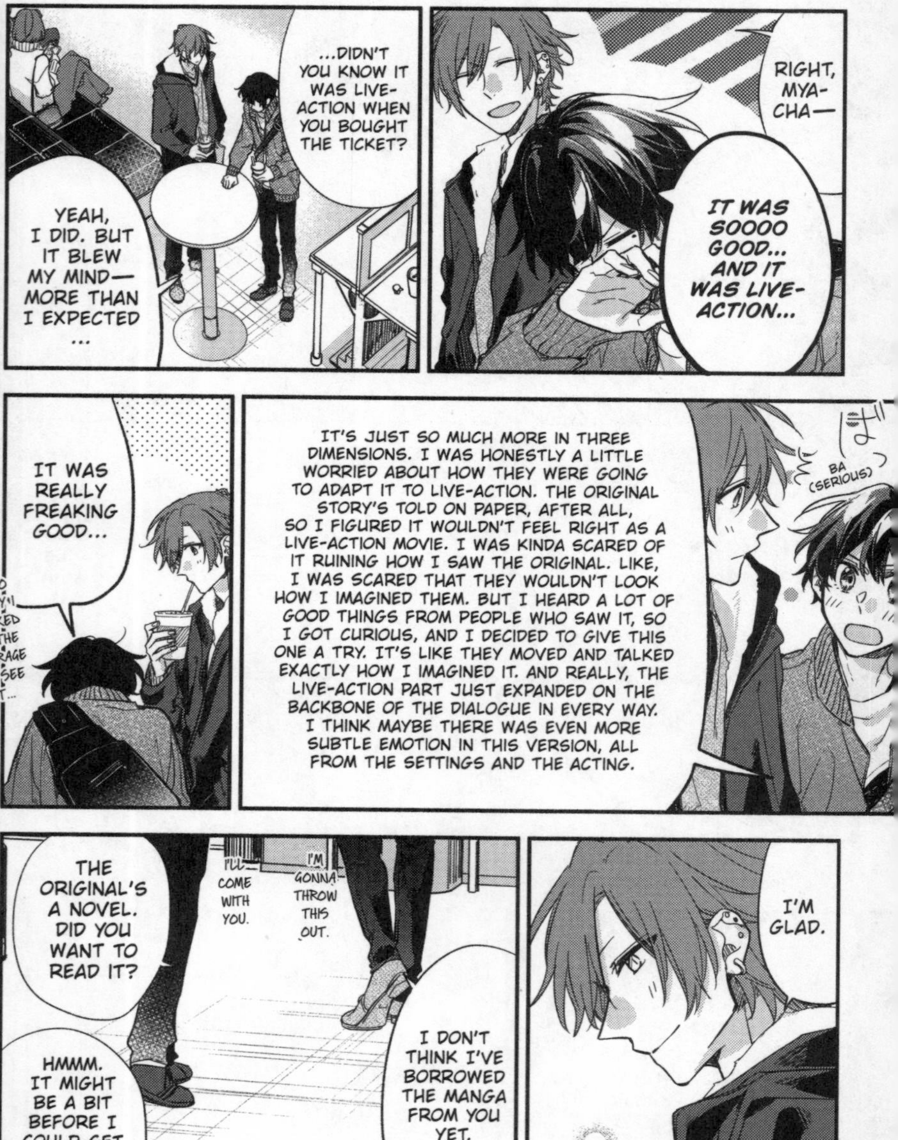
RIGHT, MYA-CHA—
IT WAS SOOOO GOOD... AND IT WAS LIVE-ACTION...
...DIDN'T YOU KNOW IT WAS LIVE-ACTION WHEN YOU BOUGHT THE TICKET?
YEAH, I DID. BUT IT BLEW MY MIND—MORE THAN I EXPECTED...
BA (SERIOUS)
IT'S JUST SO MUCH MORE IN THREE DIMENSIONS. I WAS HONESTLY A LITTLE WORRIED ABOUT HOW THEY WERE GOING TO ADAPT IT TO LIVE-ACTION. THE ORIGINAL STORY'S TOLD ON PAPER, AFTER ALL, SO I FIGURED IT WOULDN'T FEEL RIGHT AS A LIVE-ACTION MOVIE. I WAS KINDA SCARED OF IT RUINING HOW I SAW THE ORIGINAL. LIKE, I WAS SCARED THAT THEY WOULDN'T LOOK HOW I IMAGINED THEM. BUT I HEARD A LOT OF GOOD THINGS FROM PEOPLE WHO SAW IT, SO I GOT CURIOUS, AND I DECIDED TO GIVE THIS ONE A TRY. IT'S LIKE THEY MOVED AND TALKED EXACTLY HOW I IMAGINED IT. AND REALLY, THE LIVE-ACTION PART JUST EXPANDED ON THE BACKBONE OF THE DIALOGUE IN EVERY WAY. I THINK MAYBE THERE WAS EVEN MORE SUBTLE EMOTION IN THIS VERSION, ALL FROM THE SETTINGS AND THE ACTING.
IT WAS REALLY FREAKING GOOD...
I'M GLAD.
I'M GONNA THROW THIS OUT.
I'LL COME WITH YOU.
THE ORIGINAL'S A NOVEL. DID YOU WANT TO READ IT?
I DON'T THINK I'VE BORROWED THE MANGA FROM YOU YET.
HMMM. IT MIGHT BE A BIT BEFORE I COULD GET IT BACK TO YOU.

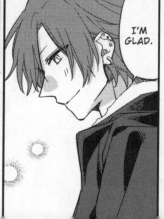

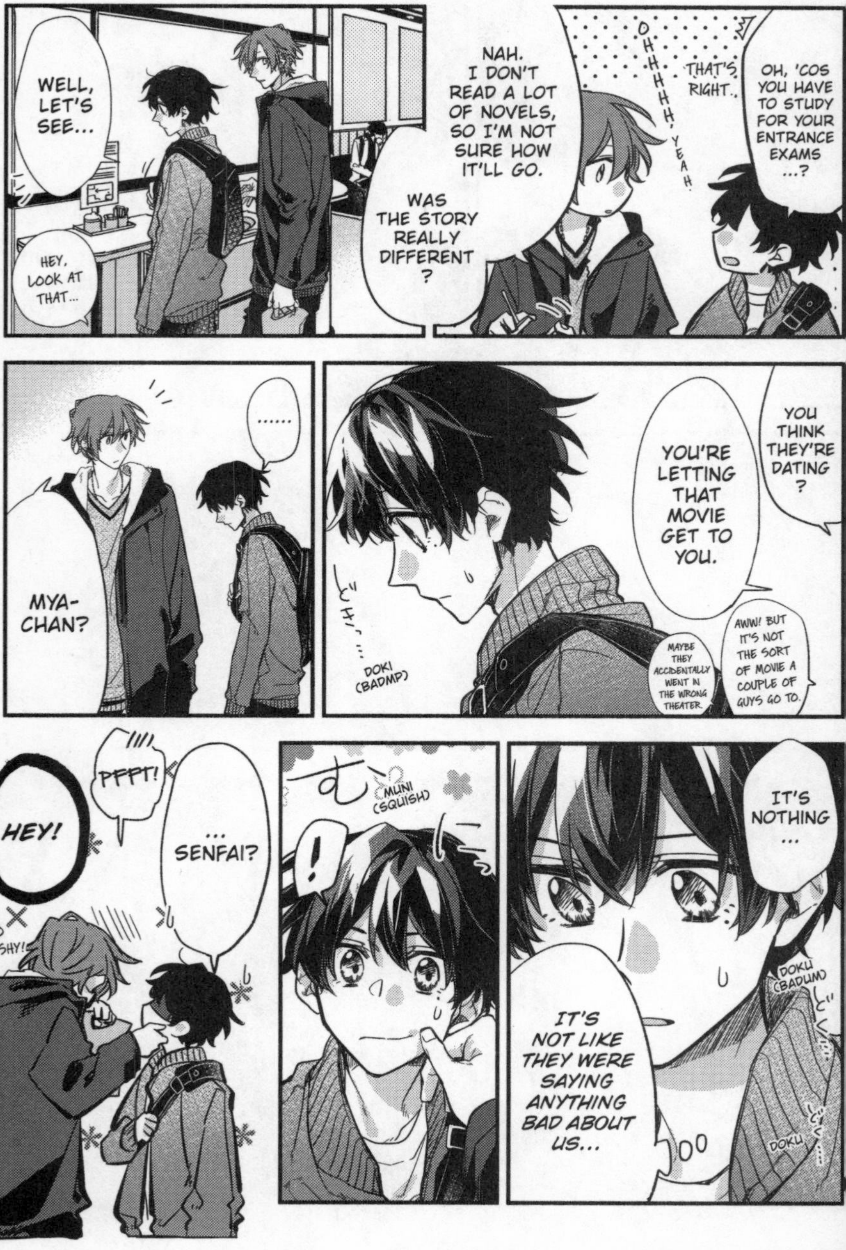
OH, 'COS YOU HAVE TO STUDY FOR YOUR ENTRANCE EXAMS ...?
THAT'S RIGHT..
OHHHHHH, YEAH
NAH. I DON'T READ A LOT OF NOVELS, SO I'M NOT SURE HOW IT'LL GO.
WAS THE STORY REALLY DIFFERENT?
WELL, LET'S SEE...
HEY, LOOK AT THAT...
YOU THINK THEY'RE DATING?
YOU'RE LETTING THAT MOVIE GET TO YOU.
AWW! BUT IT'S NOT THE SORT OF MOVIE A COUPLE OF GUYS GO TO.
MAYBE THEY ACCIDENTALLY WENT IN THE WRONG THEATER.
DOKI (BADMP)
......
MYA-CHAN?
IT'S NOTHING ...
DOKU (BADUM)
IT'S NOT LIKE THEY WERE SAYING ANYTHING BAD ABOUT US...
DOKU
む
MUNI (SQUISH)
!
PFFT!
... SENFAI?
HEY!
SO SQUISHY!

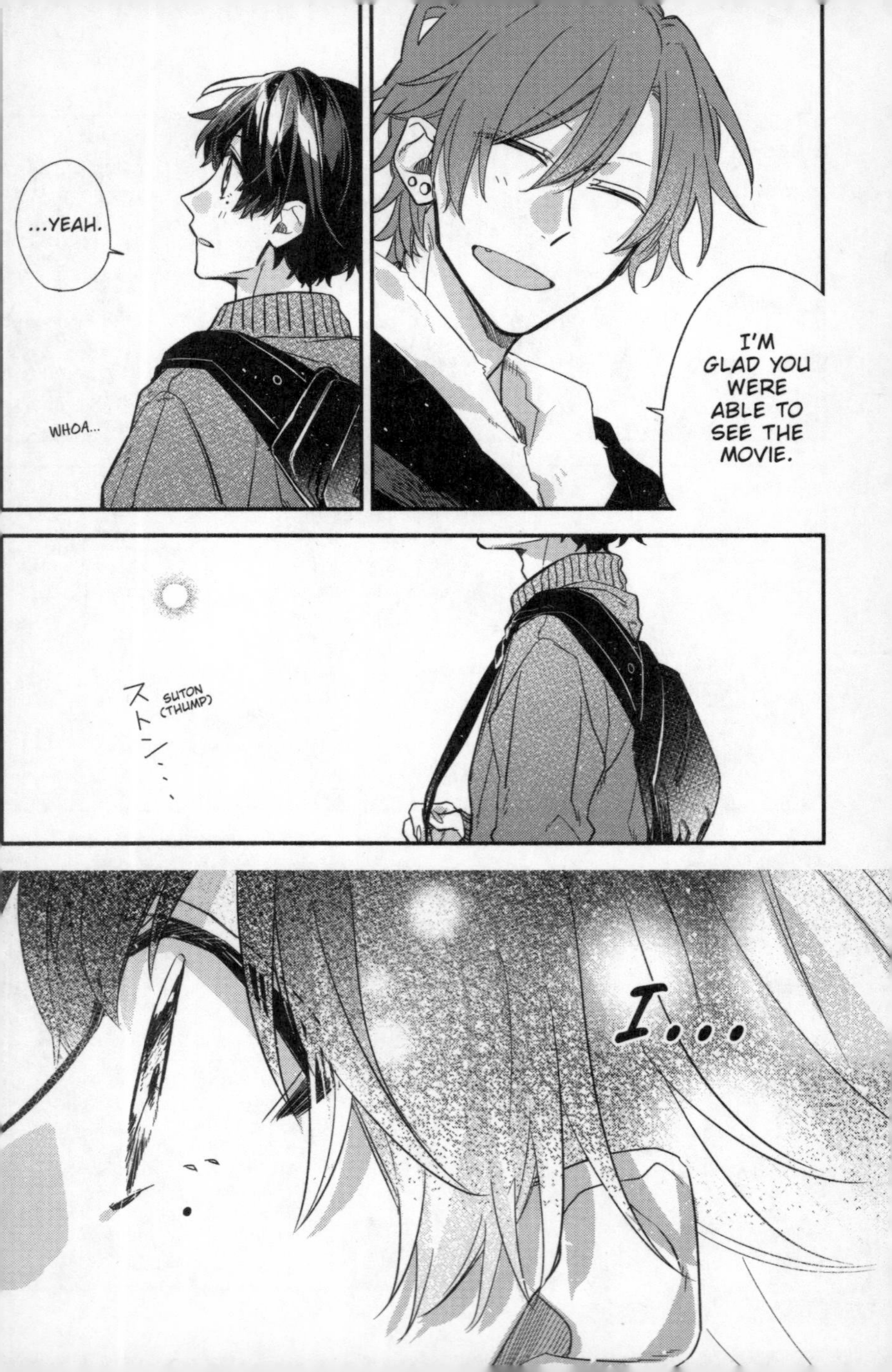
I'M GLAD YOU WERE ABLE TO SEE THE MOVIE.
...YEAH.
WHOA...
ストン
SUTON (THUMP)
I...

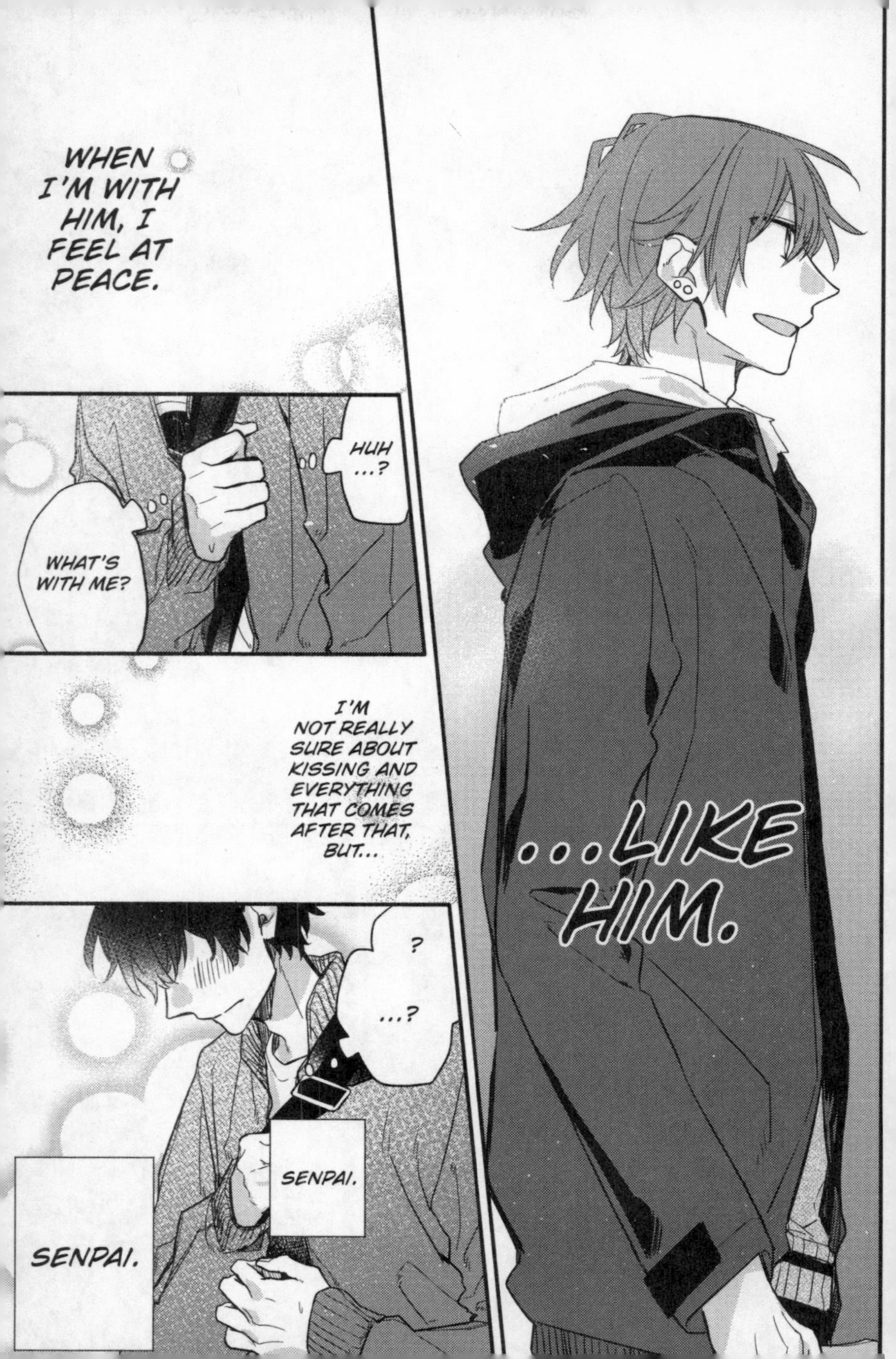
WHEN I'M WITH HIM, I FEEL AT PEACE.
HUH ...?
WHAT'S WITH ME?
I'M NOT REALLY SURE ABOUT KISSING AND EVERYTHING THAT COMES AFTER THAT, BUT...
?
...?
SENPAI.
SENPAI.
...LIKE HIM.

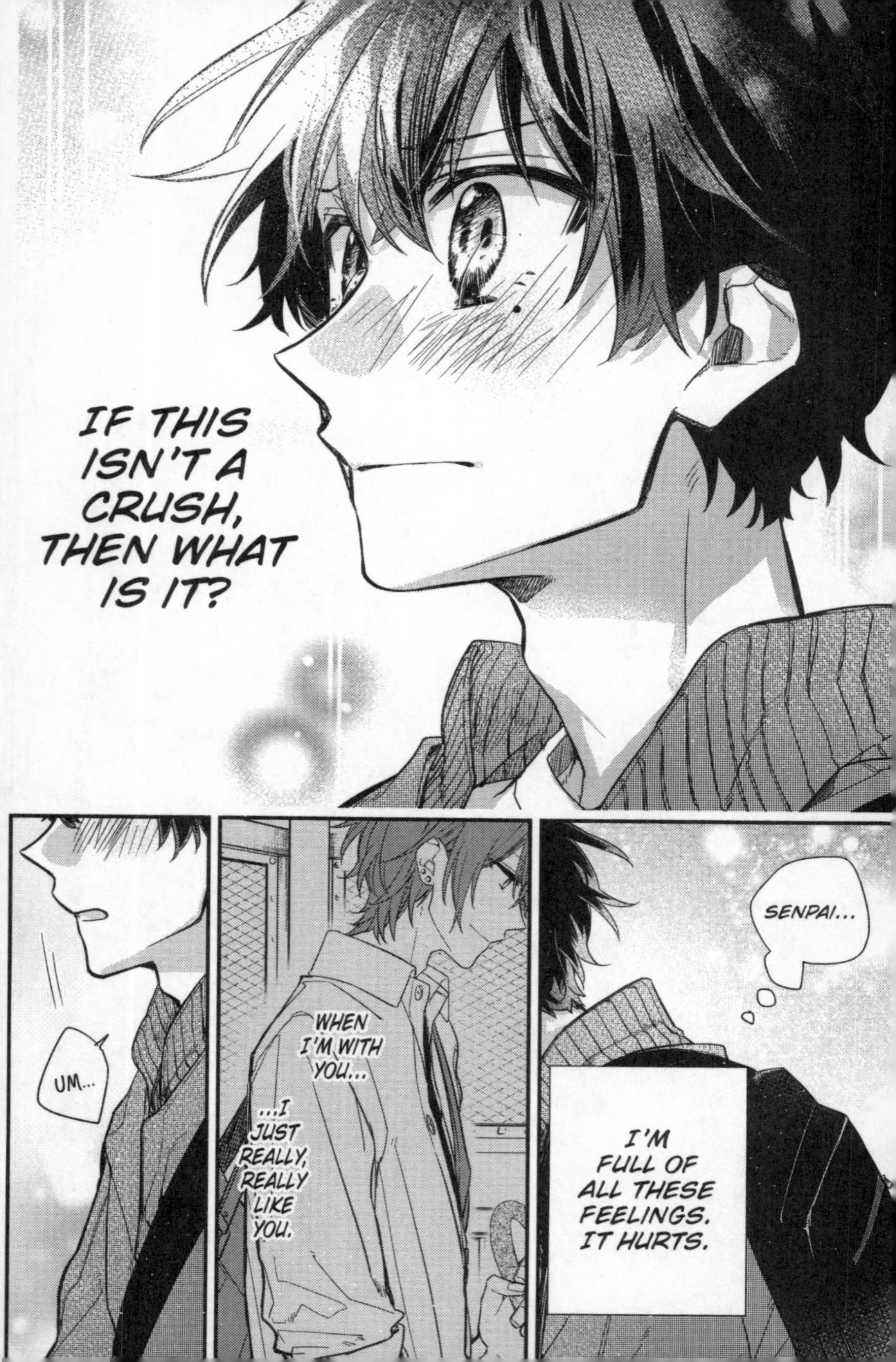
IF THIS ISN'T A CRUSH, THEN WHAT IS IT?
SENPAI...
I'M FULL OF ALL THESE FEELINGS. IT HURTS.
WHEN I'M WITH YOU...
...I JUST REALLY, REALLY LIKE YOU.
UM...

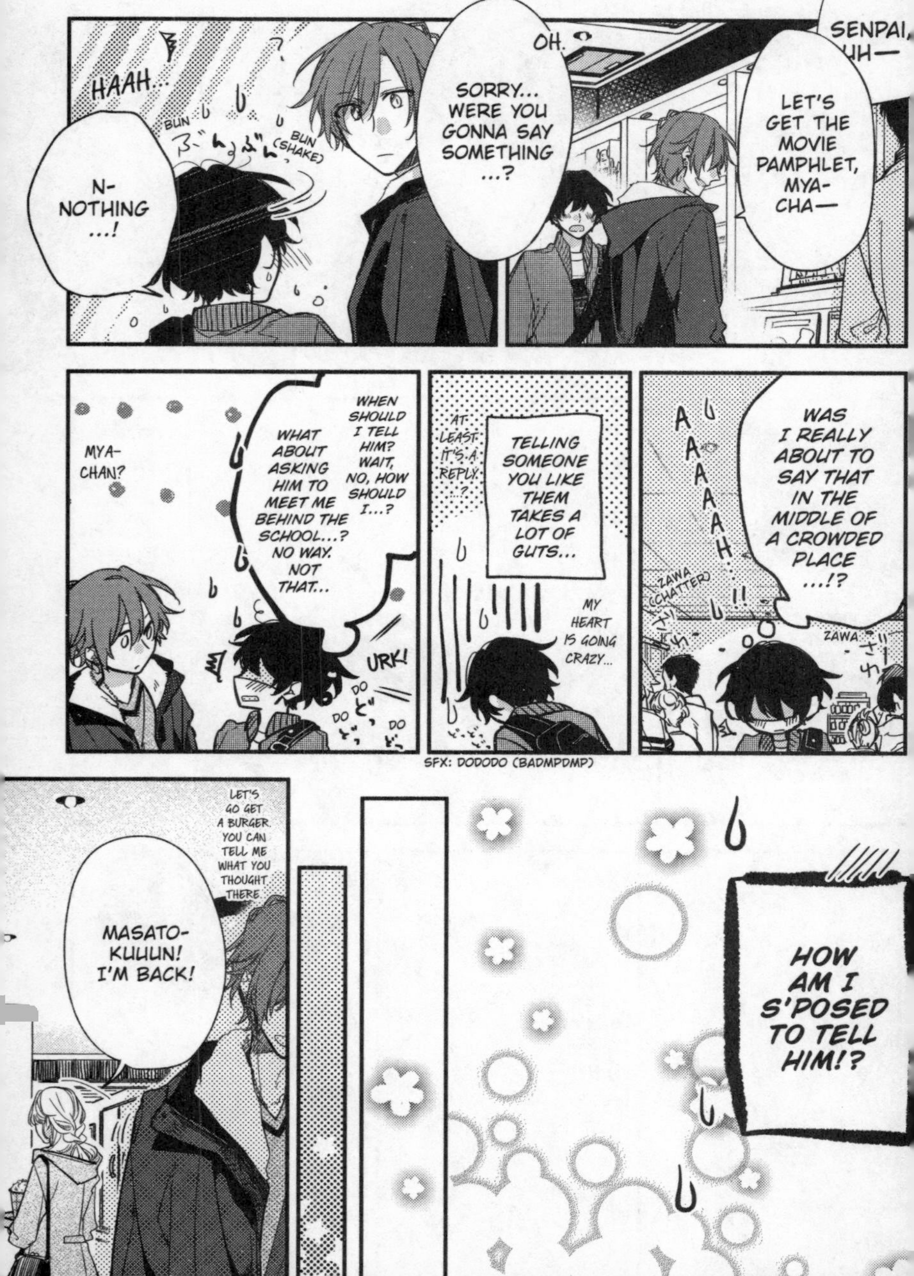
SENPAI, UH—
LET'S GET THE MOVIE PAMPHLET, MYA-CHA—
OH.
SORRY... WERE YOU GONNA SAY SOMETHING ...?
HAAH...
BUN BUN (SHAKE)
N-NOTHING ...!
WAS I REALLY ABOUT TO SAY THAT IN THE MIDDLE OF A CROWDED PLACE ...!?
AAAAAAH...!!
ZAWA (CHATTER)
ZAWA
AT LEAST IT'S A REPLY...?
TELLING SOMEONE YOU LIKE THEM TAKES A LOT OF GUTS...
MY HEART IS GOING CRAZY...
WHEN SHOULD I TELL HIM? WAIT, NO, HOW SHOULD I...?
WHAT ABOUT ASKING HIM TO MEET ME BEHIND THE SCHOOL...? NO WAY. NOT THAT...
MYA-CHAN?
URK!
DO DO DO
SFX: DODODO (BADMPDMP)
HOW AM I S'POSED TO TELL HIM!?
LET'S GO GET A BURGER. YOU CAN TELL ME WHAT YOU THOUGHT THERE.
MASATO-KUUUN! I'M BACK!

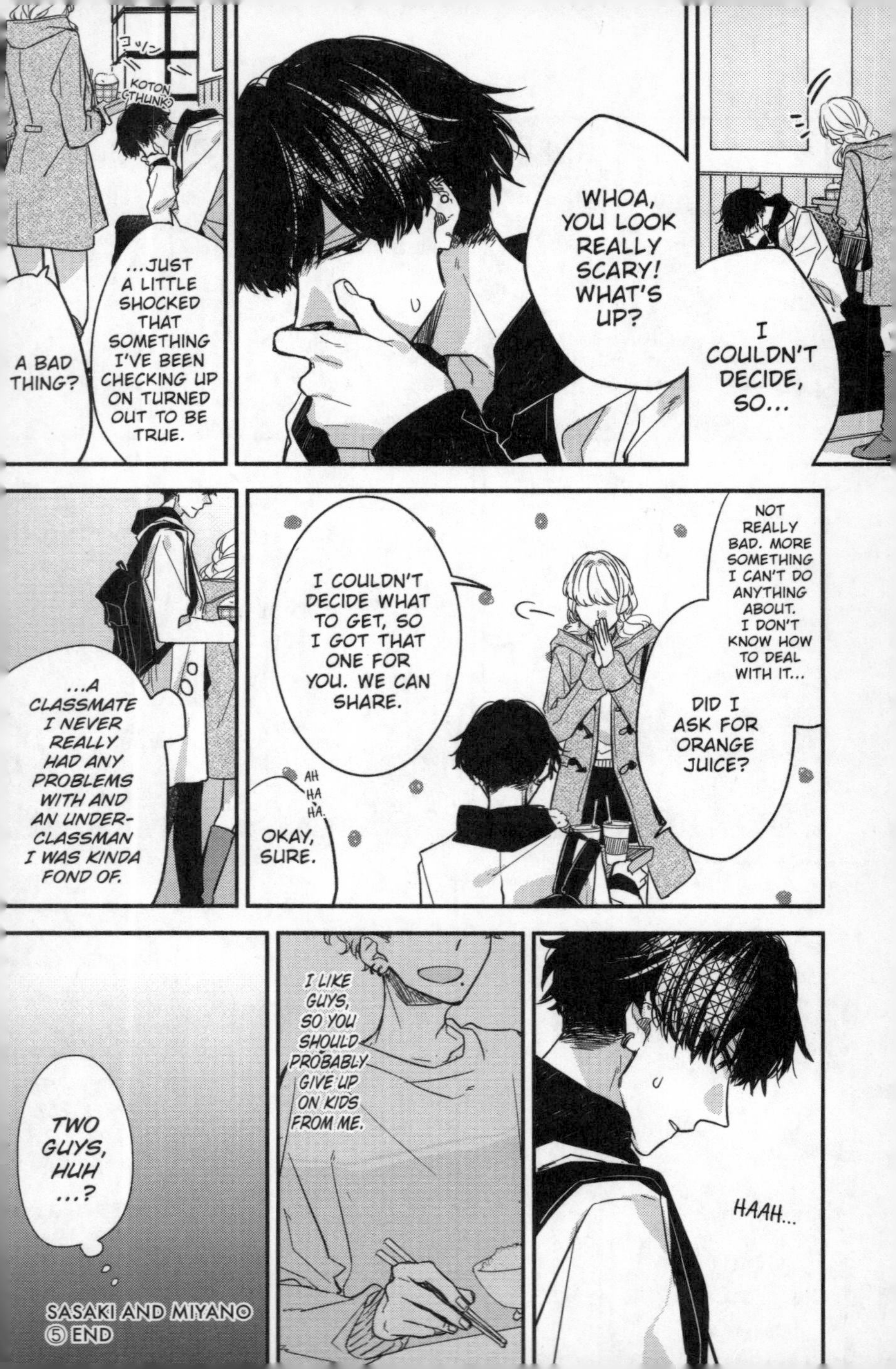
I COULDN'T DECIDE, SO...
WHOA, YOU LOOK REALLY SCARY! WHAT'S UP?
KOTON (THUNK)
...JUST A LITTLE SHOCKED THAT SOMETHING I'VE BEEN CHECKING UP ON TURNED OUT TO BE TRUE.
A BAD THING?
NOT REALLY BAD. MORE SOMETHING I CAN'T DO ANYTHING ABOUT. I DON'T KNOW HOW TO DEAL WITH IT...
DID I ASK FOR ORANGE JUICE?
I COULDN'T DECIDE WHAT TO GET, SO I GOT THAT ONE FOR YOU. WE CAN SHARE.
AH HA HA.
OKAY, SURE.
...A CLASSMATE I NEVER REALLY HAD ANY PROBLEMS WITH AND AN UNDER-CLASSMAN I WAS KINDA FOND OF.
HAAH...
I LIKE GUYS, SO YOU SHOULD PROBABLY GIVE UP ON KIDS FROM ME.
TWO GUYS, HUH ...?
SASAKI AND MIYANO ⑤ END

Translation Notes

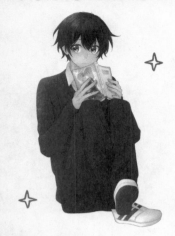

Common Honorifics
-san: The Japanese equivalent of Mr./Mrs./Miss. If a situation calls for politeness, this is the fail-safe honorific.
-kun: Used most often when referring to boys, this indicates affection or familiarity. Occasionally used by older men among their peers, but it may also be used by anyone referring to a person of lower standing.
-chan: An affectionate honorific indicating familiarity used mostly in reference to girls; also used in reference to cute persons or animals of either gender.
-senpai: A suffix used to address upperclassmen or more experienced coworkers.
-sensei: A respectful term for teachers, artists, or high-level professionals.
no honorific: Indicates familiarity or closeness; if used without permission or reason, addressing someone in this manner would constitute an insult.

Page 16
BL: Stands for boys' love, a genre that, as its name implies, is about romances between men.

Page 19
Hot guy: When Kuresawa asks Miyano about the presence of a "hot guy" in a manga volume, he uses the Japanese term *ikemen*, which usually refers to handsome or good-looking men. It comes from the combination of the words *ikeru/iketeru*, which can mean "cool" or "good," and *menzu*, an adaptation of the English word "men."

Page 22
Cultural festival: Japanese schools often hold cultural festivals that are open to the public. Typically, each class will plan events for visitors and other classes to enjoy. Popular activities include running a food stall, putting on a live performance, or making a haunted house.

Page 38
Duvet: Traditional Japanese bedding consists of a thin mattress made of straw or cotton and a heavy blanket similar to a duvet. Duvet was used here as a translation of "futon."

Page 48
***Kasha* (snap)**: In Japan, it is considered a violation of a citizen's right to privacy, or their "portrait right," to have their photo taken without permission. For that reason, every phone in Japan makes a shutter sound when a picture is taken. This feature cannot be turned off.

Page 53
Fanboy: A translation of the term *fudanshi*, which refers to men who are avid consumers of BL content.

Page 66
Kanji name pronunciations: The characters known as *kanji* form the basis of the Chinese writing system and were later adapted by people in Japan for their own writing system. As such, kanji characters in Japanese sometimes have more than one reading. On top of that, people sometimes use less common pronunciations for names, so it can be difficult to determine the correct pronunciation. The name confusion during the drag contest stems from the fact that "Yumi" is a much more common reading for those particular kanji than "Yoshikazu," and comes across as a rather feminine name.

Page 69
Cheongsam: An article of clothing popular in China. It usually has short sleeves, a slit in the skirt, and is designed to be form-fitting.

Page 82
Soran bushi: A well-known, traditional Japanese dance that allegedly first circulated among fisherfolk. The dance includes movements imitating the rolling of waves and the work of a fisherman.

Page 93
Geeking out: A translation of the phrase *otakubanashi*, which could be translated more literally as "talking like an *otaku*." *Otaku* is a slang term for people who are generally known as avid fans of something, such as computer *otaku* or camera *otaku*. *Otaku* by itself is typically used to refer to fans of manga and anime. *Fudanshi* can be considered BL *otaku*.

What gets him going: This phrase is used as an alternative to the Japanese word *moe*, which at its most basic roots, is used to describe the feeling of getting really excited by characters, relationships, animals, objects, or anything else fans find extraordinarily cute.

Page 103
Entrance exams: After high school entrance exams, third-years like Sasaki and Hirano have to pass college entrance exams if they plan on going to college. Not everyone attends college, but most people who are able to pass college entrance exams will, since it is seen as a status symbol and is basically a requirement to obtain a job in Japan.

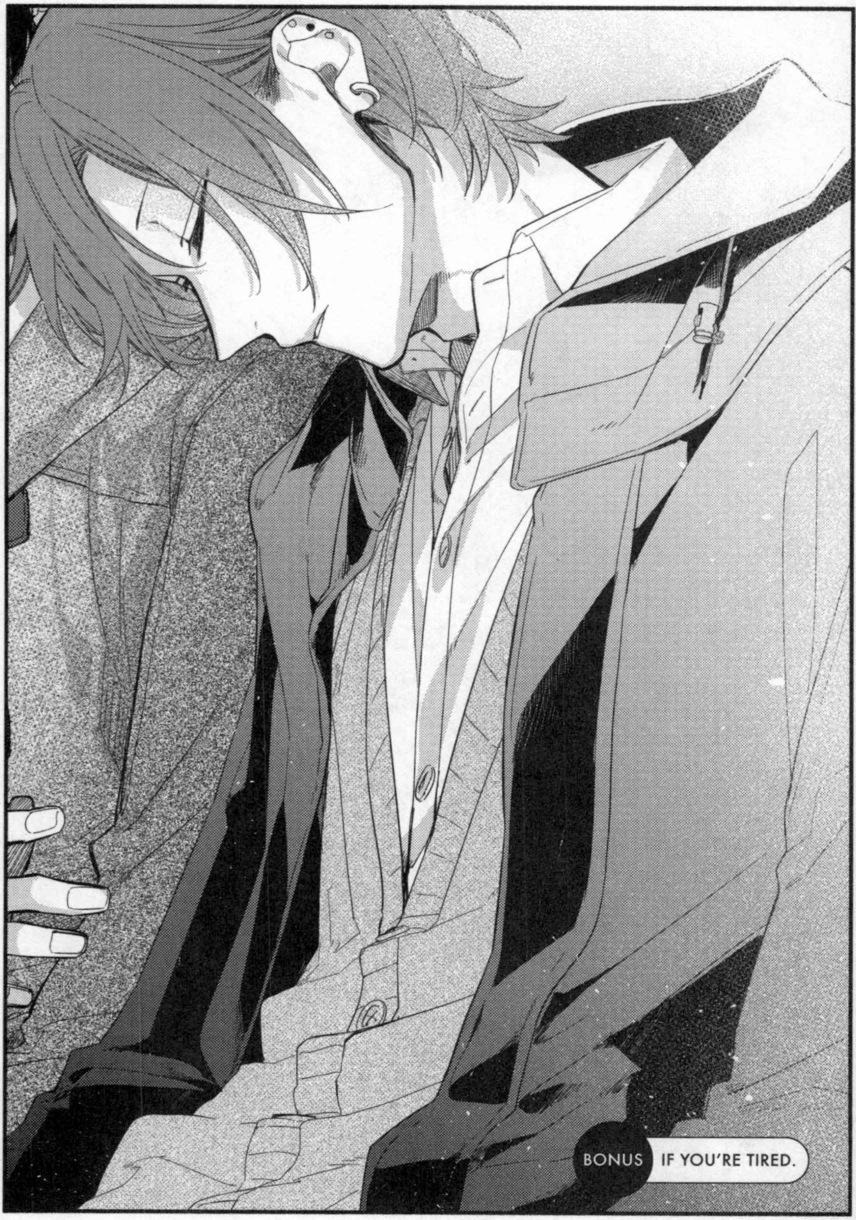
BONUS IF YOU'RE TIRED.

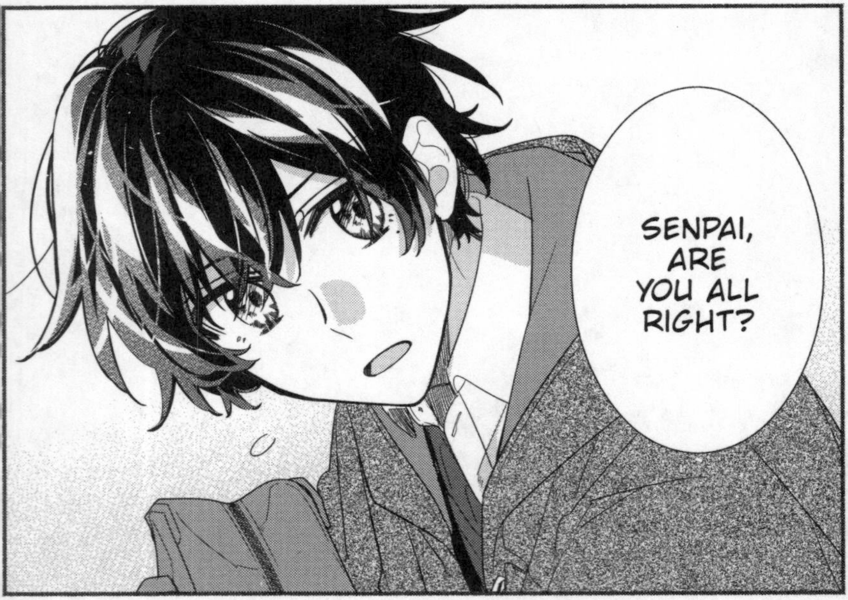
SENPAI, ARE YOU ALL RIGHT?
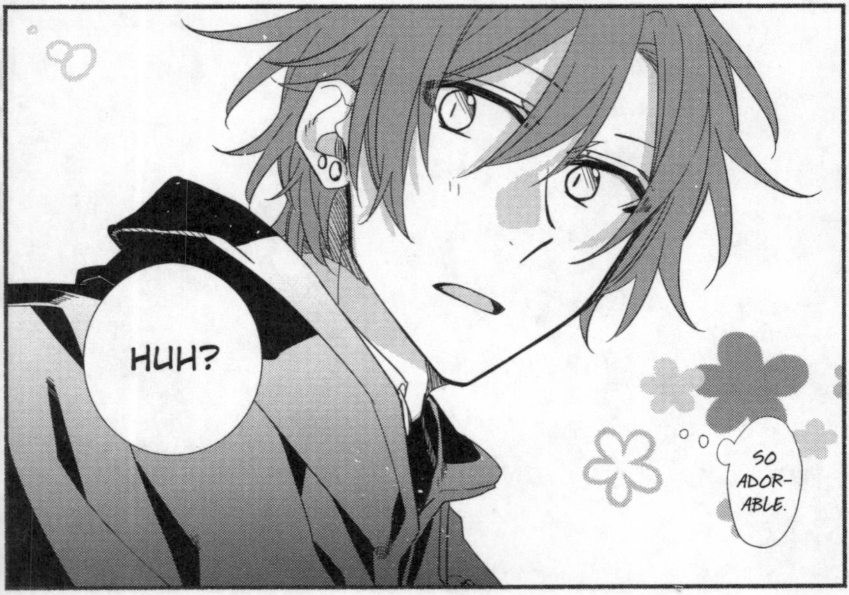
HUH?
SO ADOR-ABLE.

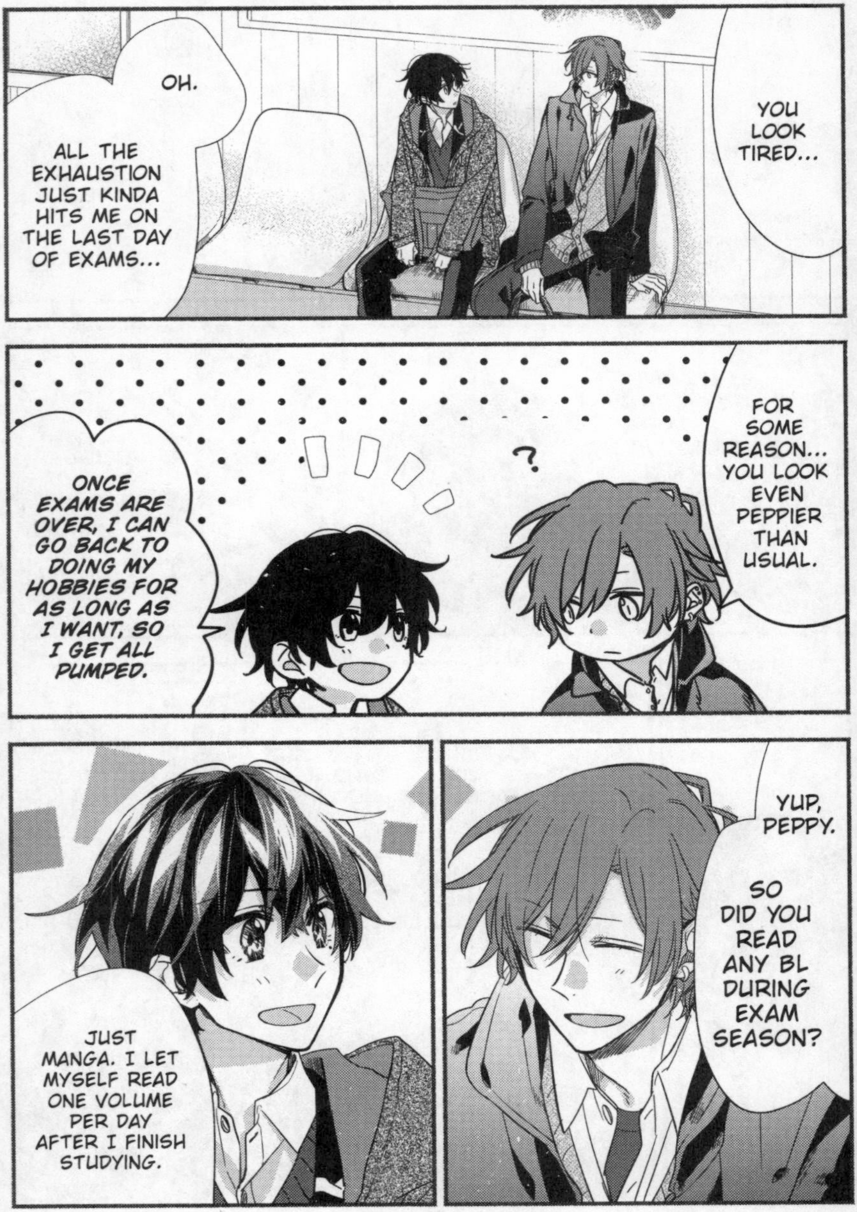
YOU LOOK TIRED...
OH.
ALL THE EXHAUSTION JUST KINDA HITS ME ON THE LAST DAY OF EXAMS...
FOR SOME REASON... YOU LOOK EVEN PEPPIER THAN USUAL.
?
ONCE EXAMS ARE OVER, I CAN GO BACK TO DOING MY HOBBIES FOR AS LONG AS I WANT, SO I GET ALL PUMPED.
YUP, PEPPY.
SO DID YOU READ ANY BL DURING EXAM SEASON?
JUST MANGA. I LET MYSELF READ ONE VOLUME PER DAY AFTER I FINISH STUDYING.

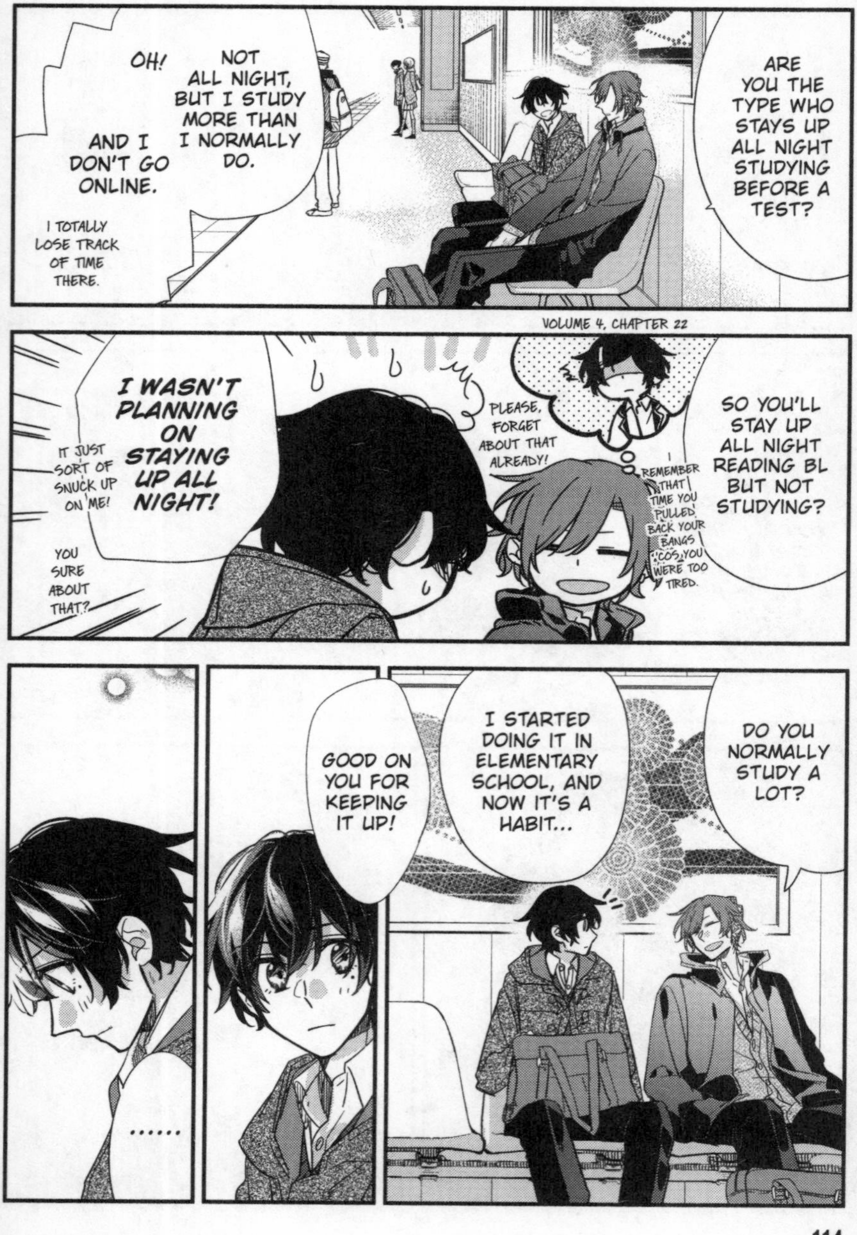
ARE YOU THE TYPE WHO STAYS UP ALL NIGHT STUDYING BEFORE A TEST?
NOT ALL NIGHT, BUT I STUDY MORE THAN I NORMALLY DO.
OH!
AND I DON'T GO ONLINE.
I TOTALLY LOSE TRACK OF TIME THERE.
VOLUME 4, CHAPTER 22
SO YOU'LL STAY UP ALL NIGHT READING BL BUT NOT STUDYING?
I REMEMBER THAT TIME YOU PULLED BACK YOUR BANGS 'COS YOU WERE TOO TIRED.
PLEASE, FORGET ABOUT THAT ALREADY!
I WASN'T PLANNING ON STAYING UP ALL NIGHT!
IT JUST SORT OF SNUCK UP ON ME!
YOU SURE ABOUT THAT?
DO YOU NORMALLY STUDY A LOT?
I STARTED DOING IT IN ELEMENTARY SCHOOL, AND NOW IT'S A HABIT...
GOOD ON YOU FOR KEEPING IT UP!
......

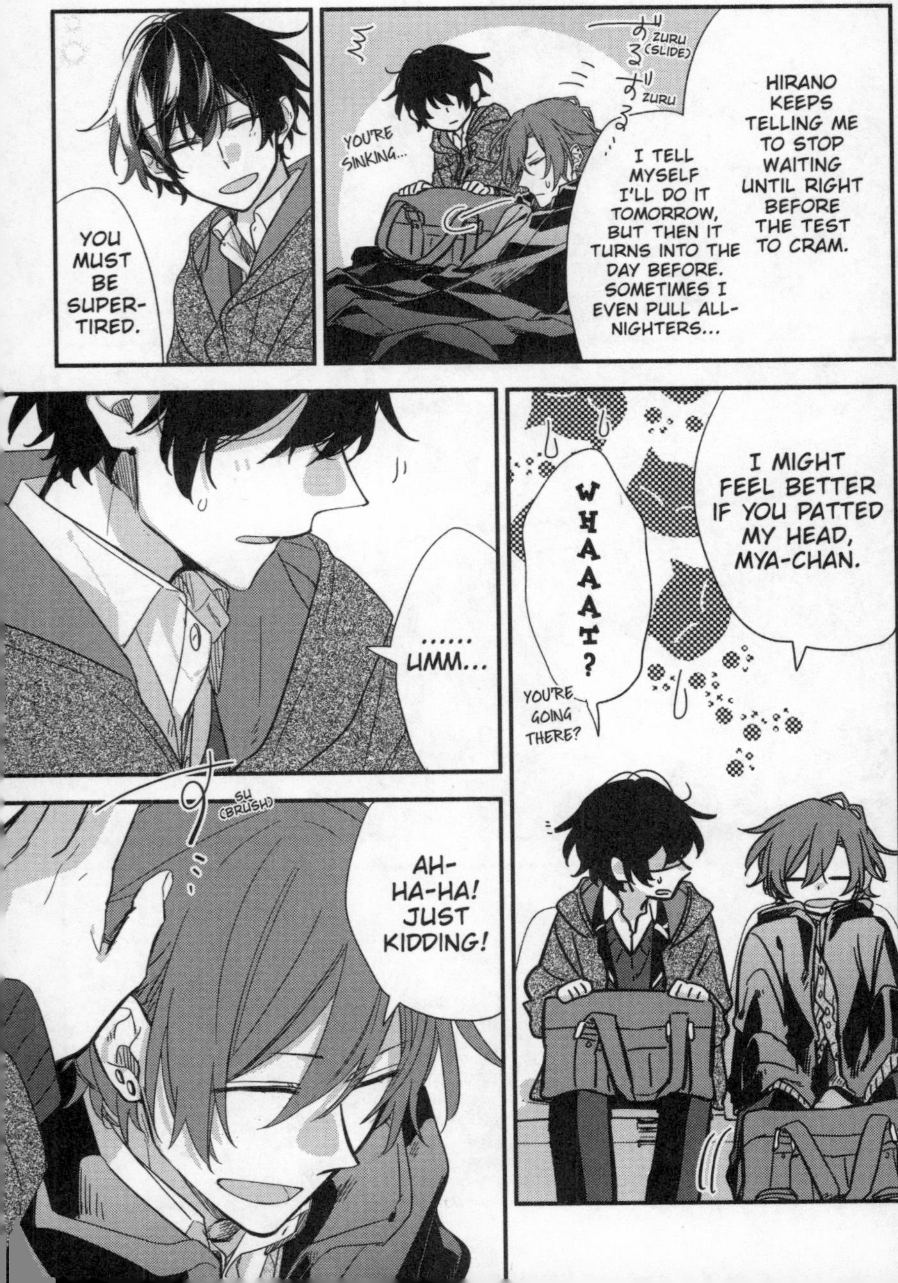
HIRANO KEEPS TELLING ME TO STOP WAITING UNTIL RIGHT BEFORE THE TEST TO CRAM.
I TELL MYSELF I'LL DO IT TOMORROW, BUT THEN IT TURNS INTO THE DAY BEFORE. SOMETIMES I EVEN PULL ALL-NIGHTERS...
ZURU (SLIDE)
ZURU
YOU'RE SINKING...
YOU MUST BE SUPER-TIRED.
I MIGHT FEEL BETTER IF YOU PATTED MY HEAD, MYA-CHAN.
WHAAAAT?
YOU'RE GOING THERE?
...... UMM...
SU (BRUSH)
AH-HA-HA! JUST KIDDING!

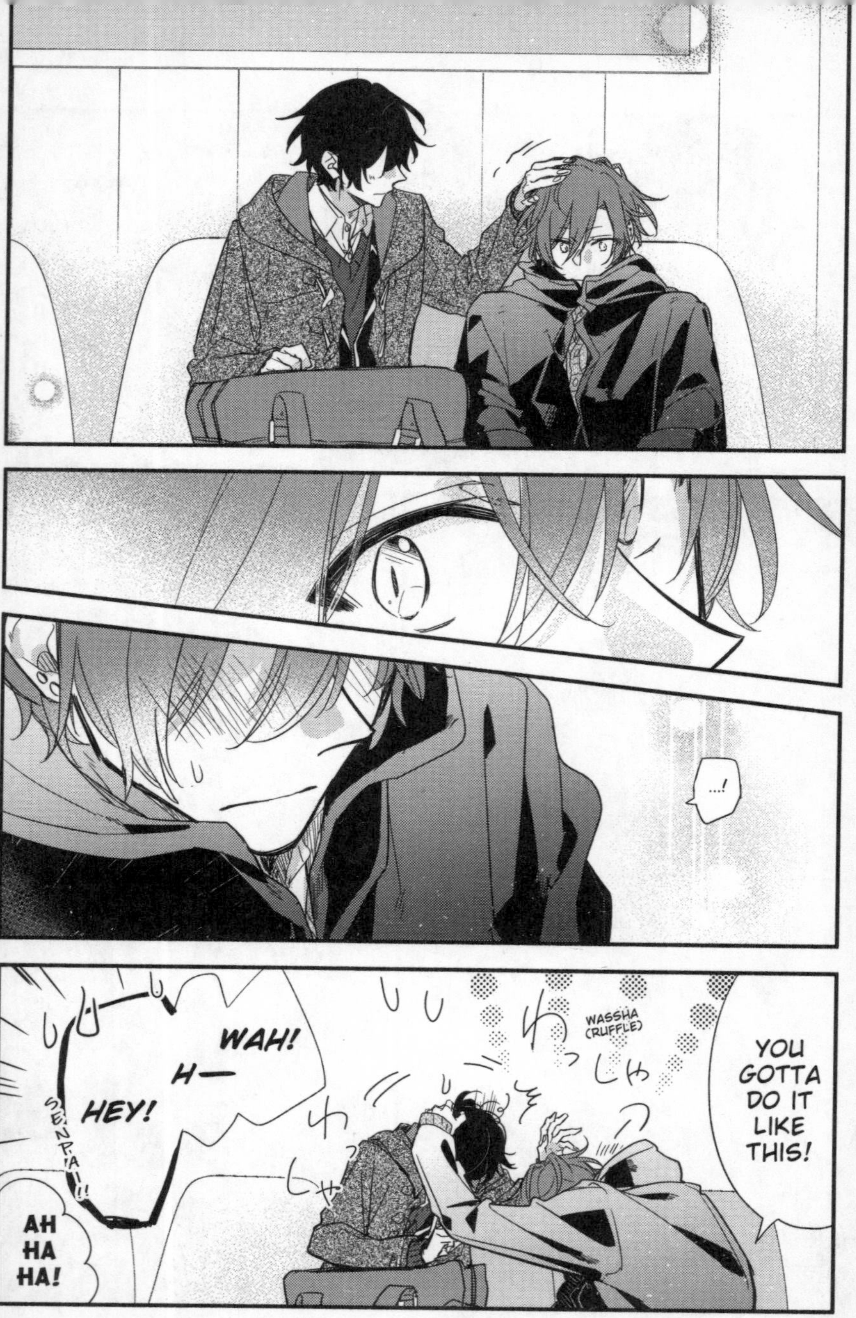

...!
YOU GOTTA DO IT LIKE THIS!
WASSHA (RUFFLE)
WAH!
H— HEY!
SENPAI!!
AH HA HA!

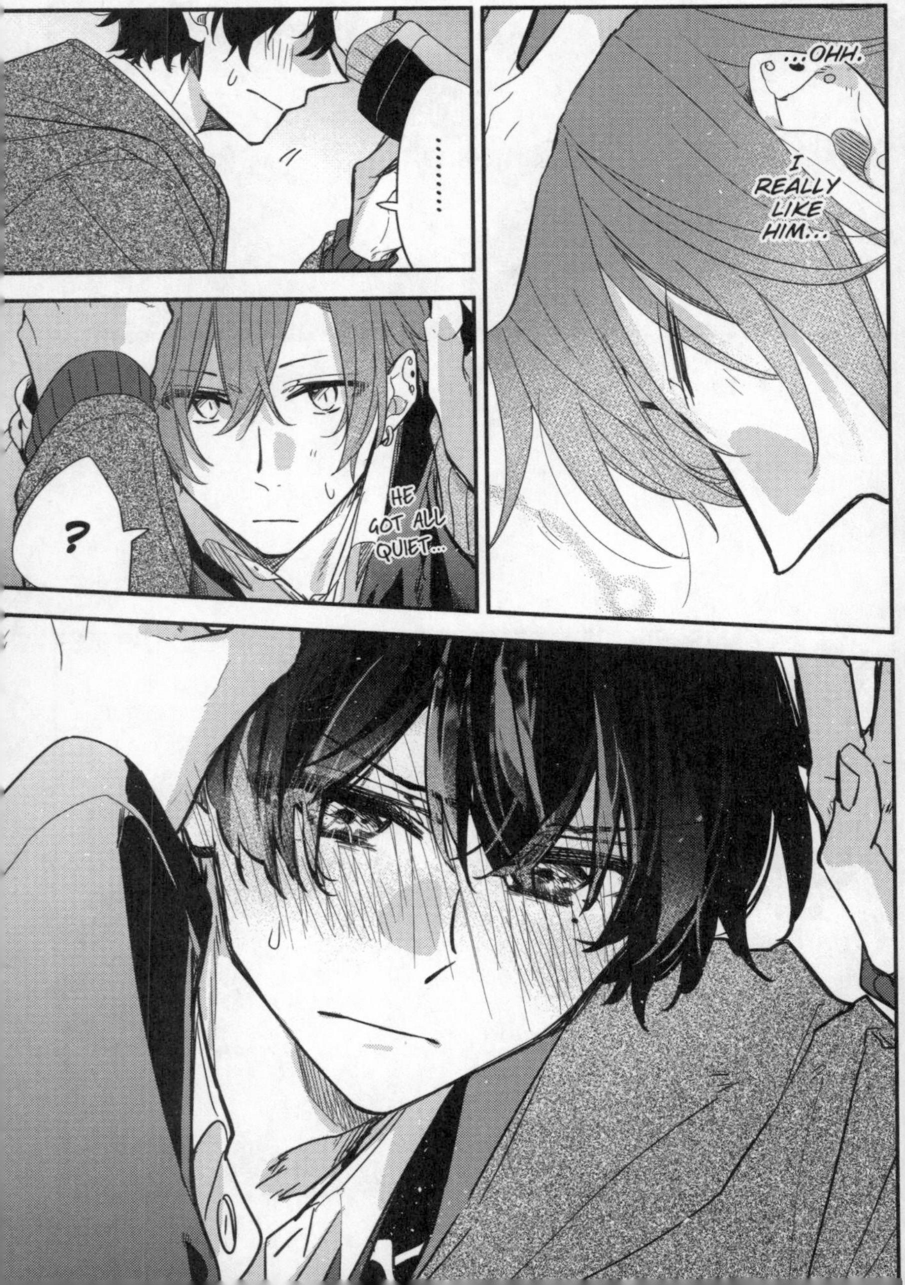
...OHH.
I REALLY LIKE HIM...
......
?
HE GOT ALL QUIET...

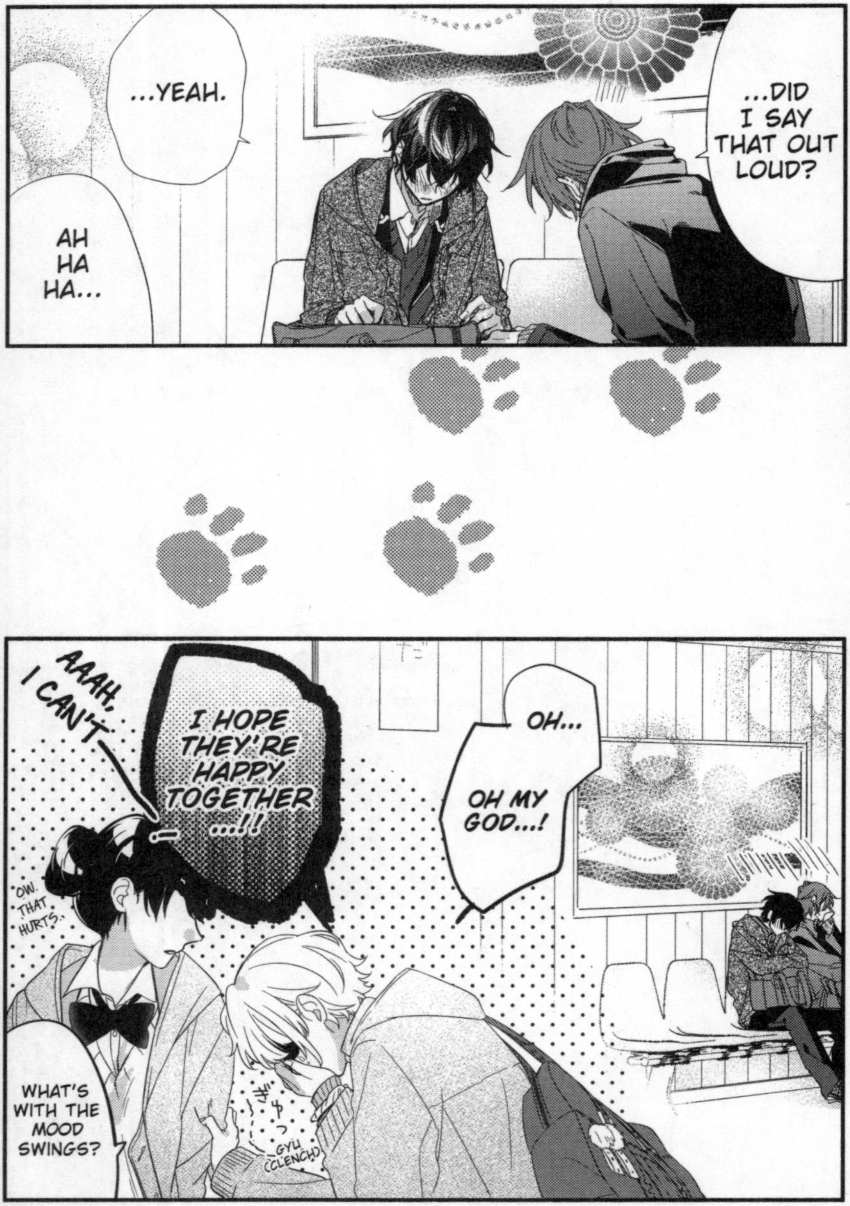
...DID I SAY THAT OUT LOUD?
...YEAH.
AH HA HA...
OH...
OH MY GOD...!
I HOPE THEY'RE HAPPY TOGETHER ...!!
AAAH, I CAN'T
OW. THAT HURTS.
GYU (CLENCH)
WHAT'S WITH THE MOOD SWINGS?

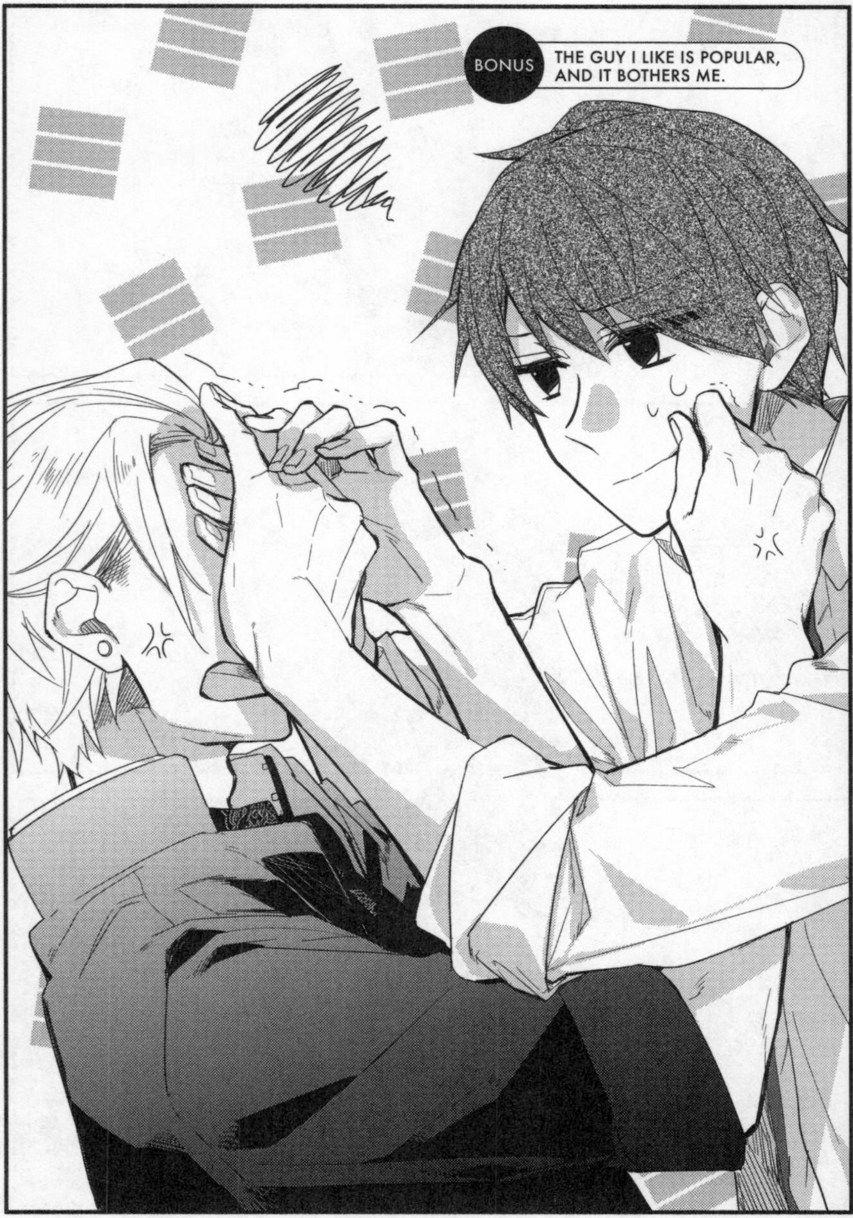
BONUS
THE GUY I LIKE IS POPULAR, AND IT BOTHERS ME.

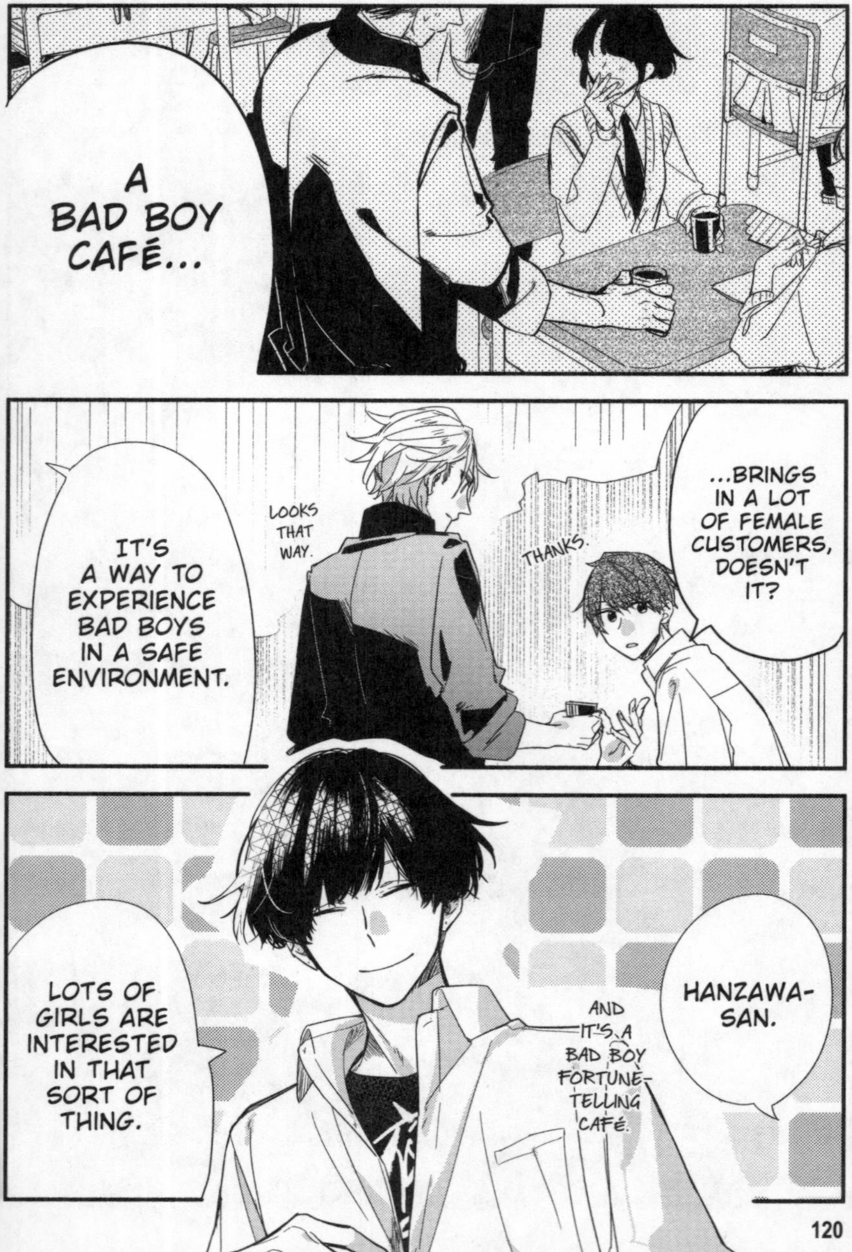
A BAD BOY CAFÉ...
...BRINGS IN A LOT OF FEMALE CUSTOMERS, DOESN'T IT?
THANKS.
LOOKS THAT WAY.
IT'S A WAY TO EXPERIENCE BAD BOYS IN A SAFE ENVIRONMENT.
HANZAWA-SAN.
AND IT'S A BAD BOY FORTUNE-TELLING CAFÉ.
LOTS OF GIRLS ARE INTERESTED IN THAT SORT OF THING.

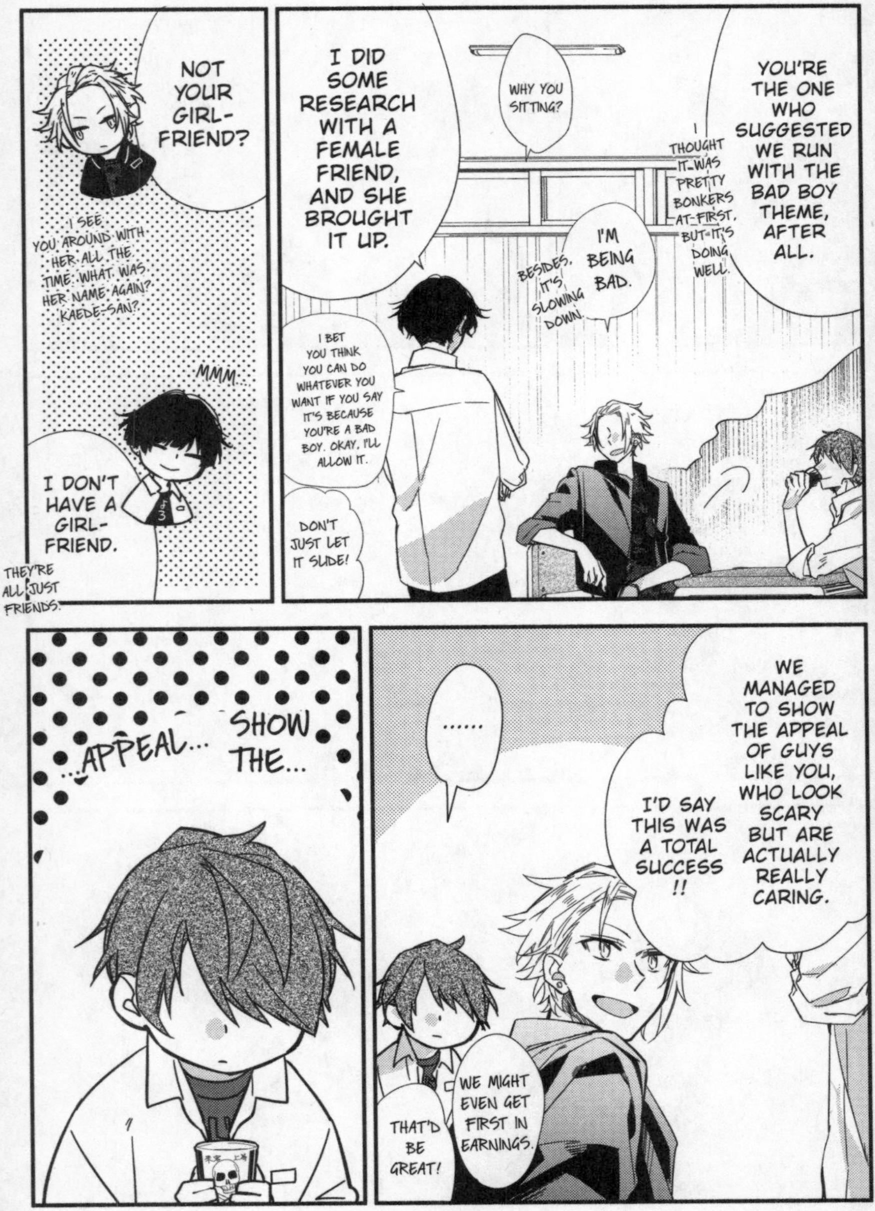
YOU'RE THE ONE WHO SUGGESTED WE RUN WITH THE BAD BOY THEME, AFTER ALL.
I THOUGHT IT WAS PRETTY BONKERS AT FIRST, BUT IT'S DOING WELL.
WHY YOU SITTING?
I'M BEING BAD.
BESIDES, IT'S SLOWING DOWN.
I DID SOME RESEARCH WITH A FEMALE FRIEND, AND SHE BROUGHT IT UP.
I BET YOU THINK YOU CAN DO WHATEVER YOU WANT IF YOU SAY IT'S BECAUSE YOU'RE A BAD BOY. OKAY, I'LL ALLOW IT.
DON'T JUST LET IT SLIDE!
NOT YOUR GIRL-FRIEND?
I SEE YOU AROUND WITH HER ALL THE TIME. WHAT WAS HER NAME AGAIN? KAEDE-SAN?
MMM...
I DON'T HAVE A GIRL-FRIEND.
THEY'RE ALL JUST FRIENDS.
WE MANAGED TO SHOW THE APPEAL OF GUYS LIKE YOU, WHO LOOK SCARY BUT ARE ACTUALLY REALLY CARING.
I'D SAY THIS WAS A TOTAL SUCCESS!!
......
WE MIGHT EVEN GET FIRST IN EARNINGS.
THAT'D BE GREAT!
SHOW THE...
...APPEAL...

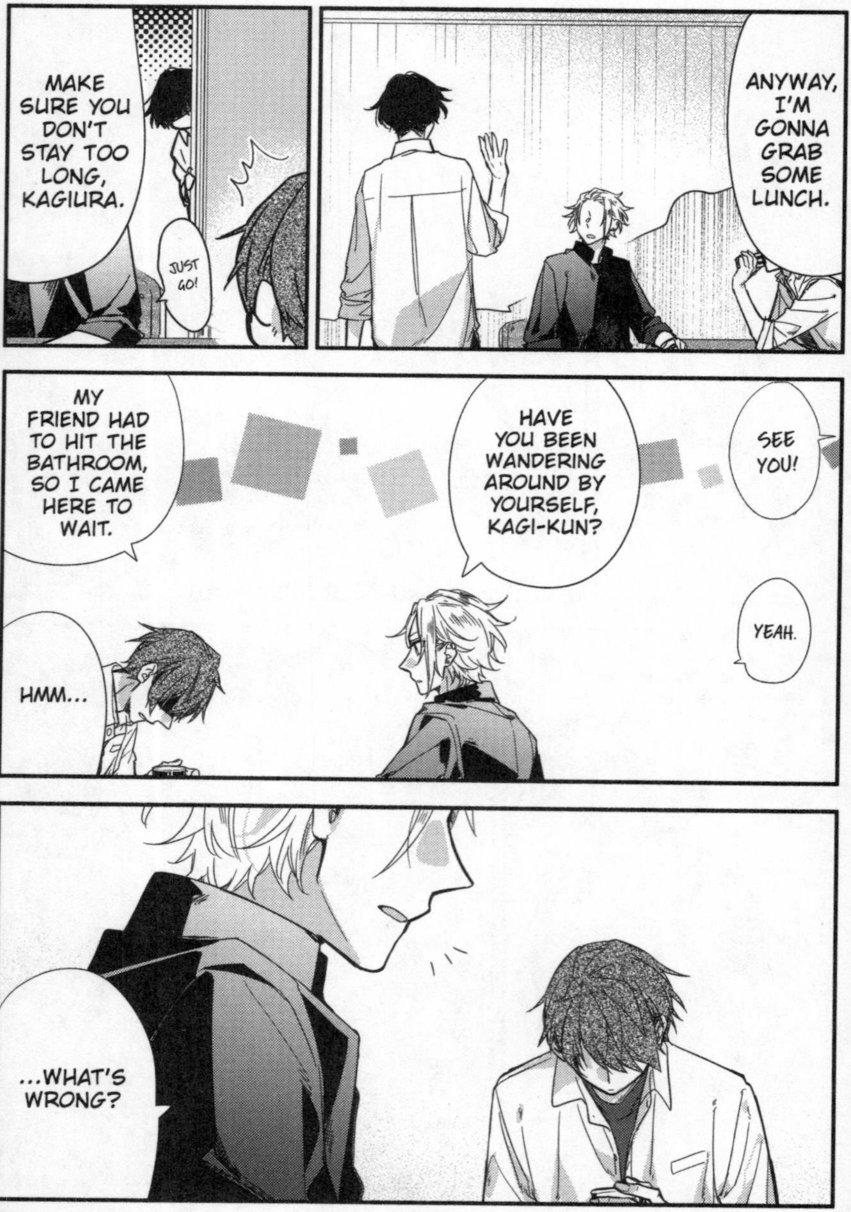
ANYWAY, I'M GONNA GRAB SOME LUNCH.
MAKE SURE YOU DON'T STAY TOO LONG, KAGIURA.
JUST GO!
SEE YOU!
YEAH.
HAVE YOU BEEN WANDERING AROUND BY YOURSELF, KAGI-KUN?
MY FRIEND HAD TO HIT THE BATHROOM, SO I CAME HERE TO WAIT.
HMM...
...WHAT'S WRONG?

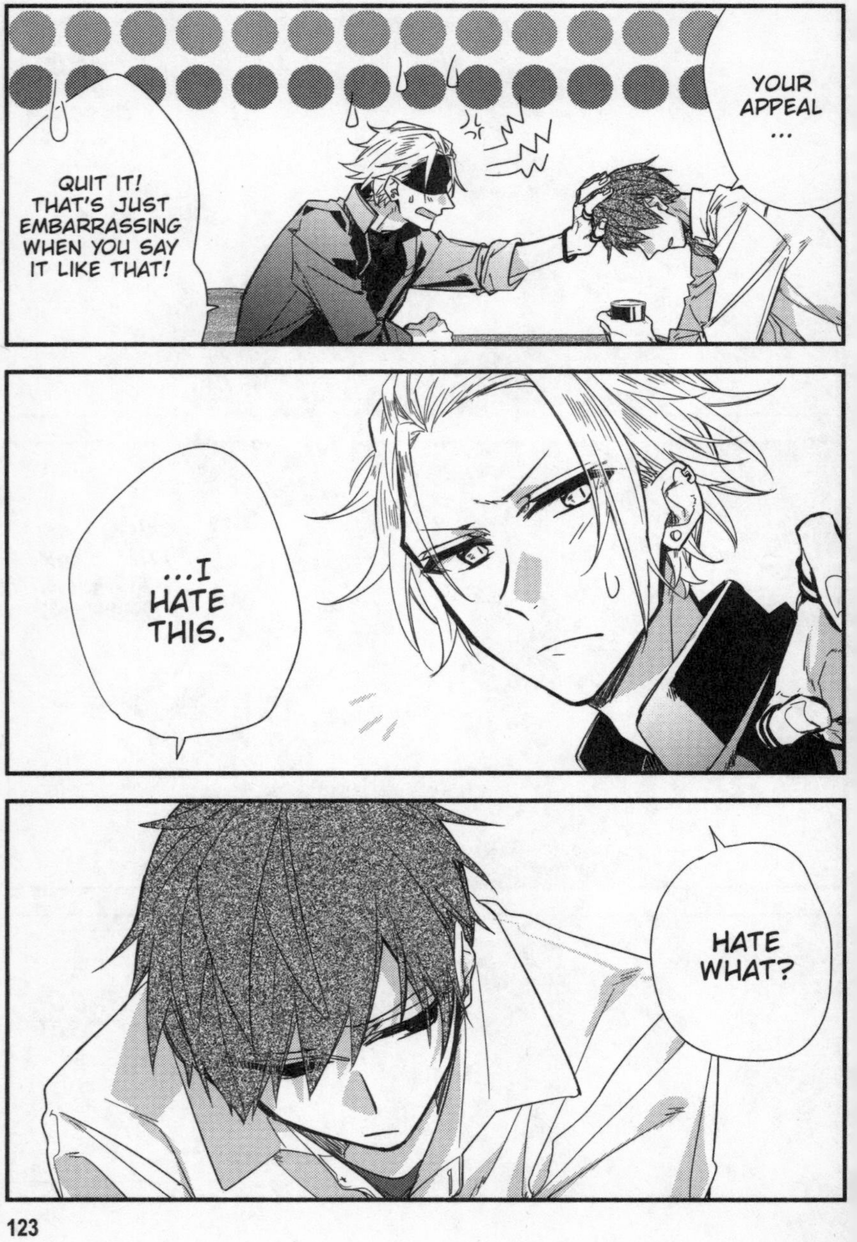
YOUR APPEAL ...
QUIT IT! THAT'S JUST EMBARRASSING WHEN YOU SAY IT LIKE THAT!
...I HATE THIS.
HATE WHAT?

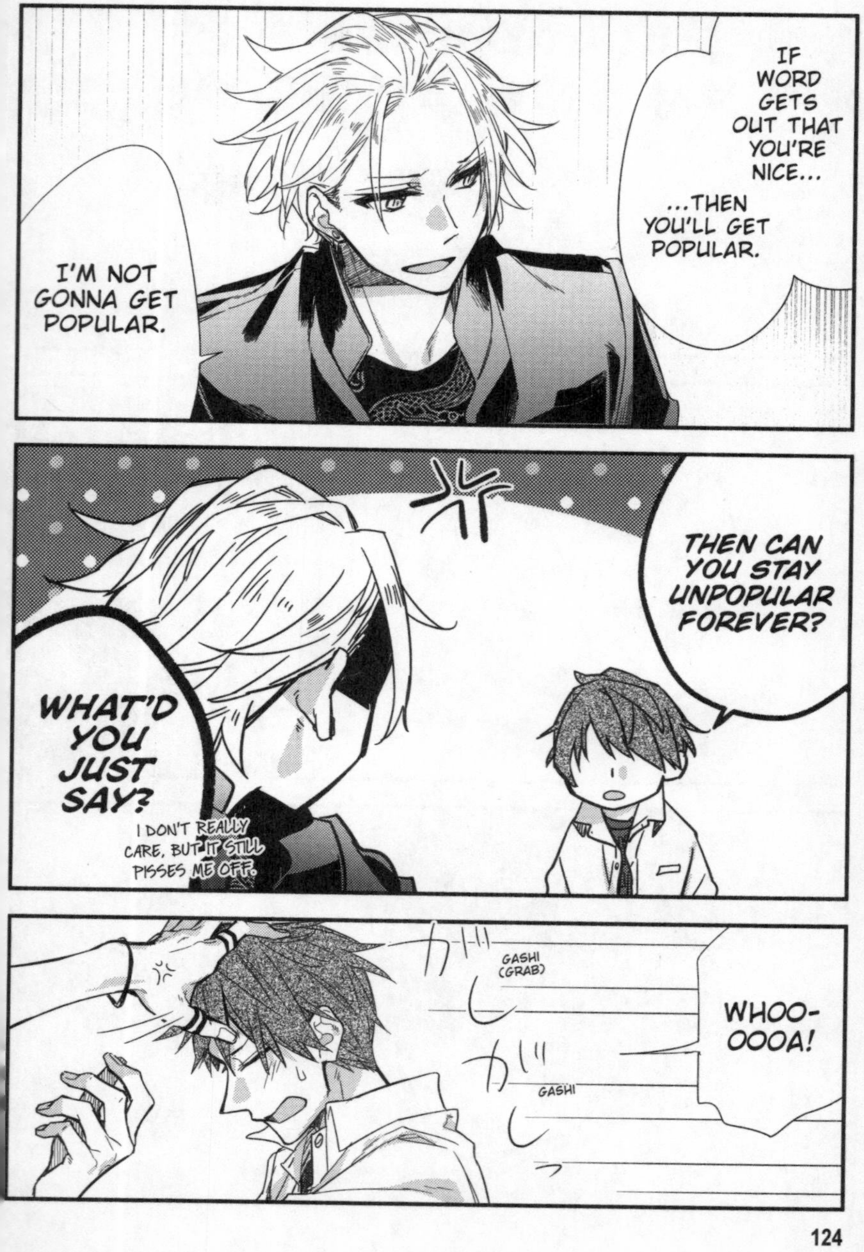
IF WORD GETS OUT THAT YOU'RE NICE...
...THEN YOU'LL GET POPULAR.
I'M NOT GONNA GET POPULAR.
THEN CAN YOU STAY UNPOPULAR FOREVER?
WHAT'D YOU JUST SAY?
I DON'T REALLY CARE, BUT IT STILL PISSES ME OFF.
WHOO-OOOA!
GASHI (GRAB)
GASHI

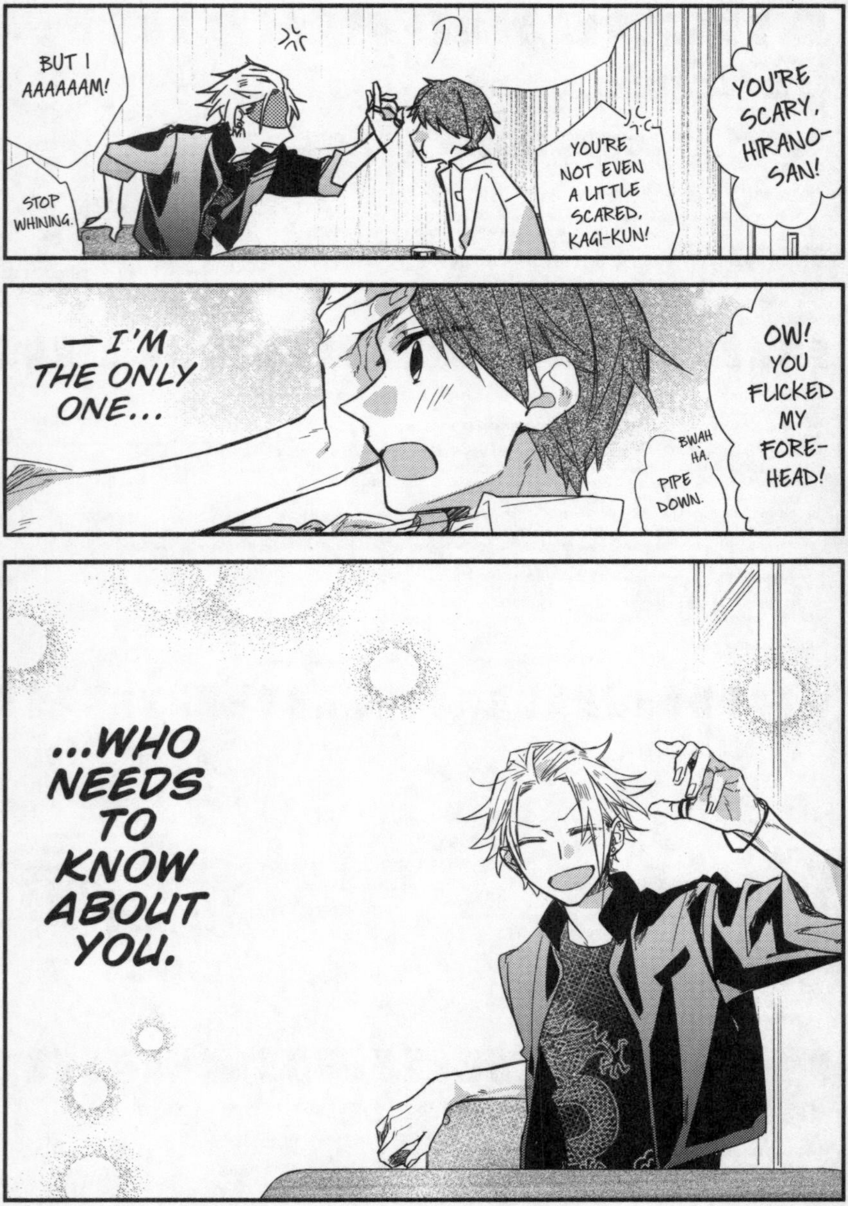
YOU'RE SCARY, HIRANO-SAN!
YOU'RE NOT EVEN A LITTLE SCARED, KAGI-KUN!
BUT I AAAAAAM!
STOP WHINING.
OW! YOU FLICKED MY FOREHEAD!
BWAH HA.
PIPE DOWN.
—I'M THE ONLY ONE...
...WHO NEEDS TO KNOW ABOUT YOU.

SASAKI AND MIYANO
AFTERWORD NEWS

6/27/2019 ISSUE

HELLO! I'M SHOU HARUSONO.
THIS IS VOLUME 5! THANK YOU SO MUCH FOR JOINING ME YET AGAIN!
I WAS THINKING I DIDN'T HAVE ENOUGH SPACE IN THE AFTERWORD, SO I FIGURED I'D TRY OUT DOING IT NEWSPAPER-STYLE.
I'M STILL NOT QUITE SURE THAT I'LL HAVE ENOUGH SPACE, THOUGH.

I OBSCURED SOME LINES OF DIALOGUE WHEN THESE CHAPTERS WERE FIRST RELEASED WITH STUFF LIKE "—, ——!"
SO IF YOU READ THE STORY BACK THEN, I'D LOVE IT IF YOU TOOK ANOTHER LOOK AT THE COLLECTED VERSION NOW.
IT'S NOTHING THAT HAS ANY RELEVANCE TO THE MAIN STORY.

THIS VOLUME IS WHERE MYA-CHAN FINALLY FIGURES IT OUT.

WHEN I MAKE MANGA, I'M ALWAYS THINKING ABOUT STUFF LIKE THE SCENES I WANT TO DRAW AND
HOW I WANT THE CLIMAX TO GO. I'M THE TYPE WHO'S ALWAYS WORKING TOWARD THOSE THINGS.
I HAVE A HARD TIME CONTROLLING MY URGES AND SOMETIMES GET A BIT AHEAD OF MYSELF, SO SOMETIMES
I GET BACK ROUGH DRAFTS FROM MY EDITOR COVERED IN RED AND COMMENTS LIKE, "WHOA...SETTLE DOWN."

I'M PRETTY SURE THAT'S HOW SASAKI AND MIYANO HAVE MANAGED TO REALLY SAVOR THEIR TIME TOGETHER. (THANK YOU!)
I KIND OF FEEL LIKE BOTH THE CAMERAMAN AND THE EDITOR. AND I FEEL LIKE I'M BEING PRESSED
TO RELEASE ALL THE FOOTAGE THAT I'VE CUT TO HIDE THINGS.

THE NEXT VOLUME SHOULD HAVE THE SCENE WITH THE VERY FIRST IMAGE I HAD OF SASAMIYA AS A COUPLE,
SO I'D REALLY LOVE IT IF YOU'D JOIN ME FOR THAT.
OH, AND NEXT VOLUME ISN'T THE END. I'M PLANNING ON KEEPING THIS GOING.

VOLUME 1 OF THE MANGA ADAPTATION OF THE SPIN-OFF STORY *HIRANO AND KAGIURA* CAME OUT AT THE SAME TIME AS THIS BOOK!
IT'S BEEN RUNNING IN *MONTHLY COMIC GENE*. IT'S FULL OF VERY PRECIOUS SCENES.
IT'S THE MANGA ADAPTATION, SO IT SAYS VOLUME 1 ON THE COVER, BUT IN TERMS OF CONTENT,
IT'S MORE OF A CONTINUATION OF THE NOVEL *HIRANO AND KAGIURA*.
WE DECIDED TO MAKE IT A MANGA FOCUSING ON JUST THOSE TWO, SO I WASN'T REALLY SURE WHAT WOULD HAPPEN TO THE BONUS STORIES
I ALWAYS DRAW ABOUT HIRANO-SAN AND KAGI-KUN IN THIS SERIES, BUT IT WOULD BE SAD TO JUST STOP DOING IT, I REALLY, REALLY WANTED
TO DRAW THEM, AND I WANTED TO LEAVE SOME STUFF ABOUT THEM BLANK, SINCE I HAVEN'T DECIDED HOW THEIR STORY IS GOING TO DEVELOP
IN THE FUTURE. SO I INCLUDED A LITTLE BIT OF THEM AGAIN THIS TIME.
BONUS STORIES ARE PROBABLY MY FAVORITE THING ABOUT MAKING MANGA.

AND AS FOR THAT DRAMA CD THAT WE RELEASED AS A SPECIAL FREEBIE——
WELL, NOW FRONTIER WORKS IS PUTTING OUT A FULL SASAKI AND MIYANO DRAMA CD! THE AMUSEMENT PARK STORY IS ALL NEW.

WE'RE ALSO GOING TO BE PUTTING OUT OFFICIAL SASAKI AND MIYANO MERCH TOO!
(FOR MORE INFORMATION, SEE THE OFFICIAL SASAKI AND MIYANO TWITTER ACCOUNT @SASAKIANDMIYANO !)

ANYWAY, I HOPE
YOU'RE ABLE TO JOIN
ME AGAIN FOR THE
NEXT VOLUME!

(I'M SO GLAD I HAD
ENOUGH SPACE!!)

YEN PRESS
150 WEST 30TH STREET, 19TH FLOOR
NEW YORK, NY 10001

EVERYONE INVOLVED IN THE
PRODUCTION OF THIS SERIES ALWAYS
DOES SUCH A WONDERFUL JOB MAKING
IT HAPPEN. MEANWHILE, I'M ALWAYS SO
SLOW, AND THEY'RE ALL SO PATIENT
ABOUT WAITING FOR ME TO FINISH UP
MY PART! I REALLY CAN'T THANK THEM
ENOUGH FOR THAT!
IF YOU'RE INTERESTED, PLEASE
DO CHECK THEM OUT!

ALSO, IF YOU HAVE ANY FEEDBACK,
I'D LOVE TO HEAR IT.

2019.6.
SHOU HARUSONO

Special Thanks

MY EDITOR MIKU SAKURAZAWA-SAMA, MY ORIGINAL EDITOR RYOU HIROUCHI-SAMA, EVERYONE FROM THE EDITORIAL DEPARTMENT,
THE DESIGNERS FROM KAWATANI DESIGN, THE DESIGNERS FOR THE MAGAZINE EDITION,
THE SALES DEPARTMENT, THE PRINTERS, FRONTIER WORKS, EVERYONE INVOLVED IN PRODUCTION AND SALES,
AND THE PEOPLE WHO WORKED ON THE DRAMA CD,
MY FAMILY AND FRIENDS, MY ASSISTANTS TSUBAKI KUROAYA-SAN (BACKGROUNDS) AND YUUKI-SAN (DOUBLE-CHECKING),
EVERYONE ON TWITTER AND PIXIV WHO CHEERED ME ON, AND EVERYONE READING THIS MANGA!

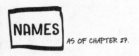

NAMES

AS OF CHAPTER 27.

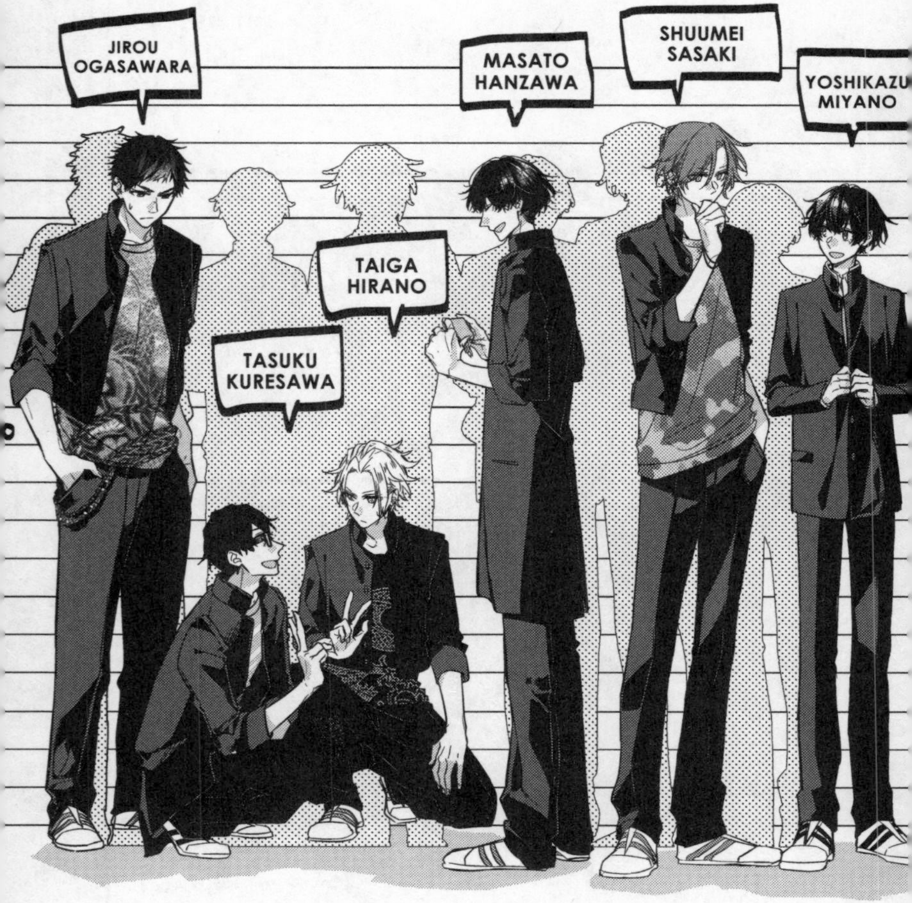
YOSHIKAZU MIYANO
SHUUMEI SASAKI
MASATO HANZAWA
TAIGA HIRANO
TASUKU KURESAWA
JIROU OGASAWARA

CULTURAL FESTIVAL DATE—COTTON CANDY EXPERIENCE VERSION

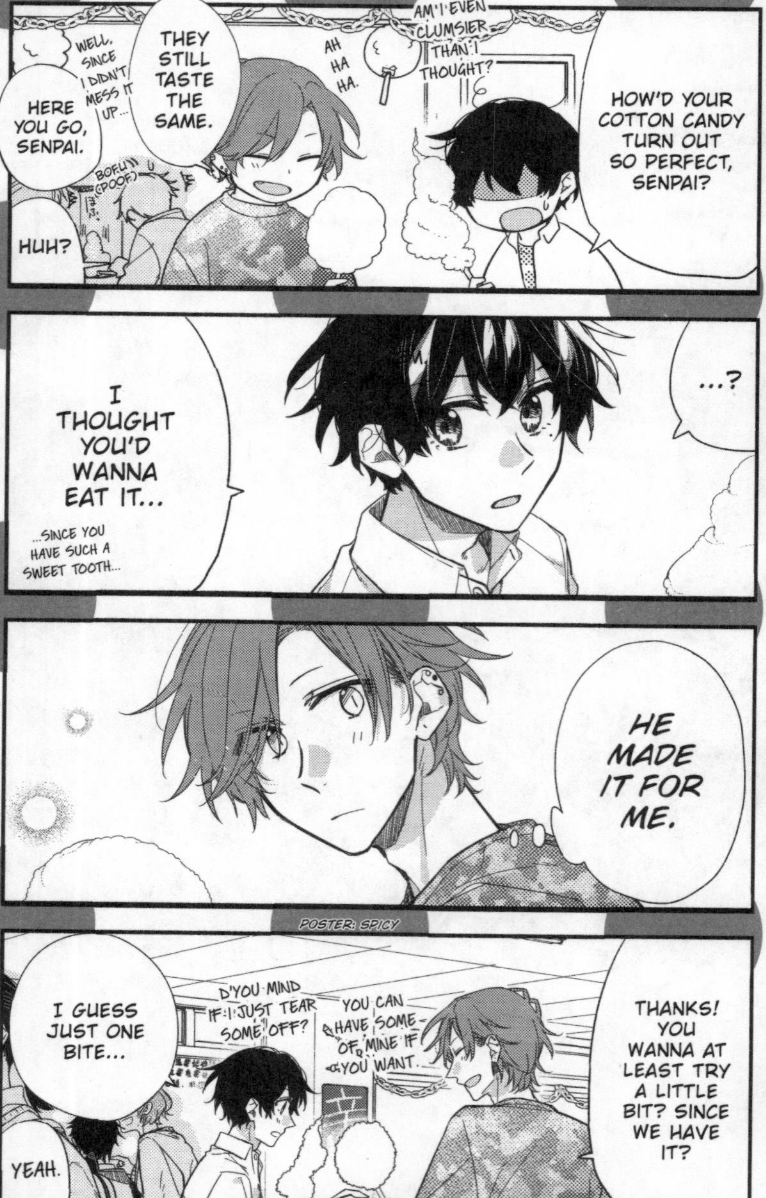
HOW'D YOUR COTTON CANDY TURN OUT SO PERFECT, SENPAI?
AM I EVEN CLUMSIER THAN I THOUGHT?
AH HA HA.
THEY STILL TASTE THE SAME.
WELL, SINCE I DIDN'T MESS IT UP...
HERE YOU GO, SENPAI.
BOFU (POOF)
HUH?
...?
I THOUGHT YOU'D WANNA EAT IT...
...SINCE YOU HAVE SUCH A SWEET TOOTH...
HE MADE IT FOR ME.
POSTER: SPICY
THANKS! YOU WANNA AT LEAST TRY A LITTLE BIT? SINCE WE HAVE IT?
YOU CAN HAVE SOME OF MINE IF YOU WANT.
D'YOU MIND IF I JUST TEAR SOME OFF?
I GUESS JUST ONE BITE...
YEAH.

WANTING TO EAT TOGETHER.

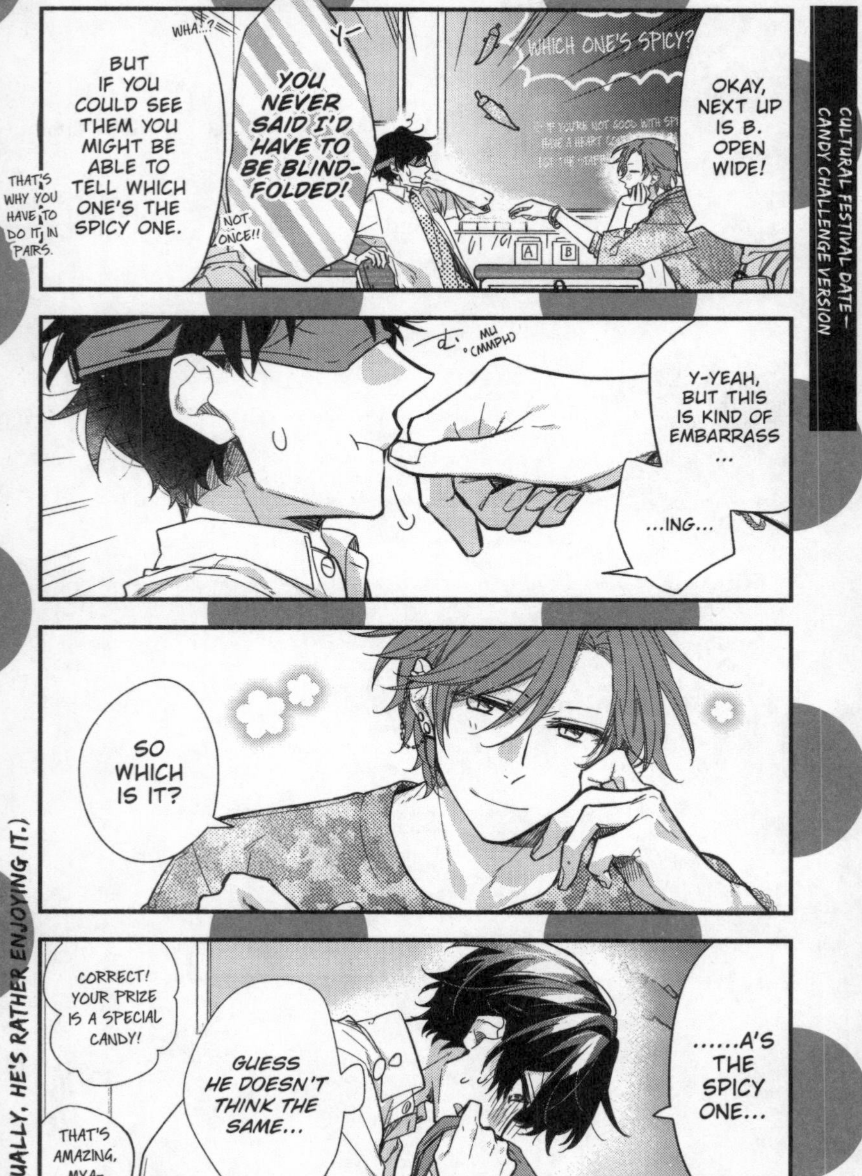
CULTURAL FESTIVAL DATE—CANDY CHALLENGE VERSION
OKAY, NEXT UP IS B. OPEN WIDE!
WHICH ONE'S SPICY?
Y-
YOU NEVER SAID I'D HAVE TO BE BLIND-FOLDED!
WHA...?
NOT ONCE!!
BUT IF YOU COULD SEE THEM YOU MIGHT BE ABLE TO TELL WHICH ONE'S THE SPICY ONE.
THAT'S WHY YOU HAVE TO DO IT IN PAIRS.
Y-YEAH, BUT THIS IS KIND OF EMBARRASS...
...ING...
MU (MMPH)
SO WHICH IS IT?
......A'S THE SPICY ONE...
GUESS HE DOESN'T THINK THE SAME...
CORRECT! YOUR PRIZE IS A SPECIAL CANDY!
THAT'S AMAZING, MYA-CHAN.
(ACTUALLY, HE'S RATHER ENJOYING IT.)

Sasaki and Miyano

05
Shou Harusono

Translation: Leighann Harvey | Lettering: DK

SASAKI TO MIYANO Vol. 5
©Shou Harusono 2019
First published in Japan in 2019
by KADOKAWA CORPORATION, Tokyo.
English translation rights arranged
with KADOKAWA CORPORATION, Tokyo, through
Tuttle-Mori Agency, Inc., Tokyo.

English translation © 2022 by Yen Press, LLC

Yen Press
150 West 30th Street, 19th Floor
New York, NY 10001

Visit us at yenpress.com ★ facebook.com/yenpress ★ twitter.com/yenpress
yenpress.tumblr.com ★ instagram.com/yenpress

First Yen Press Edition: April 2022

Yen Press is an imprint of Yen Press, LLC.
The Yen Press name and logo are trademarks of Yen Press, LLC.

Library of Congress Control Number: 2020949643

ISBNs: 978-1-9753-4190-9 (paperback)
978-1-9753-4191-6 (ebook)

10 9 8 7 6 5 4 3 2

WOR

Printed in the United States of America